QUALITY ASSURANCE for COMPUTER SOFTWARE

QUALITY ASSURANCE for COMPUTER SOFTWARE

Robert Dunn
ITT Avionics Division

and

Richard Ullman
ITT Avionics Division

McGraw-Hill Book Company

New York   St. Louis   San Francisco   Auckland   Bogotá
Hamburg   Johannesburg   London   Madrid   Mexico   Montreal
New Delhi   Panama   Paris   São Paulo   Singapore   Sydney
Tokyo   Toronto

Library of Congress Cataloging in Publication Data

Dunn, Robert, date
Quality assurance for computer software.

Bibliography: p.
Includes index.
1. Computer programs—Quality control.
I. Ullman, Richard. II. Title.
QA76.6.D844   001.64'25   81-664
ISBN 0-07-018312-0   AACR2

1 2 3 4 5 6 7 8 9 0   KPKP   8 9 8 7 6 5 4 3 2 1

The editors for this book were Barry Richman and Stephan
Parnes, the designer was Elliot Epstein, and the production
supervisor was Thomas G. Kowalczyk. It was set in Trump
by University Graphics.

It was printed and bound by The Kingsport Press.

Contents

Preface

Software engineering — the organized, "scientific" approach to computer software development — originated in the late 1960s. Quality assurance of product development goes back to the 1950s. To judge by the rate with which innovative techniques are being introduced to both fields, neither has fully matured. For our part, we rather like working in an emerging discipline; what could be duller than knowing all the answers? More important, the expanding forms of quality assurance and software engineering made it inevitable that sooner or later they would rub up against each other.

As we see it — and it is heartening to note that this is becoming the prevailing view — software quality assurance is the mapping of the managerial precepts and design disciplines of quality assurance onto the applicable management and technological space of software engineering. In the transfer, familiar quality assurance approaches to improving control and performance metamorphose into techniques and tools different from those to which the quality community is accustomed. For its part, software approaches to the production and maintenance of computer software are given new form as well as procedural efficiency. Yet both communities, to their mutual advantage, can easily relate to this concept of software quality assurance.

In stating that this is becoming the prevailing perception of software quality assurance, we have tacitly admitted to the existence of other views. There are those within the world of computer software who feel that better software will result simply through an increased commitment to adopting the practices of software engineering. They ignore the profit realized from the application of quality methodology. Conversely, there are, within quality, people who feel that all that is required is their overseeing software's conformance to its own development and maintenance standards; this without regard to the content of those standards.

No. Software quality assurance can be constructive, can avoid being a bureaucratic impediment, only by drawing upon fundamental concepts of both software engineering and quality assurance. It is the resulting amalgam which we set out to describe and whose many ingredients can be seen in the road map to the balance of the book, which is provided toward the end of Chapter 1.

If, in our description, we seem to have given software quality assurance a better defined structure, to which goal we immodestly confess, it is only because the timbers had already been hewn. The number of people who have contributed to the constituent elements of software quality assurance is surprisingly large, considering the relative youth of both of the disciplines from which it derives. The references at the end of each chapter contain but a fraction of the names of those who, directly or indirectly, have shaped our views, and to whom we are grateful.

The act of presenting software quality assurance in the form of a book involved fewer people, and it is possible to acknowledge by name the help received from those who were most prominent in giving us their time and insight: Phil Crosby, Steve Dunn, and John Tarrant. None of this, of course, would have mattered without the dedication and patience necessary for the preparation of a manuscript, for which we owe a special debt to Patty Siegendorf.

Robert Dunn
Richard Ullman

August 1980

Part One
Introduction

Chapter 1

How Did a Nice Discipline like Quality Get Mixed Up with Computer Software?

In the competitive environment in which we operate, management is continually faced with the challenge to organize or develop resources in the optimum manner to satisfy customers and stockholders. The computer revolution has intensified this challenge by making new major demands on people and organizations throughout the industrial world. The more progressive companies have been able to meet this challenge by changing their philosophies, attitudes, and organizations to keep pace with the times. However, one of the least understood areas in product development today is that of computer software. Management seldom has the proper training, experience, and understanding to properly evaluate the methods used to control software efforts. Yet control is of paramount importance. The history of software development is a chronicle of overruns in dollars and months, continued beyond delivery to include the operational life of software as well.

This observation is not unique, but is recognized within government and industrial organizations everywhere, as the proliferation of computers invades our financial structure, the control of our manufacturing processes, the equipment vital to national defense, our everyday life (appliances, automobiles, etc.), and even the manner in which management decisions are made. Moreover, we can expect the use of computers to expand at ever-increasing rates over the next decade as their cost per unit of computation continues to drop dramatically.

There is considerable concern, then, to fashion effective methods of managing the anticipated quantum jump in computer use; of even greater criticality, of managing the software efforts that will accompany this expansion. This book addresses the contribution that can be made by quality assurance, the discipline most overlooked by those who have sought to tame the software monster, yet one that we feel exerts favorable effect far out of proportion to its cost.

A HISTORICAL CASE FOR SOFTWARE QUALITY

Before dealing with software quality assurance, we shall briefly examine the larger field of quality control, starting with its early beginnings and continuing on to its modern practice. By tracing quality's evolution from primitive origins to its present reflection of today's technological society, this examination will lay a foundation for the development of parallels to software.

Table 1-1 depicts the evolution of quality control. It indicates that prior to the era of mass production, quality control was strictly an inspection function.

TABLE 1-1 Evolution of Quality Control

Time period	Quality control implementation	Remarks
Pre-20th century	Inspection by the producer	Pride in workmanship
1916	Introduction of quality control by Bell Labs	First formal programs
1920–1940	Standardization and inspection	Necessitated by mass production
1940–1950	Introduction of statistical quality control	To economically control more complex and higher output manufacturing processes
1950–1970	Formal programs encompassing all facets of design and development	More prevalent in defense-type organizations
1970–1978	Product liability and product safety, management recognition	Expansion of quality control into all industries
1978–	Introduction of computers into products evolves into software quality assurance for all software	

Even today, there are elements within industry that persist in thinking of quality as an inspection function. Nothing could be further from the truth. Back in the early days, the responsibility for inspection of a product was that of the artisan who made it. The inspection was not consciously performed as a formal and separate action; it was simply made to be sure that the item met the artisan's personal high standard of workmanship, and also that it was precisely what the customer had ordered. An analogy may be drawn at this juncture with the early software designer: the accuracy and effectiveness of the software was dependent on the designer's diligence, ability, and personal standards of quality. We will explore this thought in greater detail in later chapters.

As the industrial revolution took hold and the mass production of products became commonplace, the need for standardization of production and inspection methods gained acceptance. This was coupled with formal programs that were necessary to the planning and management of these efforts. As the operations became more complex, so did the need for increased controls to provide uniformity of the product. Acceptance and rejection criteria had to be established. The need for economical methods for applying these controls and criteria led to the adoption of statistical concepts in the control of the manufacturing processes.

As the quality function became more sophisticated and its effectiveness in dealing with more complex problems and controls became more obvious, enlightened managements began to realize the importance of the function. This receptive attitude enabled the more progressive and innovative members of the quality profession to develop and convince management to support programs such as that which was introduced into the ITT system by Philip Crosby, who was the first to hold the position of vice-president and director of quality of ITT, Worldwide. His quality policy was established on the following basic credo:

> Perform exactly like the requirement — or cause the requirement to be officially changed to what we and our customers really need.[1]

The corporate policy which ensued assured that a quality management function was established in each ITT system unit to make certain that the following objectives were met:

- Acceptance and performance requirements of products and services are met

- Cost of quality goals for each ITT unit are achieved

- Consumer affairs, product safety, and environmental quality programs are implemented and properly directed

- Quality personnel are provided required communications and training

In practical terms, the foregoing policy is applied and accomplished by first establishing the quality function within the unit organization, independently from manufacturing or engineering, thus avoiding the inevitable emasculation which would otherwise result.

In manufacturing units, product acceptance at all levels (incoming, in-process, and final, both in manufacturing plants and at installation sites) is conducted by the quality department. Product acceptance includes inspection and final test operations and the necessary planning activities, such as test engineering, to make it effective. For units involved in service activities, conformance of the service to requirements is determined by the quality department, using inspection, quality auditing, and other techniques. Results of these actions are reported in order to assure corrective action to prevent repetitive defects and to provide management data.

THE SCOPE OF QUALITY

All necessary quality engineering functions (such as inspection and test planning, test equipment selection, test procedures, software, test programming, conformance audit planning, supplier quality control, data collection and analysis, formal corrective action and follow-up, reliability programs, product qualification, calibration of equipment, analysis and control of returned products, inputs to design reviews, inputs to new product planning, and status reporting), as well as necessary monitoring functions, are implemented by quality in coordination with engineering, manufacturing, technical, and other applicable functional areas. Qualification testing is conducted on all new products, associated documentation, and processes to assure conformance of the product with all requirements of the applicable specifications.

If we consider software, too, to be a product, whether it stands alone or is part of a product that would in any case fall under the purview of quality, the foregoing description of the quality arena applies no less to computer software than to goods and services. However, for the most part, the quality community is not yet tooled to serve the needs of software.

We have touched lightly on how the concept of quality has grown from the pride in workmanship of artisans to a sophisticated management function in modern manufacturing or service industries. As a modern management function, the quality organization must remain aware of all technological changes which will have an influence on the operational policies and levels of sophistication of quality and must position itself to react properly to such changes. In the past, managers have always been faced with changing technologies in the products being produced. However, up to this time the changes have in most cases occurred in hardware; classical quality methods have always applied. We are now facing a basic conceptual change in our products. These products are becoming more and more dependent upon computers (under which name, for convenience we include microprocessors), and they, in turn, are dependent upon the software that is resident within them. Professionals in the quality field must address this change, but this is not as straightforward as was the transition from various hardware technology levels. Moreover, as has already been noted, there is a need for quality's participation in independent software as well.

We have also to consider the software professional, who must recognize, as many already have, that software has become too prominent in our society to be developed and maintained in the informal, casual atmosphere of software's beginnings. We posit, too, that it is the responsibility of upper management, to whom both software and quality report, to marshal all of its resources in the control of software cost, schedule, and reliability.

Later pages of this book will discuss the problems peculiar to computer software, the quality solution to these problems, methods of implementing a software quality program, and new developments in establishing quality standards for software. Viewed in the large, software quality will result from the participation of software management, quality management, and upper management. To enable all interests to understand the quality solution proposed, Part 2 provides a glimpse of the software world to those who have had no previous exposure.

THE NEED FOR SOFTWARE QUALITY ASSURANCE

Not unlike the growth in the influence of quality and the manner with which it now performs its essential functions, computer software has grown from the casual preparations of small programs affecting few people to the development and maintenance of program systems involving the participation of dozens, even hundreds of people, affecting thousands more; and as the size of software projects has escalated, new techniques have evolved for accomplishing and controlling the efforts. Software quality assurance is concerned with all computer software. Nowhere, however, is the influence of software more vividly demonstrated than in the class of applications referred to as *embedded software.*

Computers, whether microprocessors or "maxi" computers, which are an integral part of an instrumentation system (e.g., aircraft autopilot, oil refinery control system, department store point-of-sale system, microwave oven), are said to be embedded within the system. Such computers connect directly with sensors, control devices, unique keyboards, or unique display devices. The software that drives these computers is also said to be embedded. Unlike most computer applications, where the computer controls the input of data, embedded software must process data in *real time*, that is, at rates determined externally to the computer.

No system is of greater quality than the quality of its parts, and if one of the parts is a computer, then the quality of the program controlling that computer will affect the quality of the entire system. Computer programs, whether embedded or not, can, and nearly always do, have latent defects. These defects can cause the performance of a system to degrade, as in forcing overly long response times in an online reservation system; or they can cause a system to fail utterly, as when erroneously enabling a missile self-destruct mechanism during the launch phase. (A more complete "chamber of software horrors," including voting systems that awarded the wrong candidate the office, and a warehouse data base system that lost track of 15 tons of frozen liver, is given by Glenford Myers,[2] whose less humorous, but more important, contributions to software quality will be encountered in Part 3.)

For some time now, there have been computer programs embedded within instrumentation systems. However, with the development of microprocessors of considerable logical and arithmetic power, we are witness to a rapid increase in the number of systems and equipments, from video games to large military systems, containing one or more computers. Indeed, increasingly, we see the software embedded within these exerting an influence on the performance of the systems equal to or greater than that of the hardware. The corollary, that the quality of the product is as much vested in the software as in the hardware, is easily drawn. Parenthetically, we may infer from this that the value of the quality community, at least within the electronic and aerospace industries, will be maintained at its present level only if that community has prepared itself to cope with the quality aspects of embedded software. We may note that at present the specific problem of software reliability is being addressed principally by those who develop software, with scant regard to traditional quality disciplines. This is, of course, reminiscent of our nineteenth century artisan of Table 1-1.

As dramatic as the failures (and cost overruns) of embedded software may be, we are concerned with all software. There is no class of software that has not plagued management with cost and schedule disasters, premature obsolescence, and customer dissatisfaction. Software quality assurance is a three-forked challenge: a challenge to software development to accept the control philosophies of quality, a challenge to upper management to recognize that its own purposes will be served by early funding of quality participation, and a challenge to the quality community to acclimate to the practices appropriate to this relatively new technology.

HARDWARE VS. SOFTWARE: SIMILAR BUT DIFFERENT

Accepting the challenge of software quality requires some rethinking of the manner in which quality assurance can be effected. While quality engineering can capitalize on its position of independence from the development process, even as it does in the hardware environment, it must recognize that there are inherent differences between software and hardware that will affect the practices that quality engineering employs.

For one, we note that much quality assurance effort is related to the certain knowledge that hardware degrades with use. Software, on the other hand, can be expected to improve. Once a program bug is found and corrected, it remains corrected. Thus, the concept of mean time before failure, although applicable to software, must be interpreted in a new sense.

Perhaps the most prominent quality assurance role has been in inspection of hardware, where the effort expended is mainly to assure that the original design is being correctly copied in production units. There is no such need in software quality assurance. After a program has been judged acceptable, there need be no concern for the ability to copy it precisely.

Hardware can warn that a failure is likely to occur soon. In the electronic world, for example, one can, as part of quality assurance throughout the life cycle, periodically measure pulse shapes, power supply ripple, and other characteristics for evidence of an impending malfunction. Software will give no such warnings.

Hardware can be built of standardized components, from devices to complete assemblies, the reliability of which are known. For the most part, software contains few program elements with which there has been prior experience.

To repair hardware is to restore its original condition. The repair of software results in a new baseline (i.e., product definition) condition, with the consequence that program documentation must be updated if the success of future repairs is not to be jeopardized.

In general, equipment can be tested over the entire spectrum of operational conditions in which it will perform. [With the complexity that will attend very large scale integrated (VLSI) circuits, this may soon no longer be the case.] Thus, at least at present, the performance aspects of equipment may be completely verified by test. The number of discrete states that software can assume is so great that exhaustive testing is impossible.

For quality engineers, the sum of these differences between hardware and software implies the message that while traditional quality assurance disciplines may apply, the practices will have to differ, and most specifically, will have to emphasize the concept of built-in quality, of "doing it right the first time."

BUILT-IN QUALITY

For computer software, built-in quality is the result of a number of interdependent technical and managerial techniques and tools. This is the substance of Chapters 5, 6, 7, and 8, which follow the introductory material of Chapters 2, 3, and 4, which we recommend to readers who have little experience with software. The role of the independent quality auditors, intertwined with the elements of built-in quality, is best seen in Chapter 9. The quintessential role of quality is to focus its attention on the establishment of standards conducive to quality, and to audit the fidelity to which these standards are adhered. All too often, software is produced under the most trying of schedules. Authorization to start a project may slip. Systems analyses and simulations required to define the system concepts may slip. Hardware availability and the readiness of new support software may slip. Only one thing never changes: the end date.

Accordingly, and *consistent with the precepts that quality is conformance to requirements and prevention of defects,* it is the responsibility of quality to act as the independent instrument of management in auditing all aspects of software development and maintenance through the review of plans, specifications, designs, test documentation, configuration control, and programming standards. Quality must also assume its traditional responsibilities in vendor surveillance of procured software, qualification and acceptance of all software, certification of tools used for software testing, defect analysis, and quality improvement analysis.

IMPLEMENTATION

The manner in which quality will operate in all these areas can best be ensured by policies and procedures much like those which quality engineering has traditionally prepared for reliability engineering and inspection. These will define the authorities and responsibilities of quality, and in detail give notice of the information to be reviewed at each audit, the mechanism with which testing will be monitored and certified, the instruments for assuring corrective action, and the means by which test and defect report records will be retained, controlled, and used. These matters are attended to in Part 4, along with the establishment of software quality assurance's credibility with the management and software communities, and the techniques applicable to the staffing of software quality assurance organizations.

Once the program is in place, a formal quality cost system should be introduced so that the effectiveness of the program can be monitored and corrective action implemented as required. The basis for this is that all are then working as an integrated group with accepted standards within the company with a common goal of producing inherently quality software.

Finally, Part 5 deals with the difficult establishment of software quality standards. It proposes no single solution, but offers a discursive introduction to evolving techniques and models that may prove valid candidates on which to base quantitative evaluation methods.

SUMMARY

1. Historically, computer software has been plagued by cost and schedule overruns during development and failures during operation.

2. Quality controls were initially introduced to industry as a response to problems attending the complexity of manufacturing operations as production evolved from that of the individual artisan to that of the modern factory. The effectiveness of these controls was achieved by their being vested in an organization separate from manufacturing, namely, quality.

3. Software, too, is a product produced by complex operations and beset with problems analogous to the early problems of large-scale production.

4. Although the disciplines of hardware quality control may apply, the practices will have to be different to address a new set of conditions:
   • Hardware degrades with time, while software improves.
   • Unlike hardware, software failures are never preceded by warnings.
   • Hardware components can be standard; software rarely.
   • Hardware repairs restore the original condition; software repairs establish a new configuration state.
   • Hardware can usually be tested exhaustively; not so software.

5. One consequence is that software quality must be built in by its developers, with the quality community acting as the independent instrument for assuring compliance with performance objectives and with development and maintenance standards.

REFERENCES

1. Philip B. Crosby, *Quality Is Free*, McGraw-Hill, New York, 1979, p. 67.

2. Glenford J. Myers, *Software Reliability: Principles and Practices*, Wiley-Interscience, New York, 1976, pp. 24–25.

Part Two
Computer Software

Chapter 2
Fundamentals of Computer Software

Thus far, we have said a great deal about the importance of computer software and how it affects society, especially industry and government. It is time to define what it is we're talking about. Computer professionals may find this to be ground previously trod too well, and may want to turn to the next chapter. Those who have no background in computers will take a quick tour through programming languages, including a glimpse here and there of what programs look like, and will receive a brief exposition on systems software, the programs that improve the productivity of programmers and computer systems.

COMPUTERS: THINGS TO PROGRAM

Since computer software is mostly a matter of computer programs, the stuff with which computers are filled, we shall start by defining a computer. For our purposes, we may ignore the more elaborate definitions and simply, if somewhat pedantically, say the following:

> A computer is an adaptive device capable of performing certain logical operations based on the state of bistable electronic devices.

Our simple definition (which excludes from our scope of interest devices such as electronic differential analyzers, aviators' slide rules, and gasoline pumps, all of which are frequently called "computers") embodies two key concepts. One is found in the word "adaptive." This is little more than a ruse to avoid being accused of using the word "programmable" before it has been defined. However, it also implies a wide range of application for computers. The other concept is the stark simplicity of hardware allowed by the definition: digital manipulation of the voltages or currents (bits) presented by electronic circuits. No more than that. The electronic hardware of a computer contains circuits to move bits from one place to another, to determine if two bits are identical, to sum two strings of bits, to test a bit to see in which of two states it is, to count bits, and so on. All primitive operations. There is little a computer can do in response to a single command that is beyond the ability of a grade school student. It is what a computer can do if given a sequence of commands that makes it the ubiquitous tool it has become. That sequence of commands or instructions, is, of course, what is meant by the word "program."

Thus, the computer. "Information processor" is a marketing term; "electronic brain" belongs to the world of pulp and science fiction. Devoid of native intelligence, an inanimate collection of interconnected electronic parts, the computer sits, awaiting the touch of its muse, the computer programmer. It is, indeed, so lacking in innate capability that it cannot even perform arithmetic calculations in ordinary decimal numbers, as can decent folk. Rather, it computes in binary numbers.

Binary numbers are those having but two numerals, 1 and 0. A binary digit is a "bit," which we just defined somewhat differently. If it is true humans learned to favor the decimal system because they have ten fingers (digits), we can easily understand why computer designers favor binary numbers for their machines. Electronic devices having discrete states generally have but two: transistors can assume the stable states of conducting electricity, or of not conducting; ferrous elements can be polarized with clockwise magnetic flux, or counterclockwise; light-sensitive devices can be saturated with light, or not.

None of this is intended to be an apology for binary numbers or for binary arithmetic. A binary number is just as useful for any calculation as is a decimal number. Both binary numbers and decimal numbers are representatives of the positional numbering system, wherein any number may be decomposed to

$$a_n R^{n-1} + a_{n-1} R^{n-2} + \cdots + a_1 R + a_0$$

where the a_i are the digits one sees in a number and R is the radix (10 for decimal, 2 for binary) of the system.

Thus, the decimal number $193 = 1 \times 10^2 + 9 \times 10 + 3$. Similarly, to convert the eight-digit binary number 11000001 to decimal, we perform the calculation

$$1 \times 2^7 + 1 \times 2^6 + 0 \times 2^5 + 0 \times 2^4$$
$$+ 0 \times 2^3 + 0 \times 2^2 + 0 \times 2 + 1$$

The three nontrivial (additive) terms are

$$\begin{array}{r} 128 \\ 64 \\ \underline{1} \\ \end{array}$$

which sum to 193

That is, the binary number 11000001 and the decimal integer 193 can both express the same number. As an integer, a binary number can be operated upon by computer hardware for the purposes of addition, subtraction, multiplication, or division. Moreover, allowing the bits that represent an integer to be used in an entirely different, nonarithmetic, sense, the binary number can be used to represent a character: a letter, a typographic symbol, or a number. In the character code used by IBM, the binary number 11000001 is used to represent the letter "a." Similarly, 11111001 represents the number "9," but only if one intends to use it that way. As an integer to be added to another, it means something else again. In brief, binary numbers can be integers, which in the nonabstract world we consider measures of something (distance, weight, number of beans), or they can represent textual characters. The difference is simply in the way they are used by computer programs, and the interpretation is at the discretion of the computer programmer.

To round out this presentation of binary numbers, we note that they can be used to represent fractional and other kinds of numbers, again, at the choosing of the programmer.

It may appear from the foregoing that computer programmers have to deal with each number or character on a bit-by-bit basis. Primitive as the intellectual power of a computer may be, programmers are spared this level of detail. Generally, they can operate on whole integers or characters at a time. That is, they can instruct the computer to add two integers together, or they can concatenate a character to the end of a string of characters previously assembled. When performing the latter operations, they usually consider each character to be represented by eight bits, as we have shown, which they call a *byte*. For the purpose of arithmetic, they like to call integers, especially if they are greater than eight bits in length, *words*. Going a step further, they refer to the maximum number of bits that can be operated upon by the simplest class of instruction as the computer's *word length*. Combining these concepts, in, say, a 32-bit word length machine, we can do 32-bit integer arithmetic, or we can operate on four characters in one instruction. With few exceptions, word lengths of contemporary computers are between 8 and 60 bits.

In the early 1950s, the computers then available could conveniently be divided into four parts: arithmetic and logical unit, control unit, input-output unit, and memory. In essence this is true today also, but there are wide variations in the make-up of each. Moreover, in some architectures the distinctions between the functions are blurred. For example, it is common today to see control partly housed in a special memory containing *microcode*, which is used to interpret the commands generally considered to constitute the computer's repertoire of instructions. That the instructions used by programmers are actually operated upon by a lower, more primitive, level of instructions is invisible to them. They may know they're there (they often don't), but so far as they are concerned, the instructions are interpreted by "hard-wired" logic to control the operations within the arithmetic and logical unit.

Memory itself is not infrequently divided into several hierarchically arranged parts. Where once internal memory (that is, directly addressable, as opposed to magnetic tapes, drums, or disks, which are accessed through input-output ports) was everywhere built of magnetic ferrite cores, today we may see high-speed small semiconductor memories containing the next group of instructions to be executed; a slower semiconductor memory or a core memory containing the larger part of the program; and, with the concept of virtual storage (of which, more later), an even lower-speed memory — perhaps a disk or charge-coupled device or magnetic bubble memory — connected through a special high speed data channel.

Architectures of today's computers vary in other ways as well. The processing load may be shared by several processing units in a *parallel processor* configuration, or, in the case where many small computers share a common data base, a *distributed processing* system. Other architectures employ a concept called *pipelining*, which effects an overlap in the execution of successive instructions. Certain configurations employ an *array processing* architecture, wherein many data items are operated upon simultaneously, and often by sets of microinstructions far more powerful (e.g., trigonometric functions) than the elementary operations with which we began this chapter. And thus it goes: where once one could visualize the microdesign of a computer without unbolting its protective panels, advancements in hardware technology and computer science have created a variety of devices all bearing the same name, "computer."

Even the packaging is marked by a wide range of concepts. The image persists, in no small measure with the help of two decades of magazine cartoonists, of computers requiring at least one wall of a large room. In fact, while the tape units, disk drives, printers, and card devices associated with large-scale computers do require considerable real estate, even the most powerful of modern computers are rarely larger than a pair of file cabinets. At the other end of the size spectrum we have microprocessors. The ubiquitous microprocessor is no less a computer than the large mainframe, as it is usually called. However, architecturally it is less complex, possesses a smaller instruction set, and is considerably slower. Between the mainframes and the microprocessors we have the minicomputers. As one might expect, the borders between the three categories are often in dispute, and one person's minicomputer is another's microcomputer.

PROGRAMS

Whatever the shape or design of a computer, it performs no useful work until it is told what to do. More precisely, how to do it. Since the computer is a binary device, we might expect that a single instruction to transfer the contents of a specific memory location to the arithmetic and logic unit might appear as a binary number:

1100110000111010.

This instruction contains an operation code to define a movement from memory to the arithmetic and logic unit, the address of the memory location, and the specific register to which the contents are to be copied.

A set of instructions to solve the problem of finding the smallest of five positive numbers might take the following awesome form, which, for practical purposes, is undecipherable save for the computer that will execute it:

```
1001110110011011
0111000111100011
1100110001010101
1001110001011010011010011
1110001110101011
00100110100011011100101011
1001101000011101000011000
0110001110100011
00100110011000001110001
0010010000011110
0111111111111111
0000000000000110
0000000000000000
```

This looks like a clear case of overkill for solving a problem that we normally attack by sight, but remember that as many times as your automobile has turned from the street into your driveway, it still doesn't know when to start the turn until you instruct it. So computers: the simplest problems may require considerable instruction.

As is painfully evident, while these binary instructions are within the communications capabilities of a computer, indeed are the only language it can interpret, they are scarcely convenient for the people who must communicate with the computer. Even looking at each of the constituent parts of each instruction separately doesn't help matters much. How many seven-digit telephone numbers can the typical person remember? How many 8-, 12-, or 16-bit binary addresses for unique data items can we expect to remember?

Early in the age of computers it was recognized that something had to be done to help programmers improve their productivity, as well as to maintain their equanimity. *Assembler languages* were invented. An assembler language permits the various operation codes to be given simple mnemonic codes, allows programmers to christen with names the locations in memory where their data is stored, and even allows other instructions to be referred to by names assigned by the programmers. In assembler language, the same problem of finding the smallest of five positive numbers might be coded as follows:

```
              LD              BIG
              STO             LEAST
    REPEAT    LDX        1    LEFT
              LD     L   1    VALUE
              S               LEAST
              MDX    L        CHECK
              LD     L   1    VALUE
              STO             LEAST
    CHECK     MDX    L        LEFT, − 1
              MDX             REPEAT
    BIG       DC              32767
    LEFT      DC              6
    VALUE     BSS             6
```

If somewhat arcane,* at least assembler language makes no unreasonable demands on the memory of the programmer. However, it is one thing to define the vocabulary of a language and its syntactical rules; it is quite another to be able to understand it. A binary electronic device, the computer is at a loss to directly execute a program written in assembler language. What is required is something that will translate the program into the computer's native binary language; that is, to transform the mnemonics into operation codes, and to assign and keep track of the addresses of labeled instructions and named data items.

The required capability is supplied in the form of another computer program called, not surprisingly, an *assembler*. Figure 2-1 illustrates the assembly process. Both the assembler, in binary code, and the program written in assembler language are loaded into the computer. The assembler operates upon each of the assembler language instructions, and, in time, outputs the equivalent program in binary code.

At this point we introduce two more terms, both of which will be used frequently in the next few chapters. The assembler language program (sometimes called the *assembly* language program) is, by definition, the *source* program. The binary program output by the assembler is called the *object* program. Frequently, for reasons that will become apparent, the object program is

---

*For those who insist upon some explanation, the column on the extreme left contains the names (labels) of program statements, constants, and allocations for data storage referred to elsewhere. The column headed by "LD" contains either symbols corresponding to machine operation codes (LD means load) or definitions of the forms of constants or storage areas. The central columns modify the operation code or provide supplementary information required for its execution. The right hand column contains either constants or the operands for the instructions — data, constants, or instruction labels with modifiers.

called the *target* program. We can now view the role of the assembler as that of transforming a source program into an object program. We can say the same thing slightly differently: the input data space upon which the assembler operates is the set of source statements, and the output data produced by the assembler is the equivalent string of object code.

The foregoing does more than add to the reader's vocabulary of software argot, it also implies the fundamental systems view of programming:

Input—Process (or Transform)—Output

That the input and output in this case are themselves programs is immaterial. From the software point of view, it is a program performing a transformation of data, whatever the set of data may represent, notwithstanding the physical fact that it is the computer that has processed the data and has processed the assembler program as well. Software people, unless reminded otherwise, see it only as the assembler processing the source program, much as they see the general ledger program, not the computer, processing the week's accounts receivable. If this seems a parochial view, we must remember that the extent to which a computer appears to imitate human reasoning is only that endowed by the program being executed within it. In any event, as we introduce programs of greater complexity than assemblers, it will become apparent that it is the software, not the hardware, that seems to be in charge of things.

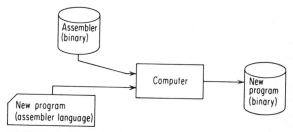

FIGURE 2-1   Process of Assembly.

If the output code of Figure 2-1 is the native binary code of the computer in which the assembly was performed, the diagram illustrates the typical assembly process. However, there is no reason why an assembler being executed on computer A cannot generate object code for computer B. Here, we refer to computer A as the *host* machine, computer B as the *target* machine, and the process as *cross-assembly*. Cross-assembly is most commonly performed in circumstances where the target machine is a microprocessor, which lacks the convenient input and output devices associated with larger computer systems.

COMPILERS

Assembler language may be more compatible with human thought processes than binary code, but it is still far removed from the way we think. For the previously offered example of finding the smallest of five numbers, it would be far simpler to instruct the computer as follows (where N is the largest number the computer can store):

```
SMALLEST = N
FOR NEXT NUMBER (NEXT RANGES 1 TO 5)
   IF (NEXT NUMBER < SMALLEST)
      THEN SMALLEST = NEXT NUMBER
      ELSE REPEAT
END
```

Now this is still not representative of the way we view a table of numbers to see which is the smallest. For one thing, our cognitive reasoning does not require the use of a formally defined and incremented index (NEXT), nor do we approach so trivial a problem in such a formal manner. However, it is certainly more intelligible than the previous solution given in assembler language. Even those who have never seen a computer program before will agree that this example might well have something to do with the relative size of numbers. Programs written in such a language can be written much faster, can be debugged (made to work) more quickly, and can more easily be understood when reexamined months or years later for the purpose of modification.

A language such as the last is called a *compiler language*.* The process of translating a program written in compiler language is illustrated in Figure 2-2. The analogy between this and Figure 2-1 is obvious. In both cases, a transforming process (compilation or assembly) is performed on a source program, and object code is output. For this reason, all language processors (i.e., compilers, assemblers, and others yet to be described) are frequently referred to simply as *processors*. This is an unfortunate term, since computers are often called processors as well. It is, however, not atypical. For a field as exacting as computation is, requiring the highest standards of precision in all matters, the practitioners have embraced a level of ambiguity in their speech and writing that has not been seen since the last general election. We shall see further examples of this as we go along.

The first compilers became available to programmers in the late 1950s. The improvement in programming efficiency should have been the major factor in their immediate acceptance. It is more likely that they rapidly gained favor

---

*The language used in the example is not, to the authors' knowlege, a real one, but was invented for the purpose of clarity. Similarly, further examples of compiler language, unless noted, will be invented for the occasion, with the intention of making the essence of the problem being solved visible to the reader who has no programming background.

because they relieved the more creative, problem-oriented, programmer from the tedium of having to contend with the detailed coding of efficient addressing schemes and with various hardware-oriented minutiae of assembler language programming. At the same time, there were programmers who resisted the invasion of the more problem-oriented approach to programming. Some took special pride in their ability to master the intricacies of computers, while others felt that their quasi-professional status was threatened by languages that could be used by the general population. It is significant that in those early days, computer programming was almost synonymous with coding. Today's emphasis on analysis and design techniques was still in the future.

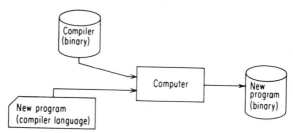

FIGURE 2-2 Process of Compilation.

Over two decades later, there are still those who argue that assembler language is preferred for professionally built software. Certainly, assembler language programs can execute more swiftly and can require less memory, *but only if well written.* Their application is still indicated for the more critical parts of certain programs that must operate in real time or are used to manage the behavior of either computers or other programs. However, as we shall see in Part 3, there is still much assembler language programming going on that is unnecessarily driving costs up and quality down.

That there remains so much sentiment for assembler language is ironic in light of the variety of languages that have been invented over the years. Each language offers linguistic and syntactical features tailored either to a class of applications (examples of classes are scientific programming and word processing) or to the inventor's stylistic prejudices. Many of the available languages have become well known to those outside the field of programming, such has the world of computation invaded our consciousness. We list here a few of the large number of languages that have proliferated during the last 20 years:

ALGOL   The earliest scientific language, and still popular

COBOL   For many years the lingua franca for business applications

LISP   A mathematical approach to dealing with the attributes of lists of things

FORTRAN The most popular for scientific and engineering applications

JOVIAL ALGOL-based, widely used by the U.S. Air Force

PASCAL Another descendent of ALGOL, achieving adherents at an ever-increasing rate

APL Succinct, but employing unconventional symbols

CMS-2 Beloved of the U.S. Navy

BASIC Easy to learn; popular in schools and colleges; often seen in small business systems

PL/1 After a hundred or so languages had gained currency, IBM decided the world was ready for its own form of Esperanto; namely, PL/1

ADA Based on PASCAL; the Department of Defense's own hope for a standard

With the notable exceptions of COBOL, CMS-2, and ADA, the names of these and dozens of other languages are, to one extent or another, generic descriptors of languages. For example, under the name FORTRAN, we have the original FORTRAN (and its dialects), FORTRAN II (and its dialects), FORTRAN IV (and its dialects), and the recently established FORTRAN 77, which has already been endowed with one extension.[1] Dialects, we might note, are usually in the form of extensions, or added capabilities, but may include linguistic modifications of the standard language forms also. If these modifications are great enough, one has not only a dialect but a language bearing another name. Thus, some consider JOVIAL to be a dialect of one of the dialects of ALGOL, and some of the dialects of JOVIAL have been given separate names (e.g., J73). In the world of computer languages, the equivalent of the evolution of Proto-Indo-European to modern English has taken place in only two decades.

Much more information on the history of the earlier languages and on their characteristics is available in Jean Sammett's book, *Programming Languages.*[2] In the years since the publication of her book, the "tower of computational babel" has continued to rise, and several of the languages that will from time to time be referred to within these pages are not covered by Sammett.

That there exists a wide variety of compiler languages is not to suggest that all are available to each programmer for the coding of his problem. A programmer may be fluent in ALGOL, but if the computer on which he is to process his data has no ALGOL compiler, he will be unable to use the language. (Unless, as is seldom the case, he has available a cross-compiler, analogous to the cross-assembler of a few pages ago.) In the most general case, the programmer and all her associates will be using one, or at most two, different compilers for their programs. For example, in a commercial electronic data processing installation, such as a bank or the management information system department of a large company, we might see both COBOL and PL/1. Even here, we might guess that COBOL is being used only for modifications of old programs; that new data processing systems are being written in PL/1. The use of a single language is conducive to simpler programming standards, avoids the duplication of utility routines (standard software components for performing common operations), and obviates the need for hiring or training bilingual programmers.

In his *Recollections of Socrates*, Xenophon attributes to Apollo the remark that "Everyone's true worship was that which he found in use in the place where he chanced to be." From a historical point of view, this is how most programmers, and also nonprogrammers who occasionally program their own problems, choose languages. The language or languages used by their employers are those that they will use. As a result, few programmers who have stayed on one job for many years are truly multilingual. Programmers may study "foreign" languages on their own, but not until they have an opportunity to put a language to use, meaning they have at their disposal a compiler for it, can they gain fluency. Similarly, it is the rare French language student who feels entirely comfortable with the language until having had to use it in a French language environment.

Carrying the analogy a bit further, programmers often exhibit an overly fond attitude toward their first compiler language. Indeed, until acquiring considerable experience with a new language, some programmers have been known to first code a program in the "mother tongue" and then translate it to the new language.

Compilers are not the only processors capable of operating on programs written in compiler languages. Another type of processor in common use is the *interpreter*. Interpreters only partly compile source language statements, leaving the balance of the translation to be performed during execution, with the interpreter remaining in the computer and completing the language processing one executable statement at a time. Quite obviously, this exacts a significant penalty on the time it takes a program to be executed. It would be most inefficient for a program that will be called upon to perform thousands of times during its lifetime. However, by leaving the processing of individual executable statements for *run time*, or the period of productive execution of a program, it is possible to present the programmer with diagnostic messages relating to program errors that are much more pertinent to the debugging process than would otherwise obtain. In the most ideal environment, both an interpreter and a compiler are available to the programmer, the one to be used during program development and the other for production. This ideal, however, is seldom found.

Of the list of languages given above, BASIC and APL are those most often implemented as interpreters. This reflects the most frequently found milieu for these languages: the direct use of computers by persons other than programmers. A student or mathematician using a computer has most likely prepared a program to solve a specific problem. After computing a satisfactory solution, the program will be discarded, thus placing the emphasis on development efficiency rather than production efficiency.

PROGRAM DESIGN

Languages are the medium in which programs are coded. It is possible, given a problem, to directly write code. Usually, however, at least some thought has to be given to what it is that will be coded. As we shall see in the next chapter, for all but the most simple problems, this thinking process is far more significant to software quality than is coding. For now, we shall take a very simple problem and see what thinking might be required.

For our problem we shall take the solution of the quadratic equation

$$AX^2 + BX + C = 0$$

As every eighth-grader knows, there are two roots, and they may be found from

$$X = \frac{-B \pm \sqrt{B^2 - 4AC}}{2A}$$

We immediately recognize that the solution can take several forms. If $A = 0$, we shall not want to use the above equation, since we do not want to require the computer to divide by zero. Moreover, there will be but one root to the equation: $X = -C/B$. However, if B, too, is zero, we shall want to avoid performing this operation. By inspection, we see that if $4AC > B^2$, the roots will be complex.

All of this implies that we cannot simply write out an equation for the solution, but that we shall have to employ *program branches* to permit alternative processing paths. The problem is still simple enough for experienced programmers, having gone through the above thinking process, to code without further intermediate steps. Less experienced programmers will probably want to sketch a diagram of their plan for the program, as in Figure 2-3.

Diagrams of this kind are called flowcharts. They are by far the most commonly used method of documenting the design of a program. Whether they are the best documentation technique is quite another matter, but we leave that for later chapters.

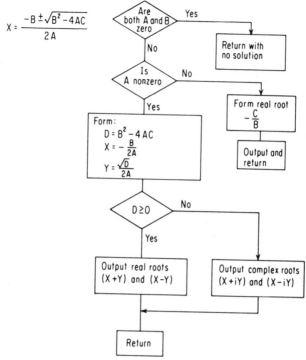

FIGURE 2-3 Solution of Quadratic Equation.

With the flowchart in front of them, the programmers now write their code. If they were using FORTRAN IV, they might code the following:

```
  PROGRAM QUADRATIC
  IOUT = 5
  IN = 2
  READ (IN,1) A,B,C
1 FORMAT (3E20.7)
  IF (A.NE.O.OR.B.NE.O) GO TO 3
  WRITE (IOUT,2)
2 FORMAT ('NO SOLUTION')
  STOP
3 IF (A.NE.O) GO TO 5
  R = -C/B
  WRITE (IOUT,4) R
4 FORMAT ('SINGLE ROOT' E20.7)
5 D = B**2-4*A*C
```

```
      X = -B/(2*A)
      Y = SQRT(ABS(D))/(2*A)
      IF (D.LT.O) GO TO 7
      R1 = X + Y
      R2 = X - Y
      WRITE (IOUT,6) R1,R2
  6   FORMAT ('REAL ROOTS' E20.7' AND' E20.7)
      STOP
  7   WRITE (IOUT,8) X,Y,X,Y,
  8   FORMAT ('COMPLEX ROOTS' E20.7'+I' E20.7' AND'
     1E20.7'-I'E20.7)
      STOP
      END
```

Note that we had said "might code the following." There are other ways the program could be coded which would be consistent with the flowchart. For example, just considering the sixth line through the last, they could have written the following:

```
      IF (A.EQ.O.AND.B.EQ.O) GO TO 2
          (main body of program)
  2   WRITE (IOUT,10)
 10   FORMAT ('NO SOLUTION')
      STOP
      END
```

It is not necessary to know FORTRAN to know that this code is not identical to the earlier one. It has been said many times that there are many ways to code a program, and this is certainly true. It is even true that there are many ways to code a program correctly. Unfortunately, there are also many ways to code a program incorrectly, but that is another matter. There are also many ways to design a program correctly. Programmers usually develop their own styles, representative of their analytic approaches to problems, and it is often possible, by inspection of the code, to determine who of the staff of programmers is the author of a program.

Nothing affects the appearance of a program as much as the language in which it is coded. The same quadratic equation problem can be coded in PASCAL as follows:

```
PROGRAM QUADRATIC (INPUT,OUTPUT);
    VAR
        A,B,C,D,X,Y : REAL;
    BEGIN
        READ (A,B,C);
```

```
IF (A = 0) AND B = 0)
  THEN WRITELN ('NO SOLUTION')
ELSE IF (A = 0)
  THEN WRITELN ('SINGLE ROOT', −C/B)
ELSE
  BEGIN
    D: = B**2−4*A*C;
    X: = −B/(2*A);
    Y: = SQRT(ABS(D))/(2*A);
    IF D ≥ 0
      THEN WRITELN ('REAL ROOTS', X + Y, 'AND', X − Y)
      ELSE WRITELN ('COMPLEX ROOTS', X, '+I', Y,'AND',X'−I',Y)
  END
END.
```

As different as the two programs may be, observe that the arithmetic operations are identical in both:

```
SQRT(ABS(D))/(2*A)
```

The rules for evaluating algebraic expressions are common to most of the compiler languages that commonly are used for scientific and mathematical application. The salient differences are found in the control structures (the means for branching, creating repetitive loops, and forming links between program units) and in the manner in which data are stored.

Compiler languages are a subset of the larger class *high order language*, usually abbreviated HOL. Other members of the class are program design languages, discussed in Part 3, and application languages. The last is a name given to a diverse group of languages employed by nonprogramming computer users. The following are examples of this group:

COGO   Solution of civil engineering problems

ATLAS   Programming of automatic test equipment

APT   Programming of automatic machine tools

GPSS   Simulation of systems of discrete events

The programs that implement the use of these languages permit the user to address a large number of problems in terms and concepts that are familiar to him. They can handle but a small fraction of all the problems that a more general compiler can. Since these tools are not used for the development and maintenance of computer software, we shall not deal further with them. We note their existence only because the term "high-order language" (HOL) is widely used at this time, often in the context of compiler languages, often in the full sense. It is yet another example of the ambiguous language peculiar to the software world.

From the term "high-order language." one might reasonably infer the existence of an opposite, "low-order language." There is, in fact, a term used to distinguish languages other than HOL, but it is more descriptive than "low-order language." Binary and assembler languages are frequently referred to as *machine-oriented languages*, or MOLs. The term implies the close relationship between a given MOL and the computer to which it is specific. COBOL compilers are available for many computer families, but each family has its own binary instruction set and corresponding assembler language.

SYSTEMS SOFTWARE

We have introduced assemblers, compilers, and interpreters as programs that, themselves, support the work of programmers. These language processors make coding, one of the noncreative tasks of program development, less tedious. Or to rephrase it, they are programming tools. There are other programs that support programmers. There are also programs that support computer operators. And there are programs that support computers themselves, in that they improve the efficiency with which computers can be used or extend the capabilities of the computer hardware. All of these programs are members of the class *systems software*. To describe the function of all members of the class would be well beyond the scope of this book. We shall, however, touch upon most of those that will enter into the discussions of subsequent chapters.

To introduce the next systems program, let us return to Figure 2-2 and the compilation process, only we shall replace the object code output of the compiler with assembler language statements. This may appear counterproductive, since previously we described the function of the compiler as the translation of compiler language source statements into code executable by the computer. Assembly language is not executable and must be processed by an assembler. Nevertheless, compilers are frequently designed to produce assembler, rather than binary, code output. Assembler output, even though it requires another processing step, can be helpful in locating the source of well-hidden bugs. Moreover, where concern for code efficiency is paramount, the assembler output can be modified ("hand-optimized") to eliminate some of the inefficiencies introduced by compilers. Thus, it is not at all uncommon for compilers to generate assembler code, and since it suits our immediate purposes, we shall assume that the compiler at hand will do so.

We need further definition of the computing environment. We shall configure the system with a cathode ray tube (CRT) output device, a printer, a disk storage device, and an alphanumeric keyboard. There may be other peripheral devices connected to the computer, but they are irrelevant. Let us now consider the steps required, using the FORTRAN program listed earlier, to find the roots of a quadratic equation.

1. At the computer panel, Carol, the programmer, operates binary switches *(toggles)* to transfer *(load)* from a disk file to the computer's memory a program that will accept characters from the keyboard and store them on disk.

2. Carol presses "GO" and enters the FORTRAN language root-solving program from the keyboard.

3. Carol next toggles binary instructions to load the FORTRAN compiler from disk. (Note: language processors are most often divided into several distinct phases, each of which would have to be treated as a separate program. Compassionately, we spare Carol this further complication.)

4. Carol then toggles the addresses of the input file (first location on disk where her input statements were stored) and the output file (first location on disk for receiving compiler output).

5. Carol presses "GO."

6. The compiler processes the input statements and generates an output file of equivalent assembly language statements.

7. Carol now toggles binary instructions to load the assembler from disk.

8. She next toggles the addresses of the input file (file on disk just generated by the compiler) and output file (first location on disk for receiving object code).

9. Carol presses "GO."

10. The computer assembles the program, generating object code in the prescribed area of disk.

11. Carol toggles binary instructions to load the object code from disk.

12. She presses "GO."

13. At the keyboard, she now enters the coefficients A, B, and C.

14. The computer executes the program within one second, displaying an incorrect pair of roots, attributable, as it turns out, to Carol's having entered a "*" instead of a "/" back in step 2.

There must be easier ways to get a wrong answer. The above is, at best, cumbersome; at worst, unproductive. Would it not be far more efficient if there were in the computer a program monitoring the entire process, automatically calling in programs from disk as needed, and assigning addresses on disk prior to the operation of each program? Given such a program, Carol, after typing her program, would need only to type a short command instructing the computer to perform steps 3 through 12. Moreover, step 1 could be replaced by another short keyboard command. To the relief of Carols everywhere, there is such a program: it is called a *monitor*, or occasionally, a *run-time supervisor*. In addition to the functions just enumerated, a monitor also performs such fairly pedestrian tasks as assigning available peripheral devices (tape drives, multiple disk drives, etc.) and performing machine use tabulations.

For computer systems containing a number of hardware and software components, the modern monitor has evolved into the manager of system resources; is, itself, fragmented into a number of parts, few of which are in internal memory at any one time. Curiously, the power of the modern software supervisory system is so great that it renders the computer hardware all but invisible to the programmers. That is, they "play" to the software of the system rather than to the hardware. This is reflected in the name that has become attached to these software systems: *operating systems*.

To programmers, the set of available systems software represents the kit of tools with which to build and test programs. Next to language processors and monitors, the *link editor*, or *linking loader*, is the tool most likely reached for. Programs are often divided into several parts. There are a number of reasons for this, some of which have a direct bearing on software quality, but for the present we shall consider only one. If a change needs to be made to a program, especially if the change is for the purpose of removing one of the many bugs (errors) that will be found during the programmers's own test processes, it is far less time-consuming to be able to revise and reassemble or recompile only a portion of the entire program, rather than the whole. Thus, if for no other reason, programmers, knowing in advance that at debugging time they will be impatient to see if each fix works, segment the program into separate *routines*. These segments are defined in formal ways that allow them to be combined for execution. Within the semantic rules of compiler languages, there are several such types. Among the names they are given are *procedure, subroutine, function*, and even *program*, each defining a specific protocol for the binding of the routine with others. The operation of combining the various routines which constitute an executable program load is the role of the link editor.

The programmers may even require the services of a link editor when they haven't segmented their programs. In our earlier examples of programs for finding the roots of a quadratic equation, both the FORTRAN and PASCAL versions included the high-level instruction SQRT. For compilation on computers that do not have square root instructions, the compiler will, upon encountering SQRT instructions, generate a transfer to a software square root routine included in the FORTRAN or PASCAL *LIBRARY* of routines. At *load time*, the link editor will see to it that the square root routine gets loaded in the computer with the (binary code) quadratic-root-solving program, and will replace, with the actual address of where it loaded SQRT, the symbolic transfer generated by the compiler.

Compiler libraries, in addition to SQRT, will contain other functions. Typical of these are the following:

- Trigonometric functions

- Finding the remainder of one number divided by another

- Forming the absolute value of a number, which, as ABS, we also used in the examples

Programming staffs will further develop their own libraries of those routines commonly used in their applications. If the root-solving program were written as a FORTRAN subroutine, to be called upon by programs requiring the roots of quadratic equations, it could be coded in this manner:

```
      SUBROUTINE QUADRATIC (A,B,C,X1,X2,Y,K)
   COMMENT:   K = 0 FOR NO SOLUTION, = 1 FOR SINGLE ROOT, = 2 FOR
   C               REAL ROOTS, = 3 FOR COMPLEX ROOTS.
      K = 0
      IF (A.EQ.O.AND.B.EQ.O) RETURN
      IF (A.NE.O) GO TO 1
      K = 1
      X1 = −C/B
      RETURN
    1 D = B**2−4*A*C
      X = −B/(2*A)
      Y = SQRT(ABS(D))/(2*A)
      IF (D.LT.O) GO TO 2
      K = 2
      X1 = X + Y
      X2 = X − Y
      RETURN
    2 K = 3
      X1 = X
      X2 = X
      RETURN
      END
```

The string of identifiers, or *arguments*, in the first line includes the coefficients of the quadratic equation, which are input to the subroutine, the values X1, X2, and Y, which are returned by the subroutine, and a *program flag*, K, which is computed by the subroutine and returned so that the calling program can interpret the result. The explanation of the flag can be found in the *comment* statement included in the code. Comments are nonexecutable statements included in code to assist programmers in their understanding of code written by other programmers, or to jog the memory of programmers reading their own code weeks after writing it.

In this example of a subroutine, we see that the statements that perform the actual computations are the same as in the earlier case. It is in the "housekeeping" statements and the logical flow that we see differences. Recall the earlier remark that there are many correct ways to write a program. We might qualify that to add that the choice of how to write a program is influenced by the form of the program.

In introducing the subroutine as an illustration of the role performed by the link editor, we seem to have digressed from the subject of systems software. Not entirely. Systems software, like any large programming systems, are built up of many subroutines, procedures, or other subprograms. More important, the sum of systems software is constituted of a number of individual executable programs. To a large extent, only those routines required for the task at hand (e.g., link editing or a specific compilation phase) are loaded in the computer memory; the balance remain on disk awaiting the supervisor's call to action. In this respect, systems software differs from the majority of programs. Most nonsystems programs, especially embedded programs, are fully resident in memory.

Having just returned from a digression, we digress again. Computers, internally, are extremely fast devices, executing instructions in a matter of microseconds. The devices attached to computers are, however, much slower, as illustrated by the following table, which lists typical operating times for some of the common peripheral functions.

Operation	Time, ms
Print a single line	60
Read a card	100
Reposition a disk read-write head	40
Allow disk to rotate into position	10
Move magnetic tape to next record	60

It is patently wasteful to allow a computer to remain idle during the 60 milliseconds the magnetic tape unit may take to fetch more input data, when, during that time, the computer has the capacity for performing 20,000 additions. Let's imagine, though, that there were two separate programs, each in its own *partition* of the computer memory. Further, that while one program waits for more input data from the magnetic tape unit, the other program has control of the arithmetic, logic, and control circuitry and continues to grind away at its task. Program TWO, finally having arrived at an intermediate result, now outputs it to the printer and prepares to settle down for a 60-millisecond wait. By this time, however, the magnetic tape unit has input the requested data to the computer for the first program's consideration, and program ONE regains control of the computer circuits. Suppose, though, that the magnetic tape unit had not yet transferred the data. Then we should want a third program to take over control. Perhaps we can best utilize the computer if we had 20 or more programs, each operating in its own partition.

Such is the reasoning behind *multiprogramming*. By making use of the natural "waits" imposed by peripheral devices, it is possible to effect what appears to be the simultaneous execution of several programs. To implement multiprogramming, a special kind of traffic policeman is needed to keep things straight and to make certain that programs don't contend with each other. Not surprisingly, this is an easier matter for software than for hardware; hence, multiprogramming operating systems.

One might wonder how much internal (real) memory is required to support, say, 20 programs. If a few of them are on the order of 100,000 bytes of storage, quite a bit is required. It is time to take another view of what we mean by memory.

Earlier, we had defined internal memory as that which can be directly addressed by a program, thereby placing it in opposition to memory (tape, disk, etc.) that is accessed through an input-output channel. To say of a program that it requires 100,000 bytes of storage really means that the program and the data it will attempt to address total 100,000 bytes. Addressing is the key, not the form of memory. External memories generally have great capacity at low cost per unit of storage. By supplementing real internal storage in a manner invisible to the programmer, the effect of a directly addressable space much larger then actually exists may be created. This is the concept behind *virtual storage*.

In a virtual storage scheme, all of the program resides in an external memory, typically disk. In a multiprogramming system, which, for practical purposes, is the manner in which virtual storage is actually implemented, all of the several programs are on disk. The program, or programs, are divided into "pages" of a few thousand bytes of storage each. One or more of the pages of each program may also be in real storage. Each time a given program location is to be accessed, the system looks to see if it is in real memory or not. If not, an address translation is performed and the disk address of the appropriate page is determined. The entire page is then transferred, via a high speed port, into real memory where it overwrites a previously transferred page. The actual addresses within a page in real memory are provided by the system. Program addresses are virtual.

Thus, in a multiprogramming virtual system with 1 million bytes of real memory, four jobs, each requiring 0.5 million bytes of storage, can run at one time.

Going a bit further, it need not only be application programs that are run from virtual memory. Operating systems also can be stored "in virtual" and brought in, page by page, as required. It then becomes feasible to run two or more operating systems at one time. If all of this esoteric systems software is beginning to get bewildering, two operating systems may seem too much of a good thing. However, an operating system can best serve the user when it is designed for the environment in which it is used. To take but two examples, the mode of operation for general ledger and end-of-the-week fiscal reports differs radically from that of the interactive scientific milieu. We have stated before that with powerful operating systems, programmers are more aware of the characteristics of the systems software than of the hardware. It should not be too surprising that the generic name given to the concurrent operation of multiple software systems is *virtual machine software.*

The concept of virtual machinery is unreal in more than the sense of a pun. To development programmers, reality is found in the communication, whether offline or online, that they have with the operating system. They refer to the operating system by name (e.g., "CMS") and give it anthropomorphic attributes: "Hey Mary, CMS is asking me where I placed the action file. Why the hell should I care?" We have actually heard a programmer, upon discovery that a latent defect in the system had caused a wasted day of fruitless and frustrating pursuit of what appeared to be a bug in the programmer's own program, say, "If I can't trust the system, who can I trust?"

With virtual machines we seem to have come a long way from the assemblers with which this discussion started. Both fall under the heading of systems software: software associated with a computing system to the purpose of improving productivity and efficiency. In addition to the few examples given here, there are compilers that partially write new compilers, programs that measure the performance of computer systems, and others. Of the "others" there are programs specific to the cause of software quality. We shall turn to these later on.

It must be recognized that not all computer software is developed on virtual machines, or even under multiprogramming, or even in compiler langauage. As there are many hardware environments for software development, so are there many software environments. The people who develop software are not all of a kind, nor are the management strategies under which they work. Software is built in many ways: some tied to the characteristics and application of the software being developed, some to historical origins, and, to an astonishing extent, some to chance.

SUMMARY

1. Computers do no work of any kind until their electronic circuits are pro-grammed to follow a specific sequence of operations. The number system of computer circuits and memory devices is binary, reflecting the several bistable devices usable for computer hardware.

2. Computer programs consist of sequences of instructions. Instructions have several parts, each coded in binary digits.

3. Since long sequences of binary instructions are difficult for programmers to form correctly, assembler languages for programming came into being. These allow the use of alphanumeric mnemonics for instructions and the naming of the data operated on. Assembler (or assembly) languages must be translated into binary code by programs called assemblers.

4. Compiler languages are one step further from binary, but closer to that of the problem being solved. In terms of programming effort, it is much more efficient to program in compiler languages. Also, preparing programs in compiler code is a less error-prone way of writing programs. To be executed in a computer, such programs must be translated by programs called compilers.

5. Regardless of the language used, code is but the implementation of a design. The basic design documentation in most common use is the flowchart.

6. Programs that are used to support the process of programming or the oper-ation of a computer system are the constituent parts of what is called sys-tems software.

7. Programs usually comprise a set of individual routines. These are bound together in the form of an executable program by a program called a link editor.

8. Monitors, or run-time supervisors, are programs that aid in scheduling the use of system resources (e.g., magnetic tape units) and system programs (e.g., compilers) so that a multiphase sequence of processes required to per-form a computational job can be run efficiently and with less opportunity for error. The more capable of these programs are given the generic name "operating systems."

9. To minimize the loss of computational power during those milliseconds when the computer is communicating with peripheral devices, multipro-gramming operating systems allow several programs to share the system; while one waits to be serviced by external equipment, another grabs hold of the arithmetic and logic circuits.

10. A virtual system provides addressable memory space beyond the capacity of a computer's real memory. The virtual addresses refer to locations on an external device (e.g., disk), totaling several times the size of real memory. The programs so stored may even include multiprogramming operating systems.

11. The power of modern operating systems is such that the environment of software development is often established less by the system's hardware than by the system's software.

REFERENCES

1. *FORTRAN, DoD Supplement to American National Standard X3.9-1978*, MIL-STD-1753, 1978.

2. Jean E. Sammet, *Programming Languages: History and Fundamentals*, Prentice-Hall, Englewood Cliffs, N.J., 1969.

Chapter 3

The Life Cycle of Software

In the last chapter we discussed the preparation of a program to find the roots of a quadratic equation. If there were distinctions between "concept," "requirements definition," and "design," they were blurred by the small effort required for each. Of programs of that size, indeed of tenfold that number of statements, one speaks of the "writing" of programs, not of formal development processes. The specifics of how the program will be used are obvious, the requirements are tacit within the context of the program's use, and the design is but a few minutes — or at the most, hours — of analysis and thought. Moreover, some design probably will overlap into the writing of code. If the program is to be used by no one other than its author, testing will be highly informal, consisting of one or two test cases for which the answers are easily arrived at without the use of a computer.

Even within a larger reference, it may be appropriate to speak of a program's having been written, rather than developed. Consider Sam, who needs a program to solve a system of linear algebraic equations. He knows how to solve them, may even know how to program the solution, but doesn't have the time to do the job himself. It is necessary for Sam to have someone else do the programming. The conceptual work has already been done, Sam previously having arrived at the system of equations as the model for scheduling the use of his company's manufacturing equipment, but now he has to write a brief specification for the performance of the program he wants. In the specification he defines the maximum number of equations, the fact that they are linear, how he will want to input the coefficients of the variables, and the accuracy he requires.

Sam gives the specification to Nancy, who now analyzes it. Nancy researches the several methods (triangular elimination, Gauss-Seidel, etc.) for their applicability in terms of computation time and accuracy. She recognizes the program must test for independence among the equations. She has to choose formats (integer, floating point, single or multiple precision) for the coefficients and variables that are appropriate to their numeric range and the required accuracies. She also thinks hard about an easy way to enter the coefficients, and arrives at a method she believes will minimize the likelihood of incorrect data entry. She then proceeds to translate the selected method of solution into an algorithm, incorporating logic for trapping outrageously incorrect input data and dependent conditions which would preclude a solution. For her own convenience, Nancy sets down the algorithm in the form of a flowchart, one of several methods she's familiar with. With this design in front of her, she fills several pages of a coding pad with the statements that will implement the design. These are entered into the computer and compiled. As Nancy expected, the compiler tells her of several errors she had made, either in writing code or in entering it, that made it impossible for the compiler to correctly process the program. These are quickly fixed. After successfully compiling the program and testing it to her own satisfaction, using test cases that she was reasonably certain would encompass the range of data, she turns the program over to Sam with an explanation of how it may be used.

Sam's approach to the scheduling problem is, with Nancy's help, so successful that he is promoted to chief corporate analyst. His first assignment in his new position is to assess the company's strategies for marketing penetration. After some research, he discovers that the strategies in use are based solely on a single set of premises about the plans of the several competitors, with no thought given to the responses that might be appropriate to other possible, if less likely, competition moves. An inveterate card player, Sam realizes he is in an N-player game, and remembers having once read about a theory of games which could be applied to economic behavior. For all his talents, mathematics of this kind is not Sam's long suit. However, he discovers that two fellows in the management information systems department do know something about it. John and Oskar now set out to find a way to model the competitive environment, using gaming strategies along the guidelines stipulated by Sam.

In time they arrive at a conceptual approach, which, of course, will require a new computer program. John and Oskar now are the ones to write a software requirements specification, which Sam, as their "customer," reviews. This is a larger software problem than the last one Sam was concerned with, and it is not only Nancy, but three of her associates as well who are assigned to implement the specification. When they are ready, the program prepared by the four is tested twice, once to their satisfaction and again against test cases submitted by John and Oskar. Still more work remains: program development of this magnitude represents a considerable capital investment, the kind that is made in the expectation of recurring return, with the consequence that the documentation prepared by the programmers is more formal, better suited to the purpose of making future changes.

The program to find the solution of the system of linear equations, like that for the quadratic equation, was "written." It was informally introduced to the programmers, and its potential use was limited. The programmer was able to complete the task without coordination with other people, and any problems inherent in the program were expected to manifest themselves quickly. The gaming problem represents a program that was *developed*. It involved three tiers of persons concerned with the program, coordination within two of those levels, and a likelihood of much future use.

Another way to view software development is to evolve it from the quintessential code and debug to a full project status. Accordingly, we first define *programming* as the translation of an algorithm (or procedure) from natural or mathematical language or a diagram into computer language, and the process of then making the translation work. We now incorporate programming in the definition of *program development*, which we define as determining the algorithm and programming it. Finally, we have *software development:*

- Analysis of the role to be performed by the program (concept)

- Program development

- Evaluation of the program against the role conceived in the first step

- Documentation sufficient for the users' needs and for maintenance throughout the life cycle

For programs that are "written," there is little interest in software quality assurance. The interest of a few people and little investment is involved. Problems will attract attention before creating serious consequences and will easily be solved. Code death will occur shortly after birth.

It is programs spawned by software development that are our concern, and, while each is different, the various phases of their life cycles have much in common. It is customary for the several phases of the life cycle of software to be depicted by a "waterfall" chart. Unfortunately, there is no agreement on how to divide the life cycle into discrete phases. To the extent possible, Figure 3-1 reflects a composite of those most prominently published.

In describing these phases, we shall attempt to define them in the most general terms of what is commonly considered good software practice. We shall, however, touch but lightly on why these represent good practice, and not at all on those techniques for implementing each phase that deliberately reflects the quality precepts of conformance to requirements and prevention of defects. These, along with the role played by the quality organization, we leave for Chapters 5 to 9. For the present, we are content to acquaint the reader of little software background with the chain of events associated with the life cycle of software.

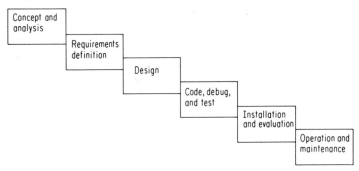

FIGURE 3-1   Software Life Cycle.

CONCEPT AND ANALYSIS

Certain problems are obvious candidates for solution by computation, and by well-established techniques at that: payroll, mailing lists, and inventory control are among those that come to mind immediately. Others are less obvious. Sam's marketing strategy assignment, improving the image of a dull photograph, and operating an urban rail transit car are representative. That a computer will be used for a member of this last group implies that an analysis of the overall problem was made, a role for the computer was established, and, in many cases, the functions of other elements of the solution (sensors, controls, people) were determined. Conceptually, the assignment to a computer of a system task or group of tasks may be reached without much understanding of how the assignment will be executed: "It seems reasonable to leave this to a computer"; "This sort of thing has been done by computers before"; "It will boil down to a lot of arithmetic"; and so forth. Analysis is required to verify that the use of a computer is a well-considered one, and to determine just how the computer will be employed.

Analysis can take many forms and extend to many depths. For Sam's problem, analysis was mostly a matter of researching the current marketing position and determining the kernel common to all the strategies; then reading as much as he could about game theory. The program itself was the analysis tool that would prove the feasibility of the approach. The final system included both the program and Sam, using it interactively with various input data sets.

Consider, though, a large telephone system requiring a discrete set of traffic handling strategies to permit automatic rerouting of excessive loads between cities. If the concept is to embed these strategies in a computer equipped with online control of the telephone switches, one had best consider simulating them in an offline mode well before continuing the development cycle. A telephone traffic program is going to be a large one, a costly one, and one that must serve a large public. One scarcely wants to wait until test or evaluation to discover that the selected method is inadequate. Therefore, it is customary to carefully simulate the effect of the processing rules that will ultimately be programmed, and to analyze the results of the simulations.

Although the simulations will themselves be performed in a computer, the simulation program can be much more modest than the final, operational program. It is not necessary to program each processing algorithm in detail (indeed, many will not even be known at simulation time), but simply the effects that the key parts of the program are expected to produce. Also, there is no need to work out the details of the interface between the computer and the rest of the system. It is sufficient to assert that status messages will arrive at a given rate and that external switches will respond to commands from the computer.

Once the computational task has been determined, it may be necessary to ascertain the amount of computer power that will be required. Obviously, this is not the case if the company's powerful mainframe computer is available and the problem to be solved is patently simple. However, if the problem is of a magnitude significantly greater than is customary, analysis of machine requirements is called for. For embedded applications, this analysis is almost always a must. The computer (or computers) to be used will be dedicated to the task, and one wants to specify hardware appropriate to the job, as best it can be sized at this early stage. The analyses must take into account memory, input-output, and computational speed requirements. Since the last two of these are a function of machine architecture, and since there is so great a variety of architectures now available, doing the job properly is no small matter. Also, there may be constraints of weight, power and heat dissipation, space, and the physical environment in which the processor must operate. Finally, if there is a decided preference for a specific programming language, the availability of a suitable compiler or cross-compiler must be considered.

REQUIREMENTS DEFINITION

Once the computational task is roughly defined and the methods generally understood, it is necessary to precisely specify what the program or programs are to do. That is, further *system-level* design must be performed, with a software requirements document as the tangible output. In the commercial and, to a large extent, systems software milieu this is normally attended to by *system analysts*. Their role is not to write code, but to specify what the code is to accomplish. For embedded applications, the requirements document is prepared by the same *system engineers* who also specify each of the other elements of the system. That is, they will have already roughly determined the function to be performed by each part of the system, including the computer, and now they must prepare detailed specifications for these functions.

The line between "requirements" and "design" is not easily drawn. One wants to draw an analogy to hardware, where one can say of an electronic amplifier that, given a stipulated input voltage, it must produce a certain output level at a specified maximum amount of distortion. How the amplifier is to perform its function need never enter into the specification. And, indeed, for many computer programs it is possible to state in the most specific of terms what it is that needs to be done without saying how the program is to be designed. Where we encounter trouble is where only the system designers understand the processing method that will produce the desired result. Here, the system designers must specify, in addition to input-transform-output, the very means of effecting the transformation.

A scientist, examining a dull photograph through a microscope, observes certain correlative properties and develops a mathematical technique for capitalizing on these to enhance the photograph. She then conceives of an electro-optical system to directly enter the quantified fine-grained structure into a computer for processing by the technique she developed. The software requirements specification she prepares will specify input-transform-output, but the transformation cannot simply be named; she must supply details of the method as well, since only she knows it. Yet, is not the method part of the design?

The kernel of the concept we are dealing with is the separation of system design from program design. We want the requirements for the program design clearly documented so that programming personnel will understand what it is they must do. From a practical point of view, if these requirements stipulate method as well as input-transform-output, no harm has been done, provided that those who specify are in the best position to do so. Where management plans break down is where the specification of software requirements reaches beyond the expertise of those preparing it into software matters better left to the discretion of software professionals. Thus we arrive at the following axiom:

> To the extent practicable, the specification says *what* is to be done, and the subsequent design documentation says *how* it will be done.

The rule serves yet another purpose. One use made of the specification, perhaps the most important from the aspects of software quality assurance, derives from its representation of tangible evidence that further software development effort will have direction. If a specification cannot be produced, further investment is obviously unwarranted. Thus, the specification, regardless of who produced it, can be the basis for a management decision, and the less design effort it contains the more timely that decision will be.

DESIGN

Software design is the name given to the set of activities that determine how the requirements will be implemented. Software design starts with an analysis of the requirements to identify any critical elements in the specification, and promising approaches to these are worked out. The various aspects of the requirements are then translated into standard software forms in the *top-level design*. The design is then further developed to the point where it can be implemented in code in the *detailed design* phase.

Top-Level Design

Personal Processor Power (PPP) is a manufacturer of home computers. With each computer sold, PPP delivers a simple operating system, an assembler, and a compiler that can process a small subset of the PL/1 language. PPP doesn't really expect the purchasers of its equipment to do much programming on their own. Rather, PPP's marketing approach is to offer a number of applications programs for which it charges high prices. PPP's technique is not quite to "give away the razor to sell the blades," but by continually adding to the list of applications it can develop each computer purchaser into a source of recurring revenue. Typical of these program products are

- Checking account reconciliation

- Bill-paying optimization tactics

- Christmas card address generator (outputs onto gummed labels)

- Pantry inventory control

- IRS 1040

The marketing department, on the basis of a nationwide survey, advises PPP to invest in an applications package to allow lonely customers to play games with their computer. The project is approved, and the product development department is given the task and funding to produce a program that will, at the user's discretion, play backgammon, bridge, or craps.

The product analysts draft a requirements specification describing the general rules for the displays it wants to see on the CRT, the techniques for human-computer interaction it believes will best simulate real-world game play, and, under the "applicable documents" paragraph of the specification, lists Hoyle as the source for the rules of the games.

The specification is, in effect, the work order for the software design group of the product development department. Their first impression of the specification is that the work to be done is too much for one person to accomplish if the program is to be ready in time to meet the marketing department's goal of the holiday season. They divide it into three major sections, each corresponding to one of the games, and add a fourth section, Executive Control, to do little more than offer the player a choice of games and provide a means of storing the status of any game if play has to be interrupted. As simple as Executive Control is, the other three sections are subordinate to it; a diagram of the first cut (or zeroth iteration) of the program hierarchy appears in Figure 3–2.

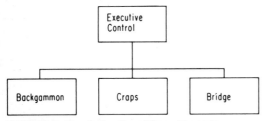

FIGURE 3-2   Zeroth Iteration of Game Hierarchy.

The top design team now analyzes each of the three main sections. Craps, they believe, will be a fairly modest program, and needs no further thought until they are ready for detailed design. Backgammon and Bridge, on the other hand, seem much more formidable. Adopting the tactic of divide and conquer, they proceed to decompose these two games into compartmented processes or segments. This allows each of these games to be handled not as a single, seemingly insurmountable problem, but as the aggregate of several smaller ones. The result is seen in Figure 3-3.

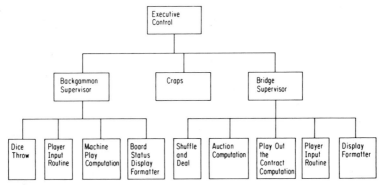

FIGURE 3-3   First Iteration of Game Hierarchy.

Here, we see the game of backgammon, as it will be implemented for a computer, divided into four separate parts: a routine to simulate the throw of dice, a routine to input the player's choice of the moves that can be made with his simulated throw of the dice, software to determine the computer's best play based on its simulated throw of the dice, and a section to display the current game status on the CRT. The four parts are not of equal magnitude in regard to programming difficulty or (anticipated) size, but, as viewed by the designers, they are of equal hierarchical rank.

Similarly, Bridge has been decomposed into five parts. Shuffle and Deal will be used to initialize each hand. Auction Computation will have to bid for three of the chairs at the table, including the human player's simulated partner. Once bidding has closed, the computer will have to be equipped either to play declarer and one of the defenders, both of the defenders, or declarer and both of the defenders. This last implies that the human player's partner has won the auction, with the result that the human player will be dummy to three computer-simulated players. In their conceptual study, the product analysts had given the merit of this considerable thought. They finally decided that a public accustomed to being told "The computer won't be able to correct the error in your balance for another month; I'll see if I can get the collection agency to ignore what the computer says" is ready to sit out a hand and let the computer have go at it. Thus, the computer will have to play a variety of roles after bidding has closed and the contract is to be played out.

Finally, there must be a way to input the player's bids and choice of cards to be played, and a display for showing each bid, the player's hand as dealt and as diminished during play, dummy, and the cards played each trick by the other "players."

At this point, the game problem has given way to a dozen or so smaller ones, but two of them, Machine Play Computation and Play Out the Contract Computation are still too complex to be grasped with a certitude sufficient to allow detailed design to proceed. A further decomposition to the next hierarchical level is required, leading to the diagram of Figure 3-4.

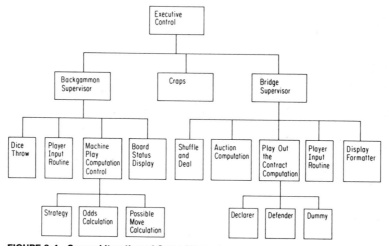

FIGURE 3-4 Second Iteration of Game Hierarchy.

Let us assume that with this second iteration, the top-level designers have decided that the principal parts of the program have been defined adequately for the purpose of those programmers who will design in detail each *module*, as we shall henceforth call each box depicted on a hierarchical diagram. However, the top-level designers are not yet finished. The modules have been identified, but as part of the top-level design a specification is required for each. The detailers need more than just a name; they must be told precisely what each module is to do. There will also be data that must be accessible to more than one module. For Backgammon, several modules will require knowledge of where on the board the pieces are. For Bridge, several modules will need to know what the contract is. Thus, the top-level design must also include a data base design to permit all of the programmers to work to the same rules regarding the manner in which data are to be stored.

As they continue to work with the temporarily frozen hierarchical design, the design team notes a reqirement common to all three games. To Throw the Dice for either Backgammon or Craps, or to Shuffle the Cards for Bridge, a software generator of random numbers is required. The designers decide to make this a *utility* module, available as a procedure or subroutine call, as was the last version (in Chapter 2) of the program to find the roots of a quadratic equation. Utilities have no hierarchical position, but they are identified at top-level design time, since they are part of the total software system. Moreover, the programming of them is part of the total development effort that is reestimated in this phase.

We shall find it necessary in later pages to refer to specific levels, or tiers, of program hierarchies. Unfortunately, there is no standard software nomenclature for these. For the purposes of this book, we shall, by our own fiat, limit all hierarchies to four tiers, and shall label them as given in Figure 3-5. The term "module" shall refer to any division, component, or element. It shall also apply to the top-module, which, to conform with some operating systems may bear the name of the entire program, but will often be known to the programmers by a title descriptive of its principal function, control.

Another result of the hierarchical decomposition is the division of the program into pieces so independent of each other that a sizable group of programmers can be applied to the further development work. This is a way of achieving schedule goals. Unfortunately, there seem to be definite limits to the number of programmers that can work on one project before a further increase in the number becomes counterproductive. We shall return to this in Part 3. To a large extent though, the breakdown of the large program into small ones is software's answer to Adam Smith's division of labor, and, except in the rare instances where the chief programmer team[1,2] concept is implemented, is the technique used to produce programs while they are still needed.

Other output of the top-level design effort includes an estimate of the memory required for each identified module (notwithstanding the likelihood that further decomposition of some modules will occur during detailed design); an estimate of execution time (machine-loading) for critical operations; an estimate of execution time by module, if applicable; and, possibly, further amplification of the program control method if this is not implicit in the specifications of the control modules.

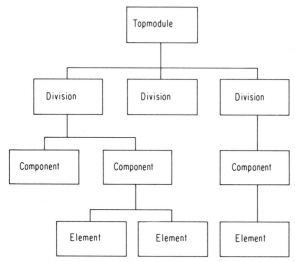

FIGURE 3-5   Labeling of Hierarchial Tiers.

A final word on the documentation of the top-level design: considering this phase as the transfer of the attack of a large problem into a set of attacks on small, more manageable problems, the documentation represents the mapping of that transfer. There are many techniques for documenting the overall design. The valid ones reflect this underlying purpose.

Detailed Design

Each of the PPP programmers assigned to a module or group of modules begins his detailed design by studying the top-level design documentation relevant to the module he is working with. Some of the programmers were members of the top-level design team, while others are new to the project. After each feels confident he understands what the module is supposed to do and how it will fit in with the other parts of the program, he, like Melvin, who has been assigned the programming of Craps, proceeds to continue the decomposition process.

Had Melvin thought that Craps was complex enough to warrant it, he might have further decomposed the modules into smaller ones. Mel likes to work with smallish amounts of code, say 200 or fewer source statements, at a time. During his debugging phase, working with modules of that size, he will seldom have to work with more than three sheets of program listings. Moreover, when making a change in the code, rather than having to recompile all the code he will have produced, he will be able to recompile only a part, since there is no need to recompile unaltered modules.

However, Mel was confident that Craps was of small enough scope that it ought to remain a single module. Even so, as he produces his detailed design, it is yet another process of decomposition; this time with a logic flowchart* as the principal representation of his design.

The specification for Craps had called for the computer to represent the house, and the player to be the only bettor. He will always roll against the house. After his first roll, if neither craps nor a natural, the player is to be given the opportunity to place a second bet behind the line. The odds for each point the player rolls for have been stipulated (2 to 1 for a 4 point or a 10 point etc.); 2, 3, and 12 have been identified as the craps numbers; and 7 and 11 as the naturals. The specification also calls for the player, on starting the game, to input the size of the bankroll he wishes to play with. Should he go broke, he will not be permitted credit. The house is to have unlimited ability to pay off, so that regardless of the length of the player's runs of good luck, there will be no need to terminate his fantasy.

In his first decomposition of Craps, Mel comes up with an almost trivial model of the program he will code. Figure 3-6 shows only three elements† of the program, and a symbol representing the return to Executive Control.

Initialize represents input of the starting bankroll, and, based on that number, a simple calculation of the starting cue for the utility routine that generates random numbers. Mel doesn't believe further decomposition of the Initialize box is needed. That is, he plans to give it no more thought before he actually codes it.

Again simply means that if the bankroll has gone negative, the game terminates with a suitable message (e.g., "Okay Big Spender, move over for the next guy."); or, if the player has tired of the game, he is given the option of quitting. Again, Mel feels no further design effort is appropriate.

Shoot One Round and Adjust Bankroll, obviously the heart of the program, does require further decomposition. Mel expands it into the diagram of Figure 3-7.

Here, all but the first action, Enter Bet, require even further logical decomposition, resulting in Figures 3-8 through 3-11, each corresponding to one of the remaining four symbols of Figure 3-7.

When Mel puts them all together, he has the complete flowchart shown in Figure 3-12.

---

*The use of flowcharts here as the means of conveying design conclusions is an admission of the overwhelmingly common practice; not an endorsement of the technique. More, in Chapter 5.

†Diamond, or lozenge, shapes enclose conditions for program branches.

Mel's design documentation consisted of more than just the flowcharts. There was also his collection of notes, which for this simple a problem consisted mostly of definitions of the terms found in the flowcharts. One note, however, reflected the one mathematical analysis that Mel had needed for Craps.

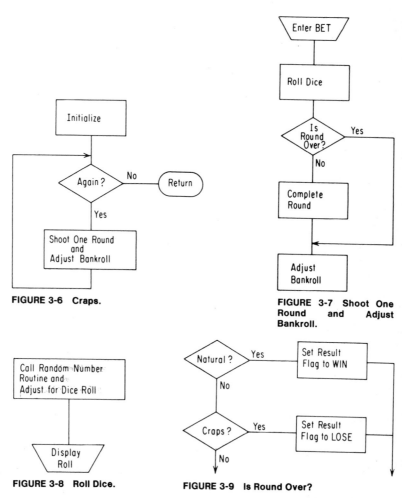

FIGURE 3-6   Craps.

FIGURE 3-7   Shoot One Round   and   Adjust Bankroll.

FIGURE 3-8   Roll Dice.

FIGURE 3-9   Is Round Over?

The specification for the random number utility routine had stipulated the range of the random function to be 1 to 32,767. Mel knew that he couldn't simply divide the range into 11 equal parts to obtain the 11 possible rolls of a pair of dice. The fact that 11 doesn't quite divide evenly into the range was less troublesome to Mel than his recognition that this simplistic method would weight equally the probability of all the rolls between 2 and 12. The obvious solution was to call for two random numbers, each time dividing the range into six parts to obtain the face number of each die separately, and then to add the two numbers. This would simulate the physical world, in which the odds of attaining a given dice roll are a function of the independent behavior of each die.

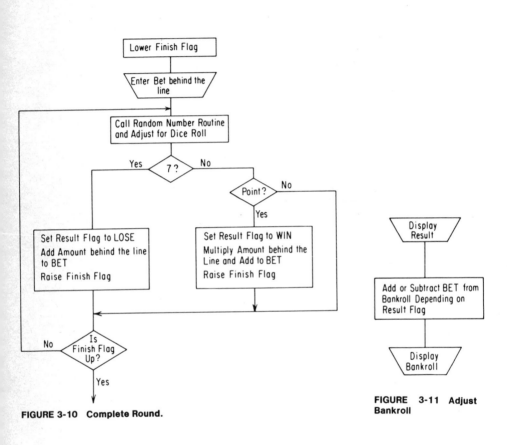

FIGURE 3-10 Complete Round.

FIGURE 3-11 Adjust Bankroll

It remained for Mel to estimate the error in his dice roll method. Since the range of the random number generator could not be divided evenly into six parts, the dice were loaded. Accordingly, Mel's documentation included his calculation of the probability of achieving each of the 11 rolls. Thus, the programming art imitating life.

Also, as part of his documentation, Mel thought it would be appropriate to sketch the displays he would provide, partly as a guide to himself during the coding phase, and partly because he expected to have that part of his design reviewed by PPP's consultant on human-machine communications.

The last item in Mel's detailed design documentation was prepared only

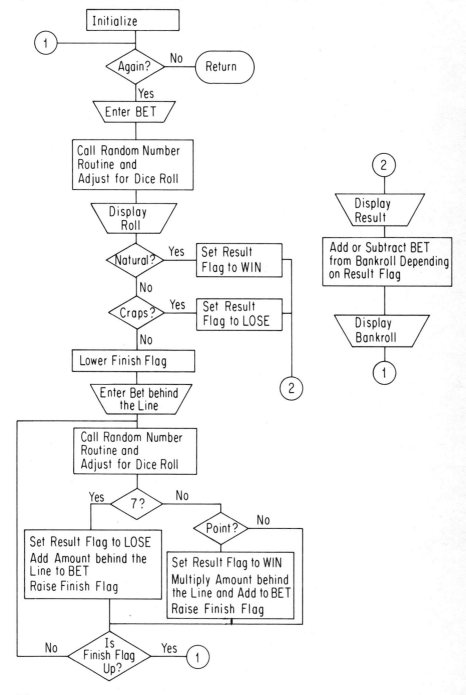

FIGURE 3-12 Craps Flowchart.

after the design was completed. This was an update of the amount of memory required by Craps. Mel did not update the execution time estimate, since this was of no consequence.

CODE, DEBUG, AND TEST

In a sense, coding is the most prominent phase of software development, generating the first output that is unique to computer software. The analysis phase is common to any development effort, hardware or software, and top-level design is patently analogous to the "black-box" design phase of systems engineering. Even for detailed design we can find patterns outside of computation: the schematic and logic diagrams of electronic engineering, or the process of determining the best method of extracting the meat from a 4-lb lobster.

Also, for the small programs that we exclude from our concern, but with which management personnel may be familiar from data processing seminars they have attended, code is often the first tangible evidence that any programming work has been accomplished.

It is unfortunate that code generation is so prominent. The effort that goes into coding is a relatively small percentage of the total spent on software development, especially when a compiler language is used. Yet management, in its search for reassurance that things are going well, is often impatient to see code, with the frequent consequence that software developers start writing code before the design has been fully worked out.

Code is usually written by the programmers who performed the detailed design that the code will implement, but not always. In certain large organizations, the coders are a separate group of people.

Regardless of who is coding, the programmers writing code work from the detailed design. They may write their code on scratch paper, sometimes leaving statements incomplete, but with enough written so that they know what the full statement should be. They will write code in this manner if they themselves will keypunch it onto cards, disk, or tape. If they use clerical help to prepare computer-readable code, they will write their code on formatted coding sheets. With modern disk file management software to make the correction of entry errors simple, a large percentage of programmers now prefer to bypass clerical help and the attendant requirement to write neatly in block letters.

Their code complete, the programmers compile or assemble it, and learn from the processor that there are a few errors to correct. With a few exceptions, these errors are those that stymied the processor in its attempt to complete the translation of the program. For example, if the code has nowhere earlier defined the variable A, a compiler will not know how to handle the command

$$Q = A$$

Another example: if the compiler expects every IF to be followed by a THEN statement, but finds an IF directly followed by an ELSE, its ability to analyze the syntax will be impaired.

Using natural language, humans communicating with each other can cope with nearly all imaginable deviations from standard grammatical structure. Language processors do not possess our cognitive abilities, thus placing the burden on programmers to communicate within the constraints of a rigid, highly formalized set of grammatical rules. Violations of these rules result in citations called "error diagnostic messages," or more commonly, if less unambiguously, "diagnostics."

What the processor cannot diagnose is a logical error made by the programmer. Quite obviously, clairvoyance is not among a processor's virtues. These errors are left for the more difficult part of debug and module test (or, as it is frequently called, "unit test").

We might distinguish between the terms "debug" and "test." They are used in conjunction with each other so frequently that the phrase "debug and test" has the ring of an old vaudeville team or a brokerage firm. Nevertheless, each of the words has a distinct meaning. *Debug* means the removal of errors discovered either by the compiler or by the test process. *Test* means execution, or set of executions, of the program for the purpose of measuring its performance. That a program was executed with no evidence of error is no proof that it contains no errors; program errors are sensitive to the specifics of the data being processed.

It is impossible to predict whether a code contains a particular error or not. However, there is a class of errors that can be depended upon to affect the accuracy of mathematical operations, and one objective of testing is the measurement of the effect. These errors are those of truncation and rounding off; the one resulting from the evaluation of functions (e.g., sin x) by a finite approximation to an infinite series expansion, and the other attributable to the finite word length available for number storage and arithmetic operations. These are not programming errors in the sense of mistakes, and if the measured errors are no greater than those predicted during the detailed design analyses, the programmers are satisfied with the test results.

In contrast to measurable errors that reflect mathematical limitations rather than programmer laxity, there are programming errors that have no effect on performance. For example, one can write code that performs no useful function. In ordinary experience who has not said, after searching hard for the name of the person shaking his hand,

"I'm sorry, I have forgotten your name."

"Black, Joe Black."

"Of course," one says, shaking ever the more fiercely, "That's right . . . Joe Black!"

In programming we have this, where BEANS(I) refers to the number of beans in the *I*th jar of beans:

```
BEGIN
   TOTAL = 0;
   I = 1;
   FOR I WITHIN RANGE OF 1 TO 10
   ADD BEANS(I) TO TOTAL
END
```

There was no need to initialize I to 1, since initialization is implicit in the statement beginning with FOR. Statements of this kind, while having no effect on the processing of data, bedevil programmers trying to understand someone else's code.

Another kind of faultless error is the statement that can never be executed. Consider this dialogue:

"Suppose you found a wallet containing a million dollars. What would you do?"

"No question about it. If it belonged to a poor person I'd definitely return it."

The computer analogy is found in

```
BEGIN
   TOTAL = 0;
   FOR I WITHIN RANGE OF 1 TO 10
   ADD BEANS(I) TO TOTAL;
   IF (I > 11)
      THEN CALL ERROR
END
```

Here, THEN CALL ERROR can never be executed. While seemingly harmless, errors like this do account for code that will never be exercised. A subsequent change to the program, perhaps to fix another error, may now make it possible to execute the statement (or in the more common instance, group of statements), leaving executable but previously untested code in the program.

The kind of error the programmer is really looking for, but hoping he will not find, is

```
BEGIN
   N = 10;
      .

      .

      .

   TOTAL = 0;
   FOR I WITHIN RANGE OF 1 TO N
   ADD BEANS(N) TO TOTAL
END
```

By adding BEANS(N) rather than BEANS(I) to TOTAL, TOTAL will be computed as 10 times the number of beans in the 10th jar. This error is typical of an absentminded slip during coding or program entry. It is less likely that it is representative of faulty logic in the programmer's thinking. Errors that reflect incorrect logic are usually more subtle. A very simple example would be the failure to initialize TOTAL to zero.

Finding one's errors can be simple or difficult, depending on the subtlety of the error. Simple ones can often be found by studying the code or by comparing the code to the design documentation. The more intractable ones require the use of diagnostic aids. The most common of these are *trace* capabilities provided by the systems software and additional program statements inserted by the programmer to output certain suspect variables. With only limited selectivity, trace routines output the results of every computation made by the program. Diagnostics inserted by the programmer permit examination of only those data areas that are of concern. If fortunate, the programmer will find in the diagnostic's output the clue to locating the error. As frequently happens, if the data areas the programmer has ordered to be output contain what was expected, then either the wrong part of the code has been scrutinized for the cause of the fault, or there is an error in the logic of the program.

There are two other commonly used tools to help in the diagnosis of errors. These are invoked at breakpoints in the program inserted by the programmer. The one outputs the contents of all the machine registers and status flags, and the other outputs (dumps) selected blocks of memory. The presentation of these is usually in the form of octal or hexadecimal numbers, rather than binary, which takes excessive space. Octal (radix of 8) and hexadecimal (radix of 16) numbers are favored because they can be converted to binary by inspection.

The use of these two tools is more common in the debugging of assembler language programs than programs written in compiler language. In the latter case the programmer cannot so readily determine the use being made of the various registers at any given point in the program, nor know what data or program material occupies a given block of memory.

Testing a module requires that it be executed, and further requires that it be given some input data to be processed. If the module is a monolithic program, no special provision is needed to cause it to be executed. If it is a subroutine, however, as indeed most modules are, it will not be executed until it is invoked by a program (such as the top-module of Figure 3-5). A program to call the module, provide input to it, and output the results of the module's operation is called a *test driver*, or simply *driver*. This, too, must be programmed as part of the software development effort. The driver may be given the capability of generating and reporting a number of test cases, or it may have the limitation of only a single, static, test. The choice depends on the difficulty of generating dynamic tests and on the plan for the tests that will follow.

Integration

Thus far we have discussed only module level tests. Modules, unlike monolithic programs, are not by themselves going to meet requirements specifications. It is the modules operating in concert that will perform a useful function. That is, they have to be integrated.

As the word is used in the software community, "integrated" means more than the literal meaning suggests. After all, the link editor performs the relatively simple task of fusing the several modules into a unified structure. The integration phase is really that of testing to make certain that the modules of a program work together. Using a graphic model, integration is the act of testing the edges of the modules after module level tests have checked operation within the edges.

Although conceptually useful, the trouble with the model is that one might infer from it that integration is trivial; modules span finite area, while edges occupy none. However, this belies the usual experience, wherein integration consumes more work-hours of effort than the sum of all the module tests. The problem decomposition described under top-down design was presented as a means of devolving a complex, often multifaceted, problem into small problems, each easily grasped in its entirety. In integration, no matter how careful the earlier design, the complexity of the problem is reconstituted. This is not to imply that careful design does not have a favorable effect on integration; it certainly does, and we shall have much to say on the matter in Part 3.

It remains that integration is the greater part of testing. One way not to integrate large programs is to start by link-editing all the modules at once and having a go at it with one's test cases. When the tests don't work, and they won't, it will be extremely difficult to trace the failures back to specific causes. The preferred practice is to gradually integrate the program, using one of two basic approaches, or a combination of the two. These approaches, which are nearly opposites of each other, are called *bottom-up* integration and *top-down* integration.

Bottom-up integration, the older of the two, is analogous to many other forms of construction. To assemble an automobile drive train, the approach is to have separate groups of workers put together hundreds of parts to form the carburetor, clutch, transmission, block assembly, distributor, and so forth, testing each after it is built; and then to have them assemble all these major components into the whole. Similarly, in bottom-up integration, we see elements integrated with components, components with divisions, and divisions coalesced into a working program.

Referring to Figure 3-4, in the first stage, Strategy, Odds Calculation, and Possible Move Calculation are link-edited with Machine Play Computation Control and a test driver. The driver will provide various test cases that will exercise Machine Play Computation Control as supported by the other three modules. Similarly, Dice Throw and the other modules on this hierarchical level are being integrated with the modules (not shown on Figure 3-4, but presumed to have been defined during detailed design) subordinate to them. When all the tests at this level have been run successfully, Machine Play Computation Control (and its three lower level modules), Dice Throw, Player Input Routine, and Board Status Display (and any modules below them) are link-edited with Backgammon Supervisor and a new test driver.

While all this has been going on, the Bridge people have been doing their bottom-up integration. And, of course, Melvin has tested Craps. Finally, all the modules are brought together in a last series of tests. In brief, a pyramid has been built, as pyramids have always been built, from the ground up.

At the other extreme, top-down integration starts with Executive Control only. There are no other modules in the system as we know them. However, substitutes for Backgammon Supervisor, Craps, and Bridge Supervisor are link-edited with Executive Control. These substitutes, called *stubs*, are relatively simpleminded replacements for the routines whose names they bear, responding to calls from Executive Control with predetermined rote responses. A driver may still be required to provide test stimuli, but not to invoke modules under test. The mode of operation here is quite the opposite: stubs replace modules invoked by the module under test. In our example, Executive Control does little beyond offering the player a choice of games and storing game status. We see more of the test methodology at the lower hierarchical tiers. Again, we have two teams, the Backgammon programmers and the Bridge people, working independently. Figure 3-13 freezes the action at a time when the testing of Bridge is nearly complete, but Backgammon remains at an earlier stage of test. In the diagram, modules defined by double solid lines represent those that have been tested, modules enclosed by a single solid line represent those under test, and dashed lines denote stubs of the same name as the module they are replacing.

Figure 3-13 shows that Backgammon Supervisor, driven by Executive Control and supported by four stubs, is still under test. Craps has been tested to the satisfaction of Melvin and the lead programmer. At the component level, as we defined it in Figure 3-5, all of Bridge has been tested except for Play Out the Contract Computation Control, which is being tested with three stubs replacing the three elements it requires. When it has been checked out, Declarer et al. will replace the stub namesakes, and in turn be tested.

For our example, no driver is required, since the stimuli are really input by the programmers taking the roles of game players. More typically, except for the responses from stubs, a driver may be the source of all stimuli in the early stages of integration, with stimuli for the later tests provided by the input routines after they have been integrated. The integration strategy is to incorporate these routines as quickly as possible so that they can be used. Even so, since they must accommodate a variety of test conditions, top-down drivers can get quite complex, more so than we would expect of drivers used in bottom-up integration.

One might question whether the integration test for Executive Control would be any different from the module level or unit tests of that module. Not really. The integration tests might well be used to replace the unit tests. Indeed, the integration tests performed for any module upon its introduction

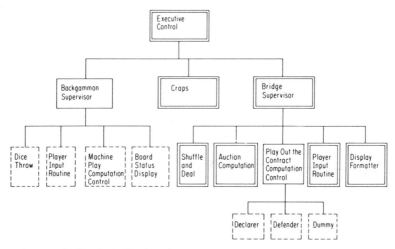

FIGURE 3-13 Top-Down Testing of the Game Program.

to the system may be the de facto module level test of the routine. This is, in fact, *true* top-down testing. What we have previously described is defined by Glenford Myers[3] as *modified* top-down testing. True top-down testing may appear more efficient than modified top-down testing, as it completely eliminates the unit test phase. This gain is mitigated, however, by an increase in the number of errors found during integration testing and the consequent increase in the length of time spent in that phase. Moreover, since integration normally involves several people, there is a multiplicative penalty of work-hours spent. Finally, there are some error conditions that modules may be susceptible to that cannot be readily tested except at the module level. For these reasons, modified top-down testing is more frequently employed.

Test schemes may employ other combinations of these techniques as well. The strategy adopted for a given program will reflect the characteristics of the program itself, the hardware and software test tools available, and the weight of precedents peculiar to the software development team. Finally, we may note that in some organizations integration is performed by a group of programmers other than those who wrote and debugged the code.

How Much Testing?

Much has been written on the topic of what represents adequate testing. Tests themselves are but jabs and thrusts used to uncover the soundness of the invisible structure of a program. Every now and again a weakness becomes manifest, and the defect is brought to light. The cumulative number of defects found at any point gives little clue to the number remaining. Yet somehow one must determine when it is appropriate to terminate the test phase.

Again, this can be a function of the type of program. For programs concerned with the processing of input limited in the number of discrete variations of the data environment, each test is concluded when each of the test conditions stipulated in the test procedure has been satisfied. This is typical of a process control program, where, although the input data may vary widely in range, there is normally but one set of measurements being processed. It is also representative of most mathematical programs dealing with continuous variables. It certainly is not typical of compilers, nor is it of programs developed to perform discrete simulations or make real-time air traffic control decisions. The number of data conditions that differ in kind as well as extent is too great to be totally delineated in a test procedure. For programs as these, one could do worse than evaluate the rate at which errors are found in response to random stimuli.

Figure 3-14 depicts the pattern of error discovery that may be anticipated for programs of this second kind when subjected to random input. Normal

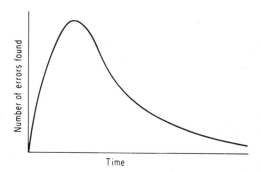

FIGURE 3-14   Error Discovery Rate.

start-up difficulties may preclude the rate of testing that will obtain later, thus leading, at the beginning, to few errors being found per unit of calendar time. As testing speed builds up, in short order an error frequency peak occurs. Assuming the number of new errors introduced by the corrections is insignificant compared to the number discovered, the rate of discovery thereafter decreases in a more or less exponential manner. There is considerable evidence that the rate of decrease is predictable enough to permit quantitative conclusions to be drawn from the discovery rate data. We shall return to this in Part 5.

As drawn, the number of new errors uncovered becomes asymptotic to a zero error condition. Since the number of errors remaining in the program must always be finite, we may expect that after several days of error-free testing, it is reasonable to decide that there are no errors left. Testing is over. It is also possible that for a variety of causes — complexity, weak structure, inadequate controls — the rate of introducing errors in the fixes approaches the rate at which errors are removed. This situation prepares the ground for a decision to terminate further testing even though the program is known to have defects. This may sound like heresy to quality managers, but not infrequently it makes good sense in the context of software.

INSTALLATION AND EVALUATION

The environment in which a program is developed is not generally that in which it will perform the service it was designed for. A compiler developed in the software "laboratory" of a computer manufacturer may be transported to hundreds of different facilities throughout the world. The compiler may have to operate under operating systems other than the one used in the laboratory, and will almost always be used with a number of different sets of peripheral equipment. When first integrated with directional sensors, radio range receivers, and control mechanisms, the program embedded in an aircraft autopilot will operate under conditions having little resemblance to those in which it was tested.

The installation of a program in conditions representative of its real service life invariably is accompanied by operational difficulties at first. These may be traceable back to defects originating in code, design, the software specification, or even the concept. In some cases, the problem can be attributed to incorrect or vague documentation. In any event, before it is possible to determine how well the program performs its function, it must be made to play as its designers intended it to. This is analogous to the earlier debugging process, except that debugging tools available for development may not exist or have equivalents in the service world. The cost of repairing a defect is much greater at the time of installation than at an earlier time.

A program may perform precisely as it was specified to operate, yet not satisfy the service environment. The user manuals may be poor. A compiler, when used for a given class of problems, may generate inefficient object code. The present position displayed by an airborne navigation program may change every 10 milliseconds, making it difficult to read. Backgammon may lose to the player too easily, or the Bridge bidding decisions may be too conservative. A program tested in an environment in which all memory is real may run much too slowly under a virtual storage system until optimized for it.

Who makes these determinations? Normally evaluation teams or selected end users. The compiler may be released to a small group of users, each in a different business field. The airborne navigation unit will first be integrated by a systems integration group in a laboratory, and then be test flown by several pilots, perhaps in several kinds of aircraft. Backgammon, Craps, and Bridge will be evaluated by many of PPP's employees, and later by friends visiting the homes of several of the PPP executives.

The object of evaluation is the determination of the usefulness of the program. This can be both qualitative (readability of the navigation display) and quantitative (statistics on navigation errors). Evaluation may not necessarily be at the discretion of the software producer; it may be written into the contract under which the software was developed. In this case it is likely that at least one evaluator will be a representative of the customer.

In the case of embedded software, evaluation of the software may not be formally distinguished from evaluation of the hardware. That is, those charged with the responsibility of appraisal are likely to be concerned with system performance, with scant regard for the contributions of individual elements of the system.

The response that is made to the conclusions reached by the evaluators is often referred to as *fine tuning*. This is the set of improvements which will resolve the problems that have been reported. Some of the changes will have been anticipated in the original design, and will be effected simply by the change of a program constant. Rarely, a major change is required before the program is declared to be operational.

OPERATION AND MAINTENANCE

During the early months of the useful life of software, despite all the testing and evaluation that have gone before, problems will crop up from time to time. In addition to operational problems associated with the suitability of the program, there are documentation errors and latent defects that have finally evinced themselves.

It is not uncommon for defects to remain hidden until prompted by an input data set never before presented to the software, or by a combination of data and operational modes. We have also to consider defects known to be in the software that, it had been hoped, would never become evident in real life: "Let's not worry about that one, Fred. Who's going to open with a bid of four diamonds?" Unfortunately, within a week of receiving his game package from PPP, Eli, recently returned from a Mediterranean cruise in which he had learned the new Minoan bidding system, did just that. Seconds later the CRT of his PPP computer started displaying lines of gibberish. Eli was able to restore order only by shutting down power and reinitializing the monitor program. Eli tried the same thing a second time. Again, the same reaction from his unseen, but simulated, partner.

On receiving Eli's letter, the PPP staff recognized that it had either to correct the bug and issue updates to all of its customers who had ordered the program, or issue a caveat for insertion in the user manual: "Opening bids of four diamonds may result in an unpredictable response."

More generally, the problems reported by users reflect defects not previously known to the authors of the program. If the problem is adequately documented by the user, it can be recreated in the laboratory, the essential step that must be taken before the cause of the problem is found. For most software, it is simple to recreate the problem. For embedded software, it may be necessary to maintain a complex hardware test fixture to provide postdelivery support.

Those persons assigned to analysis of problems reported by the user community are not necessarily the same ones who developed the program. To be sure, programmers are programmers, but for administrative purposes, program maintenance may be performed by a different department, perhaps not even colocated with the development department. For their knowledge of the programs they support, the maintenance programmers must rely on the documentation provided them by the development people. The accuracy, currency, and thoroughness of the documentation is critical to the ability of the maintenance programmer to find the source of problems.

Conventional wisdom has it that maintenance personnel will get along quite well with the design documentation required for the development phase. Since the developers supply the documentation, this attitude may simply reflect a philosophy which they initiated to serve their own purposes. What do the maintenance people have to say? Curiously, they largely agree: they want a hierarchical diagram, file formats, brief specifications of the function performed by each routine, and the like. Most of all, they seem to like flowcharts and source listings well annotated by comments. Their preference may, of course, simply reflect familiarity; the documentation they were most likely to get when they entered the field was often restricted to flowcharts and listings. Listings are in any scheme indispensable, but the merits of flowcharts are arguable.

What is surprising is that there appears to be no form of documentation unique to the purposes of maintenance. The authors have attended several symposia, well-populated with leading software figures, in which the matter of documentation through the life cycle was raised. No one was ever able to identify documentation peculiar to the ends of maintenance.

Software maintenance includes not only the removal of latent defects or the updating of documentation, but also the changes made to a program to adapt it to new operational environments. A program to compute the mean time before failure of electronic circuits, written in FORTRAN for one computer, may not directly be transportable to a second computer because of differences in the FORTRAN language specifications of two compilers. Even on the same machine, the program may have to be altered to accommodate a new, more efficient, compiler purchased to improve computer throughput. Maintenance of this kind, though frequently performed by the supplier of the software, may also be undertaken by employees of the company using the software, providing they can gain access to adequate documentation. This is frequently a problem, since software suppliers are understandably loathe to reveal their proprietary design documentation.

In the strict sense of the term, "software maintenance" does not include program modifications that are made to extend capabilities or to substitute one capability for another. Yet, such changes may be expected during the period of operation and maintenance. PPP may want to enhance Backgammon by adding the originally excluded feature of a doubling cube. A payroll program in wide circulation may be modified to include IRA pension provisions. The airborne navigation equipment may get new modules added to it to permit operation with loran as well as vortac input data. A general ledger program may be changed from FIFO to LIFO inventory accounting.

Modifications as these tend to require the full cycle of software development activity, and are most frequently undertaken by software development, rather than maintenance staffs. Indeed, it is not unusual for a development staff to spend more time on modifications of old programs than development of new ones. Software does not rust. Software that has gained wide acceptance can be expected to have a long life. It is generally cheaper to enhance existing software than to develop new systems. Also, users accustomed to programs are often unwilling to accept something else. They demand enhancements to maintain the currency of what they have. One of IBM's most popular operating systems (bearing the definitive, if somewhat presumptuous, name of OS), was at release 21.8 before being superseded by IBM's virtual systems. Each release represented an increase in capability over the previous one.

The sum effect of all this is that the overall costs of the operation maintenance phase represents 60 to 70 percent of all software costs in the United States. Thus, the ease with which software can be adapted to new situations and can be modified to include new features is of paramount importance to the suppliers and owners of software.

PEOPLE WHO PROGRAM

From the foregoing survey of the life cycle of software, it should be evident that the software business is archetypically labor-intensive. The reader who has had little firsthand exposure to software may be curious about the people who provide the labor. We shall say very little, however, since generalities, shaky under the best circumstances, seem especially difficult to apply to those who toil in the vineyards of software.

For example, consider education. If we were interested in accountants, we could be reasonably confident that most had degrees in accounting; if clergy, we could expect degrees in divinity. But programmers? The designers of systems software may have any degree conceivable, math being a favorite, and perhaps none. The more recent graduates are likely to have degrees (B.S. through Ph.D.) in computer science. Their seniors received their education at a time when computer science in academia consisted of one or two courses, probably taught by the mathematics department.

Applications programmers in electronic data processing frequently have bachelor's degrees in business or math; many are graduates of technical training schools. The more recent entrants, again, may have degrees in computer science. Scientific applications programmers have degrees in the physical sciences, math, or engineering. Again, a significant number now have computer science backgrounds. The education of the developers of real-time software shows a distribution similar to that of the scientific programmers, except that since these persons often become deeply involved in the systems aspects of the software they program, their employers tend to prefer to hire engineering graduates.

As we forewarned, these are the grossest of generalities. We know of programmers with education in music, botany, and medieval history who are doing quite well in the field. Whatever their education, there are not enough of them. Each year more men and women enter the field, and it appears that each year even more are needed. The productivity of the workers in any labor-intensive industry is always a matter of importance to management. So far as programmers are concerned, the importance is twofold: production may be limited, not by the funds available, but by the number of workers available. Productivity of each programmer is paramount; of this, more in Part 3.

In some organizations, most frequently those in electronic data processing, programming people are horizontally segregated. That is, requirements are defined by systems analysts, design — or at least top-level design — is performed by program analysts, and the term "programmers" is reserved for those writing code. Testing is performed by the program analysts, and in-house evaluation is left for the systems analysts.

The alternatives to the above are many, but most have at least one characteristic in common: software design, code, debug, and test activities are performed by a homogeneous group, although top-level design may be the responsibility of a subset of the group.

Of the professional organizations serving the software community, three dominate the field. The Data Processing Management Association (DPMA) appeals mostly to those in electronic data processing. The Association for Computing Machinery (ACM), with a scholarly quarterly among its many periodicals, draws heavily from academia, although scarcely to the exclusion of industry and government. Along with ACM's monthly *Communications*, the publications of the Computer Society of the Institute of Electrical and Electronic Engineers (IEEE) are viewed by many, regardless of specialty, as the wellspring for seminal articles dealing with technological approaches to productivity and quality.

The three organizations sponsor various symposia, hold annual technical meetings, and support regional chapters to enable their members to learn from each other. Despite this, it has been said many times that most of the people in the field of software never read a technical article or book; never attend a technical meeting. Thus although great progress has been made in the past decade to improve the productivity of programmers and the usability of their products, much of the new technology and methodology remains foreign to a majority of the practitioners.

The innovations of the past decade have, among the knowledgeable, promoted programming from an art — some would argue craft — to something akin to engineering. Indeed, the term "software engineering" was coined by Fritz Bauer in 1967 at a Brussels meeting of the Study Group on Computer Science established by the NATO Science Committee. At the meeting, Bauer, according to a letter[4] he later wrote, used the phrase " 'software engineering' in contrast to software tinkering." He was subsequently charged by the NATO Science Committee to organize a conference under the title "Software Engineering." The conference, held in 1968 in Garmisch, West Germany, is well-chronicled in a book published eight years later.[5]

If the methodology and technology of software engineering was needed in 1968, it is all the more so now. The need for software engineering practices increases with size, complexity, time and space constraints, the number of people working on the same project, and the conceptual distance between the developers and the users. With the possible exception of time and space constraints, things have only gotten worse since 1968.

Although relatively few programmers are software engineers (notwithstanding the fact that the term has a rather pleasant ring to it and has been adapted as a synonym for programmers by some who have no understanding of what it means), they have collectively overrun society with the fruit of their ingenuity, energy, and willingness to work odd hours. The fruit does, however, occasionally harbor worms.

SUMMARY

1. The computer programs that present problems of control and quality are those involving a number of people (implying considerable pairwise communication), significance to persons at a distinct remove from the developers, and an expectation of much future use.

2. Concept and analysis is the name we give to that phase of software development in which the requirement for computation and a rough notion of the role that software will play are introduced.

3. The detailed requirements for computer software are put forth in a requirements definition specification. There is a tendency, often understandable, to avoid distinguishing between requirements and design.

4. Software design may be thought of in terms of at least two sequential activities: top-level design and detailed design. The former determines the overall shape of the program, while the latter completes the scheme.

5. The tangible outputs of top-level design include the methodology of controlling program flow, division of the program into hierarchically layered subprograms called modules, memory allocations, and gross timing analyses.

6. Detailed design outputs include sufficiently detailed documentation of the control flow and data handling approaches to permit code to be written directly from the documentation.

7. The generation of code, although only one of many stages of software development, is given an unseemly amount of attention by management, who often view it as the first real output of the programming process.

8. Testing is the process of executing a program to prove performance and to flush to the surface problems that may exist in code. Debugging is the process of finding the source of problems and correcting them.

9. The test and debug phase of development is often thought of as a two-stage process: module, or unit-level tests followed by integration of modules into a working program. Integration can start at the bottom of the software hierarchical structure and work upwards (bottom-up), at the top and work downwards (top-down), or a combination of the two.

10. It is not always possible to eliminate all the bugs in a program. In the process of fixing old problems, it is even possible to introduce new ones at the same rate at which errors are removed.

11. Additional problems may arise in the process of installing programs in other computer systems or online with instrumentation systems. In the case of embedded software, installation takes on the form of another integration stage. Further adjustments are likely when the program is evaluated for its usefulness in its service environment.

12. The portion of the life cycle of greatest duration is the period of operation and maintenance. In addition to removing any defects that escaped the debugging, installation, and evaluation phases, computer programs may undergo modifications for a variety of reasons. The operation and maintenance costs may represent up to 70 percent of total software costs.

13. Despite a great diversity of backgrounds of the people who develop software, the field exhibits much professionalism. Since the mid-1960s, a movement has been growing to bring a more organized approach to the development of software. Called "software engineering," it is one of the bases on which software quality assurance is founded.

REFERENCES

1. F. T. Baker, "Chief Programmer Team Management of Production Programming," *IBM Systems Journal*, Vol. 11, No. 1, pp. 56–73.

2. F. B. Baker and H. D. Mills, "Chief Programmer Teams," *Datamation*, December 1973, pp. 58–61.

3. Glenford Myers, *Software Reliability*, John Wiley, New York, 1976, p. 184.

4. *DACS Newsletter*, September 1979, RADC/ISISI, Griffiss AFB, New York.

5. J. M. Buxton, P. Naur, and B. Randell, *Software Engineering: Concepts and Techniques*, Petrocelli/Charter, New York, 1976.

Chapter 4

The Problems

We have seen that computer software is produced by well-defined disciplines, presumably executed by bright, clear-eyed men and women. Moreover, computer programs are inherently precise and contain no mechanical or electrical parts that can degrade in performance. What can possibly go wrong?

DEFECTS

Unfortunately, just about everything. As a starter, let's consider latent defects. Of course, we do not expect that latent defects in software will take the form of latent defects in hardware. Nor can we expect that they will yield to a procedure appropriate to cracks in castings or the temperature coefficients of resistors. Yet, latent defects do exist in software. When the bank teller breaks the news to Mr. Zygote that his $100 check can't be cashed because his current balance is less than $100, and Mr. Zygote distinctly recalls depositing within the week $1500, we have to suspect the presence of a latent defect. Software troubleshooters will immediately wonder if the spelling of Mr. Zygote's name might not have placed his account at the very end of the long list maintained by the bank. This, in turn, should raise the question of the boundary performance of some of the algorithms employed in posting or sorting daily transactions. Never mind, Mr. Zygote has a problem, and likely as not that problem is a latent defect in the computer software used by the bank.

It is in the tradition of computer software that latent defects are called by any name but that. The usual designations are "bugs," "errors," or more euphemistically, "software problems." Small matter. They exist, and, indeed, are likely to continue to exist despite the efforts of quality assurance. Software quality assurance can be instrumental in markedly decreasing their number, but it is unrealistic to assume that defects can be entirely eliminated. This may appear to be a surprisingly tolerant attitude; one scarcely consonant with the historical goals of the quality community. However, as a fact of software life, no degree of quality control can assure that a computer program, save for the most trivial, can ever be placed into use totally free of "bugs."

Figure 4-1 is a model of a fairly simple computer program. The small boxes represent processing nodes of any given complexity, anywhere from the addition of two numbers to the calculation of the harmonic frequency of an airplane wing. The small clockwise arcs about each node represent program

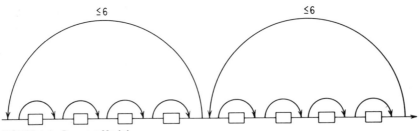

FIGURE 4-1 Program Model.

switches, or jumps around the processing nodes, with the switch settings determined by previous calculations. That is, the node either is entered or it is not, the choice being the result of some other computation within the model. The large counterclockwise arcs represent the potential for iteration, or "looping." Each group of four processing nodes may be iterated, jumps and all, up to six times; the exact number once again a function of the calculations within the model. It can be shown (and is highly recommended as an alternate to doodling during a dull staff meeting) that the number of unique paths from the one end to the other is approximately 10^{17}. That is, the model, simple as it is, is capable of generating 10^{17} discrete states.

Now, 10^{17} is a very large number. One way of appreciating its size is to say that we shall test each of these paths at the rate of one path per microsecond, or, if you will, 1 million paths per second. This may sound unrealistically optimistic, considering that we need to set up each test and record the result, but we'll go with the number anyway. At this 1-microsecond rate, in order to be ready for next week's scheduled delivery of the software, we should have started testing sometime during the reign of Alexander the Great, roughly 2300 years ago.

Thus, we can see that the number of paths that computer software can produce is too great to permit the testing of each and every one. Simply put, no technique of product inspection can guarantee the absence of latent defects. Interestingly, with very large scale integrated (VLSI) circuits, we are approaching this condition in the hardware world also; and while it is patently outside our scope, and as such will not be discussed further, we may anticipate some rethinking of the processes with which we assure the quality of hardware as well.

In brief, we cannot test computer software to the full exposure it will receive from the data (read, "real world") environment. Nearly all of the possible end-to-end processing sequences will have to go untested. It should not be surprising that some bugs will persist even after final factory acceptance testing. What actually is accomplished is the testing of the main branches of the program. In our model, we might expect that the straight through (no jumps, no loops) processing will be tested; that each jump will be tested individually; and that each half of the model will be tested with some iteration, but with a given set of jump conditions. These tests will suffice to remove all but a few of the potential errors. It is these few that remain as latent defects. As we shall see, one of the main thrusts of a software quality assurance program is to reduce the likelihood of defects ever getting into the code.

USABILITY

Latent defects are not the only problem. Many a program has been prepared and released that simply did not do the job expected of it. Perhaps the program was hard to use, required more thought than the operator was equipped to provide, or more knowledge than he was supplied with. Or even worse, it may have provided results that only represented part of the problem. If the inventory control system of a department store doesn't accommodate exchanges, because no one ever told the programmers that it ought to, how long will it be before reports of merchandise on hand are no longer current?

In the world of embedded software, we have further concerns, not the least of which is speed. We might look at a program that is intended to steer a cruise missile. If the sensor inputs (loran, inertial guidance, or whatever) occur at the rate of 10 input data sets per second, but it takes three-tenths of a second to fully process them, we can only hope that in the two-tenths of a second that the latest positional input must be ignored, the missile will not have drifted so far off course that the computed corrections will be to no avail. An otherwise splendid program, perhaps, but too slow to be of any real worth.

There are any number of ways that a computer program can be inadequate to perform the needed job. Most of the ways have been explored. The archives are full of programs that were much admired for their design concepts, but never quite became useful.

MAINTENANCE

Programs, when found to be responsive to the real application and when finally free of all bugs, can still develop problems. We have seen that software is frequently subjected to a continuing life of modifications. However, some programs are more easily modified than others. A program that is poorly documented or reflects "clever," rather than straightforward, programming techniques is hard to understand. The defects that can be introduced to code that isn't understood can be out of proportion to the significance of the modification itself. One can easily imagine the task of trying to change a program that the programmer doesn't fully grasp. Yet, modifications, or maintenance, is generally performed by programmers other than the ones who originally did the deisgn or wrote the code. Indeed, only about six months need pass between program release and first modification before even the original programmer is hard put to change code that is poorly documented or designed with obscure logic paths.

In addition to insufficiently descriptive documentation, we have also the problem of documentation that is no longer current. As the program is revised, the documentation must be revised with it so that it and the code are always in agreement. This also applies to comments within the code. It is not at all rare to find obsolete comments that mislead rather than guide.

Finally, we have the problem of finding that a change made to one function of a program unwittingly affects other functions as well. While this can be a consequence of difficulty in understanding the program, it is equally likely the result of a nonfunctional software architecture; nonfunctional in the sense that the several modules do not reflect independent performance. Modularity is not a matter of mere program segmentation. It should reflect the division of a program into a set of smaller programs (indeed, into several hierarchically related sets of smaller programs) in a manner wherein each individual program, or module, performs a unique function. In this way the set of modules will exhibit the quality of maximum mutual independence.

Unfortunately, this paradigm of modularity is not universally encountered. A maintenance programmer, altering the logic within one module which was known to perform some function, finds that the performance of another, seemingly unrelated function has been inadvertently altered. Worse, the maintenance programmer doesn't find out, but a user of the program does. The authors can recall a program that computed an optimal routing for the interconnections of a back panel of a printed wiring board cage. A year or two after constant use, the program was modified to operate on a back panel of somewhat different physical configuration. Mostly, the change involved a different scheme for identifying connector pins. Following this small change, made entirely within one module, it was found that electrical ground was no longer routed to the boards. On examination, it was learned that the altered module, which presumably only related pin identifiers to physical dimensions, also had the miscellaneous role of assigning the ground connections. Although this was properly documented, it (understandably) escaped the notice of the maintenance programmer, and the program was revised in a manner such that the secondary function could no longer be invoked.

Whatever the reasons for the difficulties encountered during program maintenance, the results are likely to be costly. Under the worst conditions, the modifications made to a program not well-suited to change, or the modifications badly made to a well-constructed program, can in time cause the program to become erratic in performance or quite nearly impossible to modify further. With a large program, it is not unreasonable to expect that a small number of new bugs will be introduced with every major modification performed. In time, however, these defects, as were those latent in the program when it was initially released for use, will be fixed. The solid line of Figure 4-2 approximates the expectations of the incidence of bugs over the life span of a program.

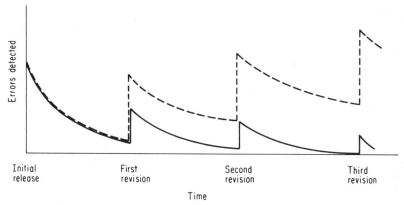

| Initial release | First revision | Second revision | Third revision |

Time

FIGURE 4-2   Error Growth.

If, however, the program is one that is difficult to modify, or if the modifications are uncontrolled, the dashed line may result, with the inevitable and costly consequence of premature code death when the only sensible management option remaining is to scrap the program and start over again.

MORE ON OBSOLESCENCE

Software construction, documentation, and maintenance practices are not the only causes of early obsolescence. The very language in which the program is written may also doom its years of use. As we saw in the previous chapter, programs often are required to operate on computers or under operating systems other than the one for which they were originally designed. The land development firm of Nemo and Ahab in 1968 purchased a minicomputer of modest capability to produce topographic maps of their development sites. The machine was programmed to compute not only the contours of the land, but also to superimpose the planned streets, canals, and clubhouses of their grand designs. A consulting firm developed the software at a cost of $30,000 in 1968 dollars. By 1978 the business of Nemo and Ahab had grown considerably, and they were no longer dealing with sites of hundreds of acres, but were acquiring huge tracts of ranchland for conversion to homesites. The old computer was no longer adequate, and the purchase of a new machine was indicated. One problem arose, however: the software was coded in the assembly, or machine-oriented, language of the old computer, and no machine currently available could execute that code.

Had the consultants used any of the more popular compiler, or high-order, languages, the problem could have been avoided, as it then would have been fairly easy to find a new computer possessing both sufficient machine power and a compiler capable of translating the program into its own machine code. Nemo and Ahab finally came to the decision that they would contract for the recoding of the program at a cost of $60,000, but in the contract they stipulated that the program be written in FORTRAN, perhaps in anticipation of their machine needs in 1988 following their purchase of the whole of Arizona.

The matter of providing machine (and, for that matter, operating system) transportability isn't quite so tidy as simply specifying an appropriate high-order language. High-order languages, or as we called them earlier, HOLs, like spoken languages, can acquire dialects, so that a program written in one dialect may have to be modified somewhat before being processed by a compiler for another computer or operating system. Worse, a program written in an HOL may still be written in a manner which reflects certain machine characteristics. The authors once bought a program, written in FORTRAN, to perform reliability predictions. The program had been developed for a computer of 60-bit word length, and with an internal character representation which allowed 10 alphanumeric characters to be packed in one computer word. Files of component failure rates were cleverly constructed to group component data in sets of 10 alphanumeric characters. This permitted the program logic to be expressed mostly in efficient word operation for the matching of component data to circuit use. Unfortunately, for the author's use, the program had to be run on a computer which packed four characters to a word. Thus, even though the program was written in a language compilable on both computers, major modifications had to be made to the program before it could be used. This could have been avoided had the program not been so cleverly constructed, but had conformed to the sense of the FORTRAN standard of the American National Standards Institute.

CONFIGURATION AMBIGUITY

No discussion of software problems would be complete without examination of the question of what it is that one has actually tested when one has tested a program. Testing takes place in the late phases of the software development cycle, well after considerable opportunity has arisen to make a number of changes to the design of the software. The prevalence of design changes during development is especially common in large programming projects, where, despite the thoroughness with which the software is initially designed in the large, the subsequent detailed design effort may reveal some inconsistencies or omissions within the overall design. Some of these may show up during detailed design, but others will await the start of testing to be found. Thus we find that a given module, having been previously tested with satisfactory results, is modified somewhat when a second module does not properly run in concert with it. This, by-the-by, can happen in either top-down or bottom-up testing. As it turns out, in our hypothetical case it is simpler to modify the first module than the second. However, a similar problem arises in the testing of a third module, and once again it is easier to modify the first. Eventually, there are several versions of the subject module to be found on various disks or tapes; each of which had at one time been the "authorized version." At this point, in any subsequent testing, the opportunity is present to include one of the earlier versions in the program load about to be tested. The situation is further compounded when one considers the periodic generation of backup files of source programs. Which version got copied?

While software documentation may lend itself to inspection by perusal of the contents, for all practical purposes the programs themselves are invisible. All that one sees is the medium on which the program is stored. This is not to say that source programs cannot be dumped onto a CRT or printer and then read, but one cannot, when looking for the floppy disk that contains the latest version, pick one up and know with any certainty that it is, in fact, the correct edition. This is especially the case if its cardboard jacket bears only the legend "Module D310, Latest Version." Of course, it is more likely that competent software professionals would have labeled the jacket "Module D310 Rev C," or "Module D310, Mar 2, 1979, 3:45 PM." Even this offers no assurance that whoever is about to use the module knows the identification of the latest version. A day-shift librarian preparing a program load for testing recalls that D310 Rev C was current yesterday, and pulls it for recompilation with other modules. Unknown to the librarian, the night-shift found it necessary to modify the module 12 hours earlier, and the current version is now D310 Rev D.

Thus far, we have only discussed source code. In actuality, the building of program loads is more typically based on relocatable object files, with only one or two newly compiled source files. This makes the problem even more difficult, since relocatable files are normally strung together in a "library" on a single disk, with the consequence that picking up the correct disk really implies picking up the current (latest authorized) version of each module. In theory, this should make matters easier. In practice it does, but only if the status of the library is updated each time one of the individual components is. This practice is one that is easily, though unintentionally, circumvented. Moreover, it is one that does not readily lend itself to auditing.

In brief, it is possible to run an entire test sequence successfully, but uselessly, because the program tested may not be the basis for the next series of tests, or may not be the program that had passed previous tests. Quality assurance, as we shall see, must be deeply involved with the test planning and the testing itself, but its involvement assures little if it cannot also verify that the tests that were performed reflected the capabilities of the program that was finally delivered.

DEPARTMENT OF SILVER LININGS

Summing up, we see that computer software can easily be the source of problems to its users and owners. It can, at delivery, be laden with latent defects, or can be endowed with them later. It can be nonresponsive to the real needs of its users. It can be difficult to modify. It can be short-lived even though its need remains. There may even be a question of what it really is, or to what tests the delivered product was actually subjected. There must be a solution, and in fact there is. It starts with the next chapter.

SUMMARY

1. The number of distinct end-to-end paths inherent in computer programs is so great that 100 percent testing is impossible. Thus, programs are frequently put into service with latent defects that may surface unpredictably.

2. It is not uncommon for programs to be designed without regard to all aspects of the operational environment.

3. Poor documentation, complex program flow, and poor modularity can each make software maintenance all but impossible; certainly more costly and error-prone than it needs to be.

4. A program written in a language unique to the computer on which it was initially intended to run will be prematurely retired if the computer is replaced. The supposed transportability of programs written in compiler languages does not always prove successful.

5. Loss of configuration control is all too easy, with the result that the program placed into service may not fully represent the software that was tested. Configuration control of software is especially difficult because code is awkward to inspect.

Part Three
The Quality Solution

Chapter 5

Defect Prevention

The quality solution for computer software rests on the foundation of those technological and managerial techniques and practices that support orderly, predictable, and controllable development and maintenance. Or, to use the term introduced in Chapter 3, on software engineering. One cannot assure the quality of software by adding gussets to stiffen it, or by derating its power dissipation, or by expediting deliveries with a private messenger service. The quality must be built in, and the only way to do so is to ensure that all phases of the development and maintenance are organized to that end.

Software engineering is a term that seems not to lend itself to definition, having, at last count, as many interpretations as there are software engineers. One can do worse than to use Barry Boehm's: "The practical application of scientific knowledge in the design and construction of computer programs and the associated documentation required to develop, operate, and maintain them."[1] We must take care to interpret "scientific" in the sense of systematic, rather than as a reference to the application of the observation of nature. Software is a product of reasoning processes, only. Other engineering disciplines derive from the natural sciences. Their products are realized in a physical sense, and the success of the disciplines may be measured against physical observations. This is a luxury unavailable to computer software. The contributions of software engineering are measurable in cost and schedule improvement throughout the life cycle, and in reliability. But the best measure of the extent to which software engineering is applied is qualitative: the degree to which development and maintenance are systematic.

Thus, the quality solution is based on a systematic approach — *any* systematic approach — to program development and maintenance. We further posit that to be systematic the approach must incorporate measurable milestones at which one can pause and verify that the work done thus far is consistent with the satisfaction of the purpose of the program and the constraints of the development environment. In the absence of a system, milestones are meaningless, and without milestones, there can be no control. Accordingly, in Part 3 we argue the concept of systematic programming and explore several of the techniques that have been applied in the achievement of that end.

In Part 2 we had said that there is more than one correct way to write a program. There is also more than one way to develop a systematic approach. In this chapter we concentrate on software development up to but not including the testing of software. It is in the phases of analysis, design, and code that the measure of software quality is most difficult to take. The approaches that are described are in some respects parallel, in other ways complementary. As a group, they represent solutions to those aspects of these phases that are most critical to quality.

It is not our purpose to attempt to touch all bases of technology; nor to recommend a single narrow course to follow. The first is far too broad in scope for the purposes of this book, while the second represents a naive presumption. Rather, in Chapter 5 we wish to acquaint managers with the sense of those development approaches applicable to the analysis, design, and coding phases that bear upon the prevention of defects and the retention of managerial control. The same philosophy is followed in Chapter 6, which is devoted to configuration control, a prerequisite for software quality in the "paper" stages of development, during testing, and throughout the postdevelopment lifetime. Chapter 7 discusses the means used to achieve purposeful, effective, and controllable testing. The use of tools applicable to all phases of the software life cycle is covered in Chapter 8. Finally, the last chapter of this section concentrates on the control of software development and maintenance, with emphasis on defect prevention and correction.

It may be observed that there is no one chapter devoted to software maintenance. Postdevelopment functional modifications are made using the disciplines that apply to the initial development. Of the two-thirds of all programming performed after initial delivery, about 60 percent is for the purpose of enhancing performance. Half of the balance, or perhaps somewhat less, is for the correction of defects, and is performed under the disciplines of Chapter 7. The remainder is a matter of adapting programs to different computers or operating systems, and is also mostly a matter of testing. The major effect on quality common to all manner of maintenance is really that of configuration control, covered in Chapter 6.

SOFTWARE DEVELOPMENT: FROM THE GENERAL TO THE SPECIFIC

In the earliest years of the software engineering era, in connection with the software of a multiprogramming system, Edsger Dijkstra defined an ordered sequence of virtual machines, A(0) through A(n). He described the software thus:

> The software of layer i is defined in terms of machine A(i), it is to be executed by machine A(i), the software of layer i uses machine A(i) to make machine A(i+1). . . . The total task of creating machine A(n) has been regarded as the machine A(0) and in the dissection process this total abstraction has been split up in a number of independent abstractions.[2]

This, the introduction of the concept of *levels of abstraction*, amounted to defining processes at one level in terms of those at the layer immediately subordinate to it. The bottom layer really is that which is machine-dependent. The top layer is the most abstract in terms of the hardware. Knowledge of the contents of any layer is concealed from all layers below it.

The idea behind Dijkstra's levels of abstraction was the attack of a very complex system (recall, this was a multiprogramming system) in a manner that would permit layer-by-layer verification of the correctness of the design. We find here also the notion of independence. Glenford Myers, writing of the system, stated:

> The purpose of the levels is to minimize the complexity of the system by defining the levels to be highly independent from one another. This is accomplished by hiding properties of certain objects of the system such as resources and data representations within each level, thus allowing each level to represent an "abstraction" of these objects.[3]

Dijkstra's levels of abstraction applied not only to a means of grappling with the complexity of design, but to testing as well. In another paper[4] on the system, he implied that it was possible to structure the design so that the test feasible for each layer would completely test the performance applicable to that layer.

We lean heavily on Dijkstra's approach to define systematic software development as that which leads monotonically from the greatest degree of abstraction (statement of the problem) to the state of no abstraction (executable code). Put a different way, systematic software development progresses with ever-increasing specificity from the general application of computer hardware to the concrete. In embodying Dijkstra's concept in the definition of systematic software development, some liberties were taken. Dijkstra's design process was, essentially, bottom-up. The use here is top-down. Dijkstra's layering was totally within the context of the technical aspects of the design. The layering concept we are primarily interested in is that which lends itself to the measurable milestones of requirements definition, top-level design documentation, detailed design documentation, and code. In a sufficiently large system, we might further layer the design phases in order to develop additional control points.

The above is not to imply that the entire process of analysis, design, and code ought not be approached as a monotonic decrease of abstraction. Indeed, this was the very philosophy followed in Chapter 3 in the iterative development of the game hierarchy and in the detailed design of Craps. From the aspects of quality assurance, however, our equivalent of Dijkstra's layers are the tangible evidence of the completion of each phase of software development.

The balance of this chapter consists of a mix of topics. Some relate to all phases of analysis, design, and code; others are necessarily peculiar to one or more specific activities, as illustrated by Table 5-1, wherein the rows represent the major topics that will be pursued. That from time to time we pause to discuss matters unique to given phases, represents not an abandonment of a comprehensive systematic approach, but a tailoring of common precepts to the attainment of each level of abstraction.

STRUCTURED DEVELOPMENT

To many people, software engineering is synonymous with *structured programming*. At this point we shall not attempt to define structured programming in any great detail, but since we shall need to refer to structure (an attribute of both software and the process that creates it) throughout this chapter, at least a minimum definition is in order.

In a landmark paper, published in 1966, C. Böhm and G. Jacopini proved that the control flow of all programs can be realized using but three constructs: sequence, condition, and iteration.[5] Figure 5-1 illustrates the three in flowchart form. Today we recognize that the significance of this transcends diagrams, but it was to flowcharts that Böhm and Jacopini addressed their paper. Since the constructs may also be implemented in programming languages, we have labeled the condition and iteration constructs with the language-oriented names commonly applied.

Sequence is obvious. The one process directly and unalterably follows the first. IF-THEN-ELSE means that IF the test (in the lozenge) is true in a boolean sense (e.g., IF the lemon is yellow) THEN process *a* is executed (the lemon is eaten). ELSE (otherwise), process *b* is executed (the lemon is left on the window sill to continue ripening). In the iterative construct, the computer will DO process *a* WHILE the test holds true. For example, DO mow the grass WHILE the month is one of those between April and October.

The full import of these constructs is not visible until one realizes that each of the boxes representing a process can be exploded into a second set of symbols, also restricted to the same three forms. This process can be continued until only primitive constructs, directly translatable into code, remain. During the process of increasing the specificity of the definitions of the processing

TABLE 5-1

		Design		
	Analysis	**Top-level**	**Detailed**	**Code**
Structured development	xxxxxxxx	xxxxxxxxxxx	xxxxxxxxxxxx	xxxx
Requirements definition	xxxxxxxx			
Refinement of estimates and staffing	xxxxxxxx	xxxxxxxxxxx	xxxxxxxxxx	
Modularity		xxxxxxxxx		
Structured programming			xxxxxxxxxx	xxxx
Design documentation		xxxxxxxxx	xxxxxxxxxx	
Languages				xxxx
A continuum of structured development	xxxxxxxx	xxxxxxxxxxx	xxxxxxxxxxxx	xxxx
Order in progress	xxxxxxxx	xxxxxxxxxxx	xxxxxxxxxxxx	xxxx

operations, the start and end of each process, as defined in the predecessor step, remain unaffected. In this manner, the design process can be started at the greatest level of program design abstraction and proceed to completion in an orderly and predictable manner. In brief, systematically.

The alternative to the restriction to the use of constructs of this kind is the unbridled use of unconditional branches, best known as GOTOs (read, "go to"). These result in program logic that is difficult to understand, impossible to formally verify, and, since they can create logic topographies (in the sense of flowcharts) approaching that of the New York City subway system, an inexhaustible source of latent defects. Putting it differently, without the systematic discipline of structured programming, with the liberty of branching at will from one logical process to any other, computer programs can be endowed with the random musings incidental to cognitive processes. Artistic, yes, but scarcely consonant with the interests of programmer productivity or software quality.

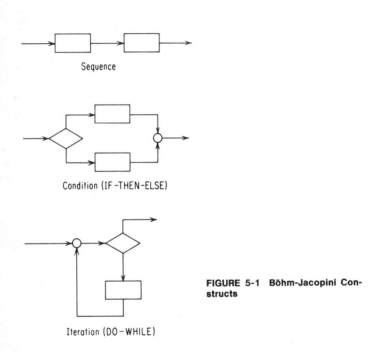

Sequence

Condition (IF –THEN–ELSE)

FIGURE 5-1 Böhm-Jacopini Constructs

Iteration (DO – WHILE)

Although Böhm and Jacopini did not concern themselves with code, the term "structured programming" is generally used today to embrace both detailed design and coding. We'll return to structured programming in that sense as it relates to the detailed design and code phases. We have introduced it now because we shall use the concept, expanded to include all phases of design (and analysis as well), from the start of the software development process.

As development proceeds from the general to the specific, data, too, can be subject to a structuring discipline to continuously refine the understanding and definition of variables, tables, and files. We shall have more to say on this, too, later. What is important at this point is the understanding that structure can encompass all aspects of software development as the single most useful concept to ensure that software development follows an unremittingly steady course from the general to the specific; that structure is the sine qua non of built-in quality.

REQUIREMENTS DEFINITION

The specification of what a program is to do is the first hard output of the development process. There are really three levels of design: systems design, top-level software design, and detailed design. In Chapter 3, we had divided the systems design into two parts: concept and analysis, and requirements definition. The end of the concept and analysis phase does not readily accommodate milestone documentation. Memoranda, hard copy output of simulations, and rough sketches of the system architecture do not represent direction for further design. The requirements definition does represent direction for further design. It is at the point where the results of analysis can be structured to form an element in the continuum of decreasing abstraction that we are first offered tangible evidence of progress.

The specification that bears the definition of the software requirements may take many forms. By one means or another, it must contain enough information to totally frame the problem that the top-level software designers are to address themselves. At this stage of the abstraction, each function to be performed by the computer should be known — and defined — to a high level of precision. The edges of the software to be designed (i.e., the hardware and software interfaces) should also be defined. Earlier, "speed," as an input datum, could be known only as speed. Now, more must be known about it. It must be specified as centimeters per second, miles per hour, furlongs per fortnight, or whatever.

Similarly, the computer hardware that will execute the software should no longer be "the computer system," but should be described in terms of the number of available memory locations, number of disk drives, and so forth. The specification must be thorough, specific to the system requirements, and accurate. It must also be readable and clear. Depending on the methods used for documenting the specifications, these twin sets of objectives may not necessarily coexist. Using traditional forms, clarity is often achieved at the expense of adequate detail. As Alfred North Whitehead said, "Seek simplicity and distrust it."

The most commonly used instrument for specifying the software requirements is text: pages upon pages of text, with amplifying tables or charts here and there, a vain attempt to stem the sea of prolixity. We do not decry the use of this traditional form. The simple fact is that *the major quality problem is not the form of the specification, but the lack or paucity of it.* However, text of this kind does not implicitly further the progress to lesser levels of abstraction. Structure does.

Specification techniques that reflect the idea of structure are known. We shall discuss three of these.

Requirements Languages

Artificial languages for the specification of software requirements are grammars tailored to the definition of the logic and algorithmic solutions that must be implemented by the software. These languages conform to the precepts of structure by confining the user to the three logic constructs described earlier.* To illustrate the idea, this is how the specification for the game of Craps might appear:

```
WHILE Player remains interested AND still has Bankroll
    accept Bet
    Roll Dice and display
    IF a Natural
        THEN Player Wins
        ELSE IF Craps
            THEN Player Loses
            ELSE declare Roll to be point and accept Second bet
                REPEAT
                    Roll Dice
                    IF Roll = point
                        THEN Player Wins with Second bet multiplied by Odds
                UNTIL Player Loses with Roll of 7 or Wins
            Adjust Bankroll and display
END WHILE
```

An underscore between words, as in Second bet, means that the words are to be considered as a single noun or verb, with the two parts separated only for readability. Words beginning with a capital (e.g., Roll and Player) are those that should be defined in a separate dictionary. Note that "point" was not capitalized, since it was defined within the pseudo-procedure, thus making a separate definition unnecessary if not incorrect.

The most apparent advantage over a traditional definition of the requirements for Craps (assuming that Craps is within anyone's tradition) is that this

---

*Some admit two more, DO-UNTIL (or REPEAT-UNTIL) and CASE, both defined later in this chapter. Others use further variations, but always adhering to the restriction of closed (single starting place, common end) processes.

presentation is both explicit and concise. The key nouns and imperative verbs are unmodified by adjectives or adverbs, and, while readability appears to suffer from the loss of the semantic niceties with which we are familiar, with experience, the reader (and writer) rapidly gains fluency. The power of the requirements language technique is, of course, trivialized by a problem as simple as Craps. Such is the nature of illustration. It must be understood that, supported by an appropriate dictionary, the individual statements may include operations that will resolve as far more than a handful of program instructions. The communicative advantages have been neatly summarized by C. Davis and C. Vick, writing of the Requirements Statement Language (RSL) used for the U.S. Army's Ballistic Missile Defense Systems: "The language represents a compromise between the desire for naturalness of expression, unambiguous communication, and machine processing."[6] These benefits notwithstanding, the salient purpose of requirements languages is the structuring they impart to the base from which design will proceed.

"Requirements languages" is a generic term. Each has its own grammatical rules. One of the best known is the Problem Statement Language (PSL) developed under the University of Michigan's ISDOS project. With its emphasis on data structures and interactions, the language has found its greatest applicability in the commercial electronic data processing world. A good summary of the language may be found in an article by D. Teichroew and E. A. Hershey.[7]

Data Flow Diagrams

Another technique used in specifying software requirements is the data flow diagram. These resemble flowcharts, but are used to define the flow of data rather than the flow of program control. Figure 5-2 shows a data flow diagram (variously called a data flow graph, a data graph, or a bubble chart) descriptive of the flow of data involved in the update of an inventory control system after a withdrawal from inventory has been made.

Note that one cannot determine from the data flow diagram which path (data flow) will be activated. This is a control feature. The diagram simply shows the paths that can be taken between the processing nodes. Persons familiar with electronic systems engineering will recognize these diagrams as being functionally identical with their namesakes as used for the documentation of electronic systems architecture.

In addition to providing a graphic technique to reduce the wordiness of specifications, data flow diagrams make it easier to determine impossible operations (recall instructions that can never be executed from Chapter 3) and data transformations that are simply incorrect. This capability is illustrated by the PL/1 procedure, DATFLOW,[8] which exposes the result of transformations that reach each node, and the uses of data at each node that can be affected by subsequent transformations.

An elaborate scheme for using data flow diagrams is that described by T. DeMarco as part of a larger structured system of defining system requirements.[9] DeMarco's diagrams contain four types of symbols:

- Data flows or vectors to portray data paths

- The bubbles, or processes, which depict the transformations of the data

- Straight lines, as compared to the free form data paths, representing files or data bases

- Rectangles for data sources or sinks outside the domain of the software being specified

Data flow diagrams for medium to large systems can cover a great deal of paper. It can be impractical to attempt to get a whole diagram on one sheet. DeMarco solves the problem by expanding bubbles on one sheet into sheets of

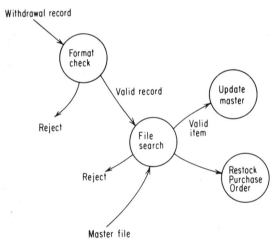

FIGURE 5-2   Inventory Withdrawal Data Flow.

their own. These are further expanded ad infinitum. This is yet another example of the use of a top-down technique in decreasing the abstraction of the system. DeMarco calls such diagrams "leveled data flow diagrams," reflecting the notion of levels of specificity.

A similar technique, also capable of graphical expansion to levels of greater detail, is the SADT system developed by the Softech people. This system has been found to be well suited to the specification of more than software. ITT Europe has used SADT for "both hardware/software systems (telephone and telegraphic switches) and non-software people-oriented problems (project management and customer engineering)."[10]

Although we have introduced data flow diagrams as a way of documenting requirements, we note that the early design stages may be undertaken as an analysis of data transformations even before the development of a modular hierarchy as had been described in Chapter 3. If so, such diagrams can be of great value to designers who need to get their thoughts on paper.

Dictionaries

Data flow diagrams and requirements language statements may name data, but more definition is required. For a diagram as simple as that of Figure 5-2, a glossary is sufficient. But even as a family of related data graphs is structured, so, too, can be the data as it becomes better defined. Beyond supporting the other techniques, structured data dictionaries have considerable merit even as independent aids to the definition of requirements. Data dictionaries can imply transformations that have taken place and can formally define the components of data sets. In his book,[9] DeMarco writes of definitions in terms of the familiar constructs of sequence, condition, and iteration. For example, he defines a flight manifest as an iteration of passenger name. Moreover, iterations can be nested for data just as they are for program flow. For example, flight manifest can generate mailing list of air travelers, and passenger name can be an iteration of alphabetic character.* When so specifying data, one has, to the extent that the interrelationships of the data become immediately evident to the software designers, largely predicted the logical manner of constructing the data base.

As was stated earlier, structured techniques are at the heart of software engineering. Perhaps because the concept of structure derives from the restrictions to closed logic constructs, the emphasis has been on the control of program flow. Nevertheless, much has been done with data, both in the analysis and requirements definition phases and in the design and coding of programs. The structuring of data, however, continues to receive considerably less attention from the software practitioners.

The Usable Specification

However the requirements are defined, a specification that will lead to quality software is one that is not so imposing and wordy that it will be skimmed over, that can be traced back to the specifications for the system problem it is intended to solve, and that is comprehensive and accurate. If it embodies structure, if it takes on the forms that are, themselves, elements of the continuum of decreasing abstraction, it will be all the better.

---

*Admittedly, this last is of a level of detail appropriate to design, not requirements; indeed, an example of how structured requirements definitions can flow into structured programming.

THE REFINEMENT OF ESTIMATES AND STAFFING PLANS

One may wonder what cost estimating and its corollary, staffing, have to do with systematic programming. Quite a bit, actually. While waiting for the system designers to complete their specifications for the software, the software designers will have to start estimating and planning the effort so that they will be able to staff it in time. The basis for their estimating will be the preliminary requirements information that they have been given during the analysis phase. Possibly, on the basis of even more preliminary information or their own interpretation of the system requirements, they may have provided management with an estimate prior to the start of the analysis phase. It is even conceivable that a programming estimate was given to management by the system designers.

Whatever the mode of preliminary, or proposal-time, estimation, the estimate should be refined as the delivery of the specification document nears; and updated again when it is received. Indeed, still more refinement will be possible as the design progresses. The logical times for these are at the milestones used to verify the design. In this manner, as the software becomes increasingly more concrete, the amount of human energy required to complete the development can be better bounded. Thus, systematic programming embraces levels of abstraction in cost estimating as well.

None of this is to dilute the requirement for accurate estimating techniques at the start of the job. The software may be entirely abstract when proposed, but the developers expect to be paid in hard cash. Still, there is no way to believe that the estimate cannot be improved as development progresses, and it must be improved to avoid overstaffing or understaffing. As we shall see, diminished returns come quickly with overstaffing. For the other side of the coin, once a development effort is understaffed, it slips in schedule, and at some point the slippage becomes irrecoverable. (Historically, the point has been when management first becomes aware that the schedule is in jeopardy. One of the goals of software quality assurance is to make potential slippages visible in time for remedial actions: increasing staff, relaxing requirements, improving the processing environment, or whatever.)

The reasons that software slippages can easily become irreversible are several, are complex, and are superbly explained in F. Brooks's classic book, *The Mythical Man-Month*.[11] We will simply summarize his thesis by quoting Brooks's law: "Adding manpower to a late software project makes it later."

Does it make sense though, to refine estimates as time goes on? Is the greater accuracy of the later estimates trivial, since some of the funds have already been spent? Yes, but up to a point well downstream in the development cycle, the milestones that represent times to stop and take stock, times to verify the latest level of software specificity, and times to reestimate the cost-to-complete occur at the natural intervals for adding staff. This is illustrated in Figure 5-3, where the width of each rectangle represents the staffing level. Figure 5-3 also shows, in a gross sense, that the closer the project is to completion, the more rapidly funds are expended.

Some may argue that no more workers are required for test than for detailed design and code. This is frequently true. There are projects, however, certainly including embedded software, where the test phases often involve persons other than the programming team. In any case, we have pyramidal staffing as a function of time, from which it is clear that the earlier that estimating errors can be detected, the better will be the opportunity for appropriate (neither too large nor too small) staffing and cost control.

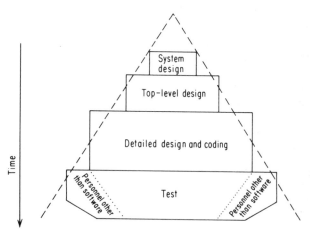

FIGURE 5-3   Manpower During the Development Phases.

One of the purposes of reviewing the development effort at discrete, measurable milestones, is to determine at the earliest opportunity any growth trends in the anticipated size of the final program. Assuming it cannot be reduced by a redefinition of the program objectives or a revised design approach, such growth predicates consideration of either increasing the size of the staff or stretching the schedule. It is common, and at a superficial level, understandable, for management to assume that staff growth, schedule slippages, or a combination of both should be a linear function of the growth of the software. They never are.

Based on earlier empirical work accomplished by P. V. Norden, who had developed a Rayleigh model for software life cycle manpower, L. H. Putnam derived,[12] for software development, the equation

$$S_s = C_k K^{1/3} t_d^{4/3}$$

where S_s = software size in number of source statements

C_k = constant based on the state of technology being applied and the type of software being developed

K = worker-years of development effort

t_d = independent calendar time for development

C_k subsumes a number of constituent factors that make presumptive calculation of it difficult. Nevertheless, the equation is of considerable interest to us. By taking the equivalent of partial derivatives and performing simple algebraic operations, J. Gaffney, Jr., and G. Heller of the IBM Federal Systems Division derived the following equation:[13]

$$\frac{\Delta K}{\Delta t_d} = -4 \frac{K}{t_d}$$

We may read this as "the rate at which development effort changes with respect to schedule is (minus) four times the ratio of effort to schedule." Thus, increasing the effort by 10 percent will provide a schedule benefit of only 2.5 percent. In short, tight schedules will be costly. There may well be an unforeseen upper economic bound to the staffing that will meet the stipulated schedule.

This is but background to the next two equations developed by Gaffney and Heller:

$$\frac{\Delta K}{K} = 3 \frac{\Delta S_s}{S_s}$$

and

$$\frac{\Delta t_d}{t_d} = \frac{3}{4} \frac{\Delta S_s}{S_s}$$

The first of these says that if the estimated program size has grown by 5 percent, the effort may have to increase by 15 percent to meet the same schedule. The second equation, surprisingly, tells us that with effort held constant, the schedule slippages will be proportionately less than program growth. In other words, management, *if warned early enough* that the anticipated program size has grown, can plan to accept a slipped delivery rather than take the cost penalty of disproportionate effort.

Now, one may argue that these conclusions are based on empirical findings. Nevertheless, their gist expresses the dismaying experience of the multitude of software managers who have applied heroic tactics to cope with software growth during the development period.

There is yet another means of recovery available to management: relax the program requirements. Sometimes whole classes of functions (e.g., an optional display or the future capability of accepting online input as well as disk input) can be omitted. Alternatively, performance objectives can be eased (e.g., replace the complex Magellan navigation model with the simpler Henry model at a sacrifice of an additional .05 percent of position uncertainty).

Another solution, applicable to real-time programs, is to reduce the data rates if possible. This won't necessarily reduce program size, but it will markedly reduce effort by making the programming easier. The effect of relaxing requirements may occasionally be achieved by increasing the available memory. The task of developing memory-bound programs is much more severe than for those for which the programmers have latitude with respect to storage utilization.

Whatever the solution, there is a far greater likelihood of its being successful if the problem is identified early. Reviews at the appropriate milestone increases of software specificity are the most, perhaps the only, reliable means of making the visibility of growth problems timely enough for appropriate remedies to be applied.

MODULARITY

One of the key activities of the top-level software design effort is the development of the modular structure of the program. The division of the problem into tiers of hierarchically related modules represents a major step toward completion of the final design. Of the technical aspects of the software design phases, we have chosen to go into modularity in some depth because the success with which software can be made modular has perhaps the most far-reaching effect on the quality of the software over its entire life cycle. It also has a direct effect on the productivity of the programming staff.

Staffing

From Putnam's equation, we saw that development effort in worker-years is proportional to the cube of the size of the program. This is a measure of the complexity implied by size alone (there are other factors that more directly affect complexity), with the constant of proportionality embedded in C_k. C_k is a function of several factors, not the least of which is modularity. Specifically, if the complexity of the program can be reduced by dividing the program into many modules, C_k is appropriately reduced. Moreover, if each of the modules can be regarded as an individual program, we can represent S_s as $S_s = s_1 + s_2 + \ldots + s_n$. Applying Putnam's equation to each of the separate programs, we have, in effect, reduced effort from

$$F(s_1 + s_2 + \ldots + s_n)^3 \qquad \text{to} \qquad f(s_1)^3 + g(s_2)^3 + \ldots + h(s_n)^3$$

This is not intended to be mathematically rigorous for two reasons: (1) C_k as it applies to s_i can no longer presume modularity, since the s_i we are concerned with are the elemental ones and will be divided no further; and (2) it would be unreasonable not to expect t_d to be much shorter for each of the modules than for the entire, integrated and tested, program. Strict mathematical sensibilities notwithstanding, it follows that modularity is a means of improving productivity, provided we can regard the modules as separate programs. Even here, we must waffle. The truth is that we can never quite reach the point of considering the modules as separate programs. That would be expecting too much of modularity. The extent that $F(\Sigma s_i)^3$ is reduced to $\Sigma f_s s_i^3$ is predicated by the degree to which we can achieve mutual independence of the modules.

An intuitive approach to the interrelationships of modularity, staff size, and total effort can be gained by anyone who has ever watched a house being constructed. When the carpenters are nailing flooring onto the joists, each carpenter at work in a separate part of the house, and the plumbers are fitting lengths of pipe together in whatever space is available to them, and the electricians are somewhere attaching cables to outlet boxes, all the workers are maximally effective. However, when the carpenters must coordinate with the plumbers and electricians to determine where holes must be cut through the floorboards, while at the same time the electricians and the plumbers need to discuss the installation of the furnace, we see minimum worker effectivity. The problem is communication. Module independence exerts a favorable effect on staffing by minimizing the need for communication among the staff once the modules have been defined. (Module independence also implies minimum communication during the development of the modular structure, as well, if the top-level design is performed using structured concepts.)

Maintenance

If the modules are independent of each other, and further reflect a strong one-to-one correspondence with specific functions performed by the program, it should be possible to alter the manner in which one of the functions is satisfied without affecting the processing unique to any other function. In the games discussed in Chapter 3, there should be no danger that an improvement made to the Strategy module in the backgammon part of the tree will have an unintended effect on any part of Craps or Bridge. However, without knowing more about the modular decomposition, we have no assurance that a change to Strategy won't affect the processing rules, as coded, of Possible Move Calculation. These modules may very well share data, exchange program flags, call common lower level routines that in some way exert control on the routine calling them, or have other characteristics that compromise their independence.

The task facing maintenance programmers is not an easy one. Let's assume that Mary has been charged with making the backgammon game, now in use on over 1000 home computers, more aggressive. She must first learn the methods and philosophies currently dictating the computer's play. She also has to understand how the program is constructed to implement these methods and philosophies. Turning to the design documentation, Mary studies the hierarchical "family tree" of modules and reads through the specifications that define the purpose of each module. She quickly narrows her interests to the module Strategy and the modules subordinate to it. The design documentation for these modules tells her the manner in which the best possible move is determined.

Mary discovers that the program's first consideration is always to minimize the number of blots that the computer has to leave. (A blot is a single marker resting on one of the locations of the board. It is vulnerable to capture if a marker of the other color can be moved to the location. A blot can be eliminated if the single marker is joined by another of the same color.) Mary wants to change this conservative play by coloring the decision with consideration of the poor strategic position that it may frequently create.

The three modules directly subordinate to Strategy are Early Game, Middle Game, and End Game. Figure 5-4 expands part of Figure 3-4 to show these,

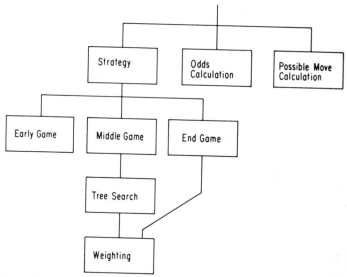

FIGURE 5-4 Backgammon Detail.

as well as the modules Tree Search and Weighting. The complaint of conservatism had been applied to the middle part of the game, and it is to Middle Game that Mary turns her attention. She finds that the most simple fix is to modify the processing of Weighting to lessen the penalty applied to those situations which result in blots.

She makes the change and runs some informal tests. After several days of making adjustments to Weighting, she performs a link-edit on the entire game system and sits down to match her wits with the computer. She wins three backgammon games in a row and is badly losing the fourth when, only a few moves from winning, the computer makes a surprisingly inept move. Mary checks back through the results of all the evaluation reports made at the time of initial release of the program and can find no report of a similar anomaly.

There is nothing to do now but study the end game processing. After considerable effort, Mary discovers the bug. Middle Game had been designed to call the random number utility routine for the purpose of occasionally setting a program flag which, passed through Tree Search to Weighting, would force Weighting into a rote response. This response, in effect, ignored all blots. It was hoped that the resultant move would be sufficiently uncharacteristic of the computer to puzzle the player. In her change to Weighting, Mary ignored the flag, since less notice would now be paid to blots, anyway. What Mary discovered about the flag was that End Game also set it, but for the purposes of establishing the rote response when blots were no longer significant to winning. Still worried about blots when it shouldn't have been, the computer defeated itself.

In effect, despite appearances, Middle Game and End Game were not truly independent of each other, but were linked through other modules.

Testing

We noted, in Chapter 3, that modern software engineering practice generally adopts a modified top-down testing regimen, integrating modules in a top-down manner after they have been unit tested; i.e., tested in isolation.

Among the purposes given for prior unit testing was the recognition that there may be error conditions to which modules may be susceptible that cannot be readily tested except at the module level. Chapter 7 will go into this in greater detail. For our present purposes, as a rationale for unit testing, we may simply consider the number of interfaces between the input routines and the modules at the bottom of the hierarchy. The processing of input data by each of the intervening modules can make it time-consuming, at best, to backtrack from the driving conditions desired for the subject module back to the input data that will generate those conditions.

The unit test of a module, assuming the module is not overly large, should be an exhaustive test; it may even be able to exercise the module in each of the discrete states of data it can produce. However, if the module is closely linked to others, as, for example, through common data areas or by a dependency on logical switches set by other modules, the test driver required to exercise it may be as large — or even larger — than the module itself. The unit test then becomes, in effect, the joint test of the module and the program used to test it. One then faces the choice of untoward costs in test support or insufficient testing.

Even in top-down testing, poor modularity can invite a visit from the pro-grammers' two-headed bête noire: cost and complexity. Prior to a module's entry into the still building system, it is represented by a stub. The role of the stub is a simple one in theory: receiving the call intended for the module it is standing in for, it provides a return logically appropriate to the arguments with which it is called. These normally are rote responses. Again, in the presence of excessive module interdependence, the stub may have to perform a set of calculations based on the current status of common data areas or the status of other logical control indicators. In the extreme, the surrogate may approach its model in complexity, in which case it, too, may have to be unit tested!

More on Independence

Modularity has been discussed as a means of dividing a large and complex problem into a set of smaller, less complex ones. It is more than an attack on complexity, it is a management hook. During the detailed design, coding, and testing phases, it permits the large, formless task called programming to be divided into a number of parts, each of which can be tracked. It is far more informative for a report to state that 45 percent of the modules have been integrated than that integration is 45 percent complete. However, if, because of excessive interdependency, integration of the next module in line requires redesign of five that were previously integrated, progress reports can still be misleading. Once again, independence is the key.

Another advantage to management that can be realized from a modular structure is the freedom it offers to create interim capabilities. As the system is building, long before the full system is operational, limited, but deliverable, capability may be desired. We shall once again use the game as an example, however trivial it may be. If it is important for Personal Processing Power to release Backgammon early, perhaps to forestall invasion by a competitor, the detailed design, coding, and testing of just the modules comprising Backgammon can proceed with the maximum practicable staff applied to that effort. These fully tested modules, with a modified Executive Control, can then be released in advance of the full game capability. Subsequent to the early release, the system can continue building with the addition of Craps and Bridge. In brief, in a truly modular structure, top-down testing, or top-down integration if you will, does not have to proceed one tier at a time across the breadth of the hierarchical tree, but in any desired directed manner, provided that no module is integrated prior to the one directly above it.

This reinforces the concept of structure, which, of course, applies as much to modular design as to any other aspect of software development. Notwith-standing the fact that the word is often used to describe a program that has been divided into more or less arbitrarily defined segments, modularity means

nothing less than the decomposition of the computational task into a structured set of programs, called modules, which exhibit minimum mutual
dependence.

Figure 5-5 depicts this graphically. The overlap area on the right represents
logical connections, fuzzy functional boundaries, and data areas used in common. This, despite the fact that, physically, the modules remain detached from
each other.

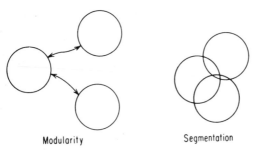

Modularity   Segmentation

FIGURE 5-5

It is unfortunate that we are forced to use so qualitative a term as "minimum mutual dependence," in defining modularity, but there is a limit to the
independence possible. Were the data processed by modules not used by other
modules, no useful purpose would be served. In the least, we must have that
linkage. If total independence is illusory, maximum independence is elusive.
We may talk about our goal, but there is no rigid scientific approach to reaching it. Nevertheless, there are techniques that can be applied.

Achieving Independence

If the decomposition of the problem proceeds in a structured manner, as was
informally presented in the development of the game hierarchy in Chapter 3,
we can be reasonably certain of attaining at least one aspect of modular independence, namely, that implied by a monotonic control gradient. A module
relinquishes control to a module subordinate to it for the purpose of performing a specific function. The called module may, in turn, call others below it,
but ultimately, program control should revert to the first module in the link
in question. After all, that module transferred control for the specific purpose
of transforming data to its own ends. Thus, in a well-structured hierarchy, one
may expect to find execution sequences in chains more vertical than horizontal. It would also be expected that the higher a module is in the hierarchy, the
more it is empowered with the capability of control; rather like a corporate
organization of people. As an example, the topmost module should be pure
control, a scheduler of the main sections of the program.

Restricting the control flow greatly reduces the need for logical links, in the form of control switches or flags, between modules. If the program is designed along structured precepts, always progressing from the more abstract to the less, the monotonic control gradient we seek will necessarily follow.

It is possible that the definitive concept of structured design, as it applies to modularity, is to be found in the article appropriately entitled "Structured Design" by W. P. Stevens, G. J. Myers, and L. L. Constantine.[14] The ideas presented, based on a decade of research by Constantine, constitute a set of general design considerations and techniques for reducing program complexity. In particular, they define the characteristics of what the authors refer to as *coupling* between modules and *cohesiveness* within modules. They also offer procedures for decomposing the computational task into a set of modules of the desired qualities.

Amplification of these procedures and the strategies behind them were published by Myers[15] in 1978 and by E. Yourdon and L. Constantine[16] in 1979. Both books describe decomposition techniques tailored to the characteristics of the problem being attacked. None of the techniques of structured design need be used exclusively for a given program. Rather, each may be used where it seems most applicable. Recall that modular decomposition starts all over again each time a module is defined. That is, the new module is decomposed further.

As effective as structured design is, it still cannot offer total independence. As we said a couple of pages back, that is impossible. We are attracted, then, to the notion of improving tolerance to dependency, and for this we turn to a tree structure. A module tree structure is one in which each module may have many modules subordinate to it, but is, itself, subordinate to only one other module. Had Backgammon, which started out as a tree structure, continued in the same vein, Mary could not have gotten herself in trouble, as she did. A tree structure inherently exhibits functional independence between branches, although this can easily be polluted by access to common data areas or by letting one branch set logical switches for another.

The problem with a tree structure is that it frequently leads to redundancy. The tree structure of Figure 5-6 illustrates this. Modules Echo and Easy, which we define to perform precisely the same function, are both needed to preserve

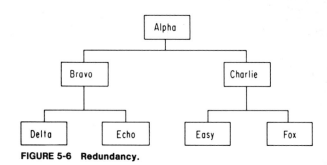

FIGURE 5-6   Redundancy.

the tree structure. In Figure 5-7, we gain efficiency by eliminating Easy, but we also lose the tree structure that afforded considerable tolerance to coupling between the Bravo and Charlie branches. A compromise can be reached by declaring all modules that are subordinate to two or more modules to be *utility routines* (much as input-output routines and trigonometric functions), seeing to it that they are designed to closely conform to the tenets of low-coupling and maximum cohesion, and providing them with the most stringent configuration control.

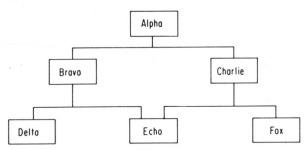

FIGURE 5-7 Redundancy Removed.

Whatever the means used, the objective of modular decomposition is to produce modules that internally have a cohesiveness that emphasizes self-sufficiency, and that externally have minimum coupling to other modules. An intuitive clue to the extent of cohesiveness is in the answer to the question, "How succinctly can we describe the module's purpose?" If we can say, "Module Xform transforms the polar coordinates of the radar sighting into cartesian coordinates," we can feel good about the module's cohesiveness. If we have to add to the definition, "and, by-the-by, compares the cartesian coordinates to the last measurement and if any is different by more than one kilometer computes the ground speed of the target," we can suspect that the purposes of modularity have been ill-served.

Coupling is the other qualitative criterion for modularity. The modular structure will be weakened if modules can directly reference a datum internal to another module, if there is extensive use of common data areas, or if parameters set by one module are used to control the operations internal to another module.

Unfortunately, we continue to deal with qualitative attributes of modularity. Although they can be neatly set forth on paper, their application as criteria usually involves at least some subjective judgment. In the absence of quantitative measures of modularity, that is, measures of the mutual independence of the modules, a numerical criterion has been advanced by a number of writers. This criterion is one that attaches to the most obvious, but scarcely most important, characteristic of modularity; namely, size. Various upper limits to the allowable size of a module have been proposed: 50 lines of source code, 100 lines of source code, 200 binary locations, and so forth.

Numerical measures are understandably attractive. However, the number of instructions in a module has no relevance to the extent to which the module is inextricably bound to other modules in the system, nor does a small number guarantee processing self-sufficiency within the module. Still, one doesn't want to totally ignore size. If independence were the only goal, it could be achieved quite easily by simply making the program a single module. Generally, a module consisting of two or more pages of compiler language source code ought to be looked at a second time to see if it should be further decomposed. This scrutiny, however, is quite apart from clamping an upper limit on size by fiat, as some have recommended.

Parenthetically, it should be noted that in embedded software, small modules may be quite harmful. It takes perhaps eight instructions to invoke a module. Let us assume that in the decomposition process two modules have been defined that together form a loop. Assuming 1 microsecond per instruction, if the loop executes 1000 times per second of real time, 16 milliseconds of each second will have been expended for the sole purpose of control transfer. It would be better to fold one of the modules into the other and buy an additional 16 percent of computer load reserve. One must, of course, be careful not to abuse the license to recombine functions if, by doing so, the complexity of the total system is unnecessarily increased.

The structured decomposition of the problem to a set of smaller problems ends when each module so defined is small enough to be fully grasped. Individually, the modules may not be complex in scope, but it is possible to program them in such a way that the final code for each replicates, in miniature, the apparent intricacy that existed prior to decomposition. Structured techniques are still called for.

STRUCTURED PROGRAMMING

What we have defined as detailed program design has, historically, followed any arbitrary route the wanderings of the programmer's mind might select. It was utterly without structure save for that which, without formal awareness of the process, the programmer gave it here and there. This is not to discount the frequency with which designs demonstrated a logical flow of control. The better programmers have alway been eminently logical people. However, these inherently structured code segments were often connected to each other in a nonchalant fashion.

What was missing was a technological discipline for ensuring the continuous use of structure throughout the design process.

The early stages of this chapter presented that discipline in the form of the three canonical constructs of Böhm and Jacopini. Each construct has but a single entry point and a single exit point. Within each construct, the process symbol can be replaced with another full construct; thus permitting the program to unfold in an iterative manner. What results is a program of inherent structural strength created by a specific self-controlling process. Moreover, the permissible constructs relate to a larger arena. McGowan and Kelly have made the observation that "each of the permissible control structures corresponds to a standard mathematical pattern of reasoning, namely, linear reasoning or substitution, case analysis, and induction."[17] There is no reason that this elegant design methodology need ever by considered inimical to the programmer's efficiency. Nevertheless, the use of structured programming in the design phase is still far from universal, with the consequence that writers still feel compelled to expound upon its virtues.

To many programmers, structured programming, as evidenced in code, is synonymous with avoidance of the GOTO. The three Böhm-Jacopini constructs make the GOTO unnecessary, so the popular belief is certainly well-founded. It has, however, led some practitioners to believe that the purpose of structured programming can be served by first designing the program in any arbitrary fashion, and then reconstructing it (usually at the expense of adding control variables) to eliminate GOTOs. While the product may lead to more readable code, it defeats structured programming's quintessential purpose of filling a role in the process of monotonically decreasing the abstraction of the system. Only by truly designing according to structured precepts, will logical flaws, with their potential of subsequent eruption as software failures, be apparent to the designer.

Perhaps the easy identification of structured programming with GOTO-less programs derives from Dijkstra's letter, "Go To Statement Considered Harmful,"[18] printed in Communications of the ACM (CACM) in 1968. Referencing Böhm and Jacopini's article, published two years earlier in CACM, Dijkstra's letter, while not the first public reproof of the GOTO, permanently coupled the concept of GOTO-less programming with the substance of Böhm and Jacopini's proof.

It is patently unconstructive to achieve the appearance of structured programming by cosmetic expulsion of GOTOs. In fact, for improving efficiency or for implementing error escapes, a good argument can be fashioned for the occasional considered inclusion of GOTOs. The definitive defense of the GOTO in structured programming is Knuth's 1974 paper.[19] Any logic constructs that adhere to closed form, single-entry–single-exit structure is suitable for structured programming. Accordingly, in addition to the three Böhm-Jacopini forms, two others have become commonplace among those who practice structured programming. These are the DO-UNTIL* (or its equivalent,

---

*Böhm and Jacopini showed that this form can be derived from the sequence and DO-WHILE constructs.

REPEAT-UNTIL) and the CASE. The full set of five is illustrated in Figure 5-8.

It is clear that the only difference between DO-UNTIL and DO-WHILE is that the test of loop satisfaction is made in the DO-WHILE before the process is executed, whereas the DO-UNTIL test is made after the processing has been completed. These two are the basic mechanisms for creating loops, or iterations. Note the difference between DO-UNTIL and the similar FORTRAN DO construction in the following example of a program segment that lists the

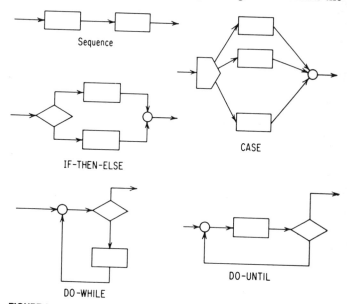

Sequence

IF-THEN-ELSE

CASE

DO-WHILE

DO-UNTIL

FIGURE 5-8 Constructs of Structured Programming.

records of a file, up to and including the last active record, which is denoted by a set of special symbols (e.g., dollar sign characters). In both cases we assume the ability to compare two vectors, Record and Last, in a single statement.

FORTRAN-like* code:

```
      DO 10 I = 1,MAXFILE
         READ (INFILE) RECORD
         IF (END FILE) CALL EXIT ROUTINE
         WRITE (PRINTER) RECORD
         IF (RECORD.EQ.LAST) GOTO 11
   10    CONTINUE
   11    . . . . . . . . . .
```

*As a further liberty, to avoid obscuring the point being made, FORTRAN format statements are ignored.

Code with DO-UNTIL form:

```
UNTIL (RECORD = LAST) DO
   BEGIN
      READ (INFILE,RECORD);
      IF (END FILE) THEN CALL EXIT ROUTINE
      WRITE (PRINTER,RECORD)
   END
```

We see that FORTRAN required an integer variable, I, and a label, 10, to create a loop. Neither the variable nor the label were in any way related to the function of the loop. The FORTRAN example also requires an explicit test to terminate and escape the loop when the last-active-record indicator is encountered. The improved readability of the structured example is its most striking feature.

The CASE construct is an extended IF-THEN-ELSE. It is not only a convenience for the programmer, it can also improve readability. A program to generate a calendar for a single month might include the following code:

```
IF MONTH = JANUARY
   THEN NDAYS = 31
ELSE IF MONTH = FEBRUARY
   THEN NDAYS = 28
ELSE IF MONTH = MARCH
   THEN NDAYS = 31

          .

          .

          .

ELSE IF MONTH = DECEMBER
   THEN NDAYS = 31
```

This can be replaced by:

```
CASE MONTH OF
   JANUARY:
      NDAYS = 31
   FEBRUARY:
      NDAYS = 28

          .

          .

          .

   DECEMBER:
      NDAYS = 31
END
```

The readability is most enhanced when the CASE construct can be used to reduce the number of nested IF statements.

It has been argued that the advantages of multiple entry points are lost to the programmer using structured programming. Specifically, it appears, at the module level, that the tenet of single-entry–single-exit does not permit multiple entries. However, this is a semantic matter, with the formalism of module entry points confused with the idea of a single entry to each logical block of code. Multiple entry points can be accommodated within structured programming provided the code associated with each entry point does not overlap (branch into) the code associated with any other entry point.

At the module's nether end, structured programming has been charged with impeding the programmer's ability to use diagnostic procedures based on subroutine returns. For example, a simple way to narrow the search to determine which module is causing the program to "hang-up" is to trap and output all subroutine returns. The problem is then known to exist in the routine called after the last one that is listed. Now this would seem to violate the precept that returns are always made to the calling module. (Single exit point implies this.) However, it is harmless to replace the return with a branch to a diagnostic module that, following completion of its processing, employs CASE-like logic to generate a transfer vector back to the calling module. Even better, modify the systems software under which the testing is being performed, to invoke the diagnostic module. The return will then be intercepted in a manner totally invisible to the module. As long as its essence is uncompromised, one need not be doctrinaire about structured programming.

Data

Computer programs are not just a matter of control logic; they are also made up of data, or more accurately, of data definitions. Even the input data they process must be defined within the program. At the code level, the definitions may be as vague as the simple allocation of space for a general purpose buffer, or they may be so precise as to imply the operations appropriate to the data. The concept of structured data extends to a development phase much earlier than coding, however. As was the case with control flow, the structuring of data starts at the higher levels of abstraction.

As an analogy, consider the design of electronic equipment. The electronic devices — transistors, capacitors, integrated chips — are the functional data of the equipment. In the early design phases, we have a circuit diagram in which the eventual employment of devices is indicated solely by abstract symbols, accompanied by the identification of the electronic characteristics of each that are relevant to the analysis of performance. The diagram will indicate the reactance of a capacitor, but not its arcing voltage or the associated parallel leakage. Subsequently, after the diagram has been analyzed and found suitable, an engineering parts list will be generated. The components gain in specificity by the designation of manufacturer and manufacturer's part numbers. C13 on the diagram now becomes Captronics part number C1234M06J, from which arcing voltage and parallel leakage may be learned. Finally, the assembly diagram is drawn, giving the location and orientation of each component, thus lending to each a uniqueness within the system.

Once again we turn to the games discussed in Chapter 3, this time to see how the definition of data may be refined. In particular, consider the display of a bridge hand. Initially, during the definition phase, the display is no more specific than Display of Hand. Later, the hand becomes 13 cards. Still later, the pictorial manner of display is defined (e.g., Queen of Hearts, or H Qn). In the detailed design phase, the display takes on the structure of a table of 13 rows, with each row containing enough character space for the selected display technique. The hand is finally made specific by the code. As was the case with program flow, at each step properties of the next level of abstraction remained hidden; no more detail was defined than was necessary to complete development of the program at the step in question.

Just as we can speak of structured constructs for program flow, we can refer to standard forms for data. From the earliest years of programming, the forms of *constants* (in a semantic sense these may not usually be considered as data, but for the present purpose they are), *variables*, variables logically associated in *tables*, and *files* have been found useful as standards. Later, certain types of data were defined: variables could be integers, reals (capable of taking on fractional values), complex, or boolean (having but two values, true or false). Each type defined the attributes and storage requirements for each datum so defined.

It is interesting to note that in terms of input and output files, programmers have for some time been accustomed to dealing with abstract data sources and sinks. Under modern operating systems, the physical devices inputting data or accepting output do not have to be defined until run time, when the job control statements, the directives to the operating system, can specify the card reader, tape unit, disk drive, or printer containing, or designated to receive, each file. Thus, the lowest level of abstraction is achieved externally to the program.

At the code level, data structuring is best accommodated by application typing. Most popular languages used for algebraic computation, such as FORTRAN and PL/1, differentiate between integers and reals, but then there is BASIC, which in its minimal form treats all data alike. At the other extreme, specificity gains when the programmer is permitted to define his own types. PASCAL comes supplied, as it were, with the types integer, real, boolean, and character. The operations permitted on each are those appropriate to the type. One cannot multiply two boolean variables, but one can form their logical conjunction. One cannot add two characters, but one can use the comparison operators (e.g., "less than," "not equal to") to determine which of two characters has alphabetic priority or whether they match. Beyond the built-in PAS-CAL data types, one then defines one's own type. For example:

TYPE

DAY NAME = (SUNDAY, MONDAY. . . . . . . .SATURDAY);

Having so declared the names of the days, one can then use the PASCAL function ORD (short for order) to operate on a variable of the type DAY NAME. Thus, if one, having previously pulled from a file a datum, TOLL RECORD, of the type DAY NAME, wants to determine if it is a week-day record,

K: = ORD(TOLL RECORD)

will return a 0 for Sunday or a 6 for Saturday. Thus, for K = 1 through 5, weekday toll rates apply.

Further, one can define sets of data and perform the boolean operations of conjunction and disjunction on them. For example, if one has declared TEN-NIS, GOLF, BASEBALL, WATER POLO to be the set of warm weather games one plays with a ball, and SAILING, WATER SKIING, WATER POLO to be one's favorite water sports, then the conjunction of variables assigned to the two sets turns out to be the only water sport (WATER POLO) one plays with a ball, and the disjunction yields the full complement of one's summer recreation.

Relating this to typical electronic data processing operations, we see that the conjunction of sets is essentially what the programmer calls a sieve, while disjunction is none other than concatenation. Here, however, they are performed without the housekeeping details of indexes, table bounds, block transfers, and the like. In effect, the compiler has been used to tailor a data structure specific to the problem.

Languages like PASCAL offer a number of other capabilities for data structuring, well beyond the scope of this book. Their contribution to the quality solution lies in their allowing certain error-prone details of data representation and handling to remain hidden from the programmer. Among these details, none presents a greater source of latent defects or wasted debugging hours than that of *pointers.** A pointer is a variable set to some specific location within a table or file to mark an entry, or set of entries of interest. For example, in what is often called a threaded list or data chain, each record contains a pointer to the location of the next record in conformance to some logical ordering scheme (chronological order of invoice receipt, alphabetic order, or whatever).

Sometimes multiple chains are maintained within a file when more than

---

*Actually, to accommodate space efficient data structures, such as threaded lists, PASCAL does permit the declaration of pointers. However, these remain bound to the data they reference, and, moreover, to preserve their functional integrity, are subject to rigorous restrictions on the operations that may be performed on them.

one logical order is important. A file of airline flights out of Chicago, physically in chronological order, may have a different chain for each airline. This permits a simple listing of all the outbound flights in the most logical order (time of day), while simultaneously providing easy access to just those departures flown by Trans Illinois Airlines. Each time a record is added to or deleted from the file, pointers must be readjusted. The opportunities for fouling the system are limited only by the development programmer's imagination. The likelihood of the maintenance programmer's being confused by the system is bounded only by the obfuscation of the design documentation.

The conceptual similarity of structured program flow and structured data has been vividly extended—by C. Hoare,[20] who has convincingly likened pointers to GOTO statements—beyond the philosophy of design abstraction levels to include code. However, analogously to the earlier caveat that structured program flow is not simply GOTO-less code, it is important to remember that structured data is more than just the elimination, or the PASCAL-like binding, of pointers.

DESIGN DOCUMENTATION

Can the manner in which software design is documented reflect the structured decomposition of the problem, or must it continue to reflect the miscellaneous assortment of charts, text, and tables that has evolved? The answer to this ponderously loaded question is, of course, yes, but only up to a point. Hierarchical modular architecture can be placed in a data base for subsequent explosion, similar to that applied to bills of material, but as an aid to grasping the manner in which the hierarchy reflects the system requirements, presentation in the form of a chart is still desirable. Tables of memory allocation by module and of machine loading by module or function remain the most effective way of communicating these inherently tabular functions. Planning documentation is still explained best by text and various time-based charts.

Still, this leaves the vast area of control flow, data flow, and data structures open to improvement, and there is no more likely candidate for improved documentation technology than control flow. As we shall see, solutions to this can entail data flow and structures as well.

Certainly, the ubiquitous flowchart leaves much to be desired. Flowcharts do not lend themselves to restrictions of form, with the consequence that they frequently spread amorphously into entangled networks that approach plates of spaghetti and meatballs in their intricacies. Worse, in trying to find one's way from one processing meatball to another, one often follows a spaghetti tube to an off-page connector, not at a logical functional boundary, but at a point dictated by the size and aspect ratio of the paper the diagram is drawn on. One can bound the topographic excesses with well-considered standards, but the application of these often requires an untoward amount of planning time by the programmer. In fact, if he, like most programmers, uses flowcharts to record his cognitive progress as he works out the detailed design, he will end, in order to meet the relevant standards, by performing the role of a drafter in totally redrawing the diagram.

Before leaving flowcharts (which we should want to do as quickly as possible), we must pause and address the venerable question of how detailed a flowchart should be, since this arises in alternative methods of documentation also. Flowcharts should certainly not be detailed to the point of one symbol per instruction. That would be unreadable. Those given to quantitative standards at all costs have suggested that each symbol should represent an average of five instructions. Except for those who advocate an average of seven or eight or ten instructions. None of these magic numbers bears directly on the matter of readability or communication of design concepts or evidence of design completion. Another school of thought holds that each decision point, or branch, should be shown. If well drawn, this will at least show structure. The problem is that the flowchart may still be so cluttered with detail that the concepts are beclouded. As a somewhat lame alternative (one is always defensive about submitting qualitative standards), we suggest that for each symbol on the flowchart the form of the consequent code should be obvious; that is, that there should be no substantive differences in the manner in which the design can be implemented in code. The weakness of this standard lies in the ad hoc subjective interpretations allowed by the qualifier "substantive." In defense, we note that use of the criterion errs mostly on the side of insufficient detail, somewhat the lesser of the two evils.

Hierarchy Plus Input-Process-Output (HIPO)

One popular attempt to overcome the disadvantages of flowcharts has been the technique of hierarchy plus input-process-output, best known simply as HIPO. To each module shown on the hierarchical charts, such as we have been referring to since Chapter 3, an input-process-output chart is prepared. This chart tabulates the elements of the input and output data spaces of the module, as well as the operations within the module that will effect the data transformations. The three sets are related by directed lines, as in Figure 5-9, which shows an input-process-output chart for the module of an inventory control system that handles deletions from stock. The module updates the master inventory file and, if the remaining inventory of items of the type being withdrawn from stock falls below a preset minimum, issues a purchase order for more stock.

Viewing a chart, one may decide that certain of the transformations should be performed in modules subordinate to the one depicted. For example, recalling the earlier description of modularity, the generation of purchase orders would seem to be a matter better handled by a separate module. Thus, HIPO abets structuring of the modular architecture. Indeed, one may write an input-process-output chart for the program, while still considered as a monolithic entity, and start structuring from the top within the HIPO documentation methodology. That is, HIPO can be more than documentation, it can be a complete design process, with documentation necessarily produced as a by-produci. A good, concise, description of HIPO is given by J. Stay in the IBM Systems Journal.[21]

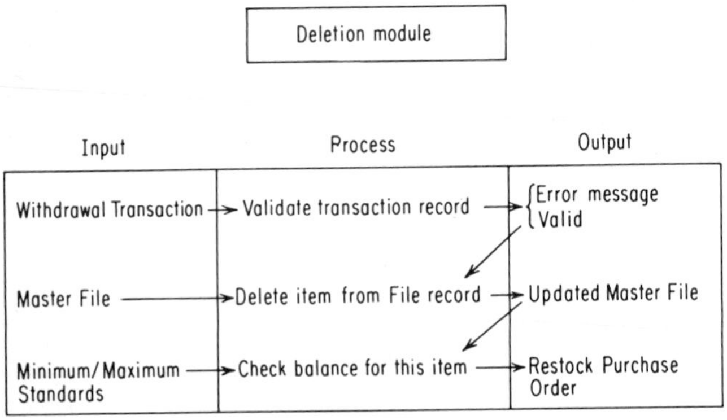

FIGURE 5-9 Input-Process-Output.

As a substitute for flowcharts, HIPO has at least one major drawback: it simply is not as good a vehicle for portraying control flow. It is well-suited to the replacement of much of the text that forms a part of the top-level design documentation, but does not always give a clear indication of *how* transformations are to be performed. For this reason, HIPO seems more compatible with problems that involve standard computational operations. HIPO makes good sense in transactional processing. It would be a relatively poor instrument for the documentation of Craps. HIPO also shares two of the disadvantages of flowcharts. For archival documentation (not to be confused with dead storage; it will inevitably be used for software maintenance), both require the services of those who can draw and letter neatly. Admittedly, this is a relatively low expense item, and, moreover, one that can often be ameliorated by computer-aided design systems. Of greater importance, neither lends itself to inclusion in a data base for simplified updating and from which software tools can perform consistency checks and various summaries.

Program Design Languages

Program design languages (PDLs) solve these problems. Whether or not software tools are implemented for them, they offer natural language statements within a structured grammar. A philologist might view a PDL as an artificial language rendered excessively pithy by its lack of semantic qualifiers and graceless by its syntactical constraints. To a programmer, a PDL is a form of pseudocode, uncompilable, and not demanding of intrinsic data and label definitions. Typically, the only permissible language constructs relevant to program flow are those selected from, or minor variations of, the five forms (Figure 5-8) used for structured programming. This may strike one as similar to the requirements languages discussed under the heading Requirements Definition. The only real difference is in the greater degree of formalism, appropriate to the level of greater specificity, that attaches to PDLs.

PDLs are frequently referred to as "structured English," a most appropriate term (at least in English-speaking countries), possibly introduced by Caine and Gordon in their 1975 paper.[22] Expressing the design of Craps in an arbitrarily contrived PDL, one can easily see how the term "structured English" has gained currency:

```
Initialize Random AND ACCEPT Bankroll
WHILE Player ENTERS 'again' AND Bankroll > 0
   ACCEPT Bet
   CALL Random
   Adjust for Roll AND DISPLAY AND Pause
   IF (Roll = Craps)
      THEN SET Bet to (-Bet)
      ELSE IF (Roll ≠ Natural)
         ACCEPT Second bet AND ADD to Bet
         SET point to Roll
         REPEAT
            CALL Random
            Adjust for Roll AND DISPLAY AND Pause
            IF (Roll = point)
               THEN to Bet ADD (Second bet x (Odds(point)-1))
               ELSE IF (ROLL = 7)
                  SET Bet to (-Bet)
         UNTIL (Roll = 7) OR (Roll = point)
      ADD Bet to Bankroll AND DISPLAY
END WHILE
```

This example should be compared with Figure 3-12, the flowchart illustrated for the program. One immediately notices that the PDL example is readable from top to bottom. This is because it is structured. There is no reason for the reader's eyes to roam about the page. More important, unless one works at writing code that does not follow the design, there is no way in which the code cannot be structured. The code represents the next level of abstraction and should follow quite naturally. In the development of the Craps flowchart, although the principle of iterative design was observed, with the design becoming more detailed step-by-step, there were no constraints laid upon the structure. Indeed, in the process of refining the design, a decision block, Is Round Over?, was expanded into two decision blocks and two processing blocks. We now realize that this is unacceptable in structured programming. We could not have done this with the PDL example.

Note, also, that in the PDL example, the Result flag has disappeared in favor of reversing the sign of the bet if the player loses. This is not a concomitant of the use of PDL. However, the use of flags contravenes the spirit of structured logic in the same sense that logic switches, passed between modules, dilute their independence. Although the Result flag could have been retained in a PDL description of Craps, it was actually easier not to.

The PDL example assumes certain conventions. Words in capital letters are reserved words. Their meaning is self-evident. Verbs and nouns with the initial letter capitalized must be defined externally in some sort of glossary or dictionary. Mostly, definition of the verbs that were used would be trivial. However, in the cases of Pause and Adjust, the definition would cover what in compilable code would resolve as several statements. In a more complex problem, with all operations scaled up in size, these would be candidates for separate routines. Odds(point) refers to the entry in the Odds table applicable to the point; for example, 2:1 for a 4-point or a 10-point. Here, the dictionary would indicate the structure of the Odds table.

Finally, the example may be compared to the requirements language example for the Craps specification, given earlier in this chapter. Note that the requirements, prepared at a greater level of abstraction, required fewer statements. In a more typical case, the ratio would be considerably greater.

The example is, as we had defined PDLs, noncompilable. However, given some additional syntax rules, such as rigid indentation conventions or the BEGIN-END and semicolons of PASCAL, it could be processed to produce a number of useful design aids. Among those that have been implemented for PDLs are the following:

- Input statement error reports
- Analysis of the relationships among the several modules or submodules
- Cross-reference of data items
- Formatted list of individual modules and global references
- Module interface compatibility errors

At least one design language, the PASCAL-based PDL2 language used for the U.S. Army's Ballistic Missile Defense Systems (see Davis and Vick[6]), can accommodate levels of specificity down to and including compilation into executable code. There is also a design language served by a processor that translates its statements into FORTRAN. This language, the Urban Mass Transportation Administration's USL, is one of ten described in an excellent state-of-the-art summary prepared for the U.S. Air Force's Electronic Systems Division.[23] We may expect that in time we shall see executable code exercised by test data automatically generated from the more abstract definition of the program given in PDL.

Neatly filling the sizable gap between requirements language and compiler language, and machine readable for the potential of processor tool support, design languages have much to recommend them over graphic techniques for the documentation of detailed design.

Software's Stepchild

Even within any single industry involved with software, there are relatively few standards for documentation accepted by the majority of the members of the industry. Electronic data processing standards are almost nonexistent. The military standards differ from service to service and even within individual branches. Process control is in even worse shape. And so it goes. This is in sharp contrast to the hard goods industries, where schematic and assembly diagrams, engineering parts lists, and bills of materials are much alike from one company to another; where the blueprints a machinist uses in one shop can be accurately interpreted by a machinist in another; where galleys differ little from one publisher to another.

This may be blamed on the relative youth of the software industry. It may also be a matter of relative necessity. If they are not copied — that is, manufactured in a production environment — most hardware designs are useless. This has driven the documentation of hardware designs. Software products, however, are cloned from the last development model, with the result that the heat has been taken off their documentation. Yet, the last, tested, proven development model is the end product of a lengthy and (presumably) orderly process of analysis, specification, design, and testing. If efficient, consistent, and informative documentation hasn't attended all phases of development, the quality of the product will be severely compromised. And then there is maintenance, for which the documentation represents a Rosetta stone for unlocking the mysteries of the program, without which the program will surely be short-lived.

LANGUAGES

One can code in a compiler language at roughly five times the production rate for assembly languages. Except for a few pathological cases, one can debug at five times the rate, also. The level of design documentation doesn't have to be quite so detailed for programs written in compiler language. (Assembly language is so arcane that a group of ten or so sequential statements are hard to relate to the rest of the program without external help.) Assembly languages open up a level of hazard, hidden by compiler languages, to programmer error; that of register and status bit manipulation. Some compiler languages lend themselves to structured programming. No assembler languages do. Programs written in assembly language can be executed only on computers that can execute the same instruction set.

Most programming is performed in compiler language; not necessarily the most quality-oriented compiler languages, but compiler languages nonetheless. Unfortunately, "most" leaves a great deal that is not so performed, including one of the classes of software most subject to cost, schedule, and reliability problems. A major part of the programming of embedded software continues to be performed in assembly language. Compiler language is gaining ground, but at a disquietingly slow rate.

One reason for this is that many embedded programs are intended for operation on microprocessors. There are few microprocessors for which efficient compilers exist, although, happily, this is changing.

Beyond the availability of compilers, we still find continued loyalty to assembly language. Two reasons are given: memory and speed. That assembly language is more efficient, at least at the pen of a good programmer, is incontrovertible. Code processed by compilers, depending upon the language, the manner in which the compiler implements the translation, and the degree of architectural dissonance between the language and the target computer, is at least 10 percent less efficient than assembly code, frequently much worse. However, it is scarcely sufficient to settle on assembly language for a project without examining the alternative.

First, is memory the principal problem? If so, is it cost or is it space, power, and heat that is the concern? It should rarely be cost any more, now that memory cells are in the millidollar range. But even the physical problem is often more fancied than real. For many programs, the greater part of memory is taken by data, not executable instructions, and modern compilers allow programmers to pack data into memory nearly as efficiently as assembly code can.

More significant is the speed problem. For this, more ingenuity is required. There are basically two approaches that may be used: hand-optimization and an occasional reversion to assembly language. The former implies a compiler that produces assembly language output rather than object code. This output will, of course, subsequently be assembled. Assuming the availability of software tools that can correlate areas of code with computational time-stress, the programmer can scrutinize the critical assembly code produced by the compiler and manually improve it. This is a form of local optimization beyond that produced by the compiler. The penalty to be paid cannot, however, be ignored: the compiler language source code no longer represents the delivered executable code. Configuration control must now be maintained for the source code, the assembly "patches," as the handwritten code is called, and the instructions for overlaying the compiler's output with the patches. Nevertheless, although the technique vitiates the benefits of compiler language, all is not lost if the speed-sensitive areas are but a small part of the program, as is usually the case. A programming adage is that 5 percent of the code does 95 percent of the work.

The other technique worth considering also assumes that the programmer can isolate the most frequently exercised code. However, instead of optimizing the compiler's output, the programmer either segregates the hard-working code in separate modules, which are then coded in assembly language, or, if the compiler permits, replaces the compiler language source statements with inline assembly language.* Combining modules written in assembly language with those coded in compiler language is hardly a novel idea. Even if speed of execution is not a consideration, the I/O primitives will be written in assembly language. Why not allow the innermost loops to be so written, if necessary?

Attributes of Compiler Languages

This is hardly the place to discuss the effect of specific languages on software quality. It is appropriate, however, to note three of the properties of languages, not covered elsewhere in this chapter, that can influence quality. We assume that it is obvious that languages that include structured control forms and data restrictions are preferred to those that do not. In the same vein, it should be clear that reliability is enhanced by language restrictions that deny one module's access to another except through the second's explicit interface.

Recursion

Recursion is a useful feature in programming for the same reason that it is in mathematics; it makes things simpler to do and, in the process, more understandable. For our purposes, this means less prone to programmer error. In mathematics, recursion is employed wherever possible. Familiar examples are the binomial coefficients and the Chebyshev polynomials. Using the latter for illustration, rather than having to grind out $T_i(z) = \cos(i \cos^{-1} z)$, with far less effort we evaluate the three term recurrence

$$T_i(z) = 2zT_{i-1}(z) - T_{i-2}(z)$$

given $T_0(z) = 1$
$\qquad T_1(z) = z$

---

*The inline capability is a function of the compiler, not the language. It is not commonly made available. The only compilers having the feature with which the authors have first-hand familiarity were written for the U.S. Navy's CS-1 and CMS-2 languages. The results were in all respects excellent.

The equivalent in software is a subroutine that can call itself.* To take a simple, and classic, example, a solution to the computation of $N!$ can be given recursively by

```
PROCEDURE FACTORIAL (N)
IF N ≤ 1
    THEN FACTORIAL = 1
    ELSE FACTORIAL = N * FACTORIAL (N− 1)
END
```

Without giving explicit direction, the programmer has, with this concise procedure, called into play the hardware-software system of stacks (first-in–last-out lists used to keep track of addresses, register contents, and interim calculations) to be relieved of tedious details. In the finest traditions of levels of abstraction, these stacks are, of course, hidden from the programmer. From a quality point of view, recursion provides an elegant technique for making the kernel of the solution clear. The natural alternative is iteration, which involves considerably more code. Recursion is mostly used in operations allied with the ordering of data or the processing of tree networks. For example, if one wanted to list all the source statements comprising the tree network represented by the game hierarchy of Figure 3-4, the simplest and clearest way would be to employ recursion. Each box on the tree represents a string of statements, one of which points to a subordinate box. Thus, the code that finds and lists the contents of each box also finds the contents of the boxes below.

Unfortunately, recursion takes more execution time than does iteration, making it unsuitable for many applications. Even then, however, if the problem lends itself to recursion, it may be profitable to write an interim recursive routine to validate a solution of inherent subtlety. It is likely that conceptual errors underlying any faults that appear will more easily be found in the simpler code. After the program is found to work correctly, if slowly, the module can be reprogrammed without recursion. The tests run earlier can then be repeated to validate the reprogramming. Not all compilers support recursion. FORTRAN, COBOL, and BASIC do not. ALGOL, PASCAL, and PL/1 do.

Verification Aids

Although not in wide use, software technology exists to affirm the processing rules of a program. These do not constitute formal validation, since they do not assure that the program's design was fully predicated by the specification, nor that the specification, itself, was correct. Nevertheless, they can provide dynamic tests of the relationships among the data.

The term *assertion testing* has increasingly been applied to these methods, which originated with R. W. Floyd's concepts of inductive assertions.[24] Floyd's

---

*We understand that computer science students at Rutgers University have suggested, for inclusion in a glossary of software terms, the following definition: Recursive. *See* Recursive.

work also underlay C. A. R. Hoare's later work on the development of axiomatic proofs of computer programs.[25] The tests made are of the expectation of the status of variables at a given point in the program. As implemented in languages, programmers are allowed to assert their belief of the condition of data for the subsequent testing of the truth of the assertion. Ignoring practical considerations of implementation, one can base a definition of correctness on assertion tests:

> A procedure is said to be correct (with respect to its input and output assertions) if the truth of its input assertion upon procedure entry insures the truth of its output assertion upon procedure exit.[26]

Invariant assertions define conditions that span entire routines, while *loop invariants* define relationships which, if true before entering a loop, must be true during and after the loop as well, and from which the condition of loop termination can be derived.

Assertions are written as boolean predicates (i.e., true or false) as, for example, in ASSERT A > B. This simple assertion can be placed within the program and compiled with other statements of the program. If the assertion does not hold — in the example, if B ≥ A — the failure is flagged.* One way of handling a failure is to cause an immediate program halt, thus preserving all data conditions for trouble-shooting. Alternatively, the programmer may be permitted to stipulate a number of allowable false assertion tests prior to the program's aborting. In other implementations, assertions may be made not only at a specific point in a program, but with the implication that they are to be applied at all relevant points. For example, the range a variable may take may be asserted. Each time the value of the variable is altered, the new value is tested against the asserted range.

Assertion testing is not yet a specified feature of standard existing languages. However, some compilers have been developed (mostly for PASCAL, to which an axiomatic definition in the sense of Hoare applies) that incorporate the feature. Moreover, preprocessors for PASCAL, and other languages as well, have incorporated assertion testing. At this writing two well-publicized PASCAL extensions that include assertion statements are evolving. One of these is ADA, which will be used for software developed for the U.S. Department of Defense. The other is EUCLID, which will have the further capability of automatically generating assertion statements for certain operations, such as checking — prior to its use — that a subscript is within its valid range.

Assertion tests have even been provided for assembly language programs. Traditionally, assembly language programmers have used breakpoints in their debugging. These are program halts at predetermined locations within the pro-

---

*A compelling parallel can be drawn to Susanne Langer's definition of a verb as a symbol: "Verbs are symbols with a double function; they express a relation, and also *assert that the relation holds*, i.e., that the symbol has a denotation."[27] (Italics hers.)

gram. There is no presumptive assurance that the selected location is at the source of error. The ALADDIN[29] debugging and testing facility allows assertions in the form of conditional (halt if assertion is false) breakpoints. It also permits the stipulation of tests similar to the range assertions discussed earlier. For example, if it is asserted that the program counter is always greater than N, a halt will occur if the computer attempts to execute an instruction in location $M \leq N$, presumably outside the program's scope.

Data Checking

The more highly typed the data structure of languages is, the easier it is to check the use of data at compile time. An attempt to multiply a datum typed as a character implies an oversight of the programmer's in naming the variable or a slip in entering the source file. If errors of this sort are not caught at compile time, they usually show up early in test. But not always. In a program written some years ago by one of the authors, it was necessary, upon entering a procedure, to initialize a passed parameter, KIND, to 1 if $KIND < 0$. The assignment statement was entered as $K1ND = 1$, rather than $KIND = 1$. The data entry error first manifested itself more than a year later. Even if the language is not richly typed, but like ALGOL, requires declaration of all variables prior to the first executable statement, errors such as this can be caught by the compiler. This is the notion of redundancy.

In a language such as PASCAL, with powerful typing capabilities that include range declarations and even unique type definitions tailored to the application, the potential for considerable redundancy exists, with the consequence that many errors will be found even before the program is actually tested. At the other extreme is the weakly typed language. FORTRAN IV, for example, types integers and reals, and then allows an integer to be multiplied by a real. This "mixed-mode" capability was absent in earlier FORTRANS, not in the interest of data structuring, but to avoid complicating the compiler design. When introduced, the mixed-mode capability was welcomed as a major convenience by programmers. It made the language more "forgiving." Forgiving of what? Programmer sloth (which is really no quarrel of ours) and programmer errors (about which we sometimes get downright irate). Forgiving languages do not enhance quality. Curmudgeonly ones do.

A CONTINUUM OF STRUCTURED DEVELOPMENT

In his famous paper, "Program Development by Stepwise Refinement,"[30] Niklaus Wirth* illustrated an iterative method of decomposing a task into subtasks into still lower level subtasks into code. The method encompassed the decom-

*Wirth is perhaps best known as the developer of PASCAL.

position of both program flow and data. Starting with the analysis of the problem, at each step his conclusions were presented in the language of ALGOL 60, as slightly augmented. The solution he developed was to Gauss' eight-queens problem, in which eight mutually hostile queens must be positioned on a standard chess board such that no queen may be captured by any other. The analysis steps consisted of successive mappings of the problem, culminating in an approach, expressed in four statements, based on trial solutions with backtracking. The grammar was that of ALGOL 60; the vocabulary required further definition. For example:

> If successful, THEN advance ELSE regress.

This is, substantially, the use of a requirements language as we discussed earlier, but used by Wirth at every step of the analysis. Also, since he had no need to communicate with others, he didn't support the language with a dictionary.

The first implementation of the method (i.e., the first design step) included the initial definition of data (e.g., *board*) as well as an outline of the program; again expressed exclusively in the augmented ALGOL 60 language. Next, the pseudo instructions were defined as procedures, which, in turn, were coded. Here, we see what, in effect, is the use of a program design language, as defined a few pages back. We may also note that the first step of the implementation also defined the modules of the program.

What Wirth described was the development of a homogeneous methodology, including the technique of reasoning each refinement, for the parallel iteration of program flow and data structure. Distinctions in the methods of performing the tasks of each phase vanish. Aesthetically, the elegance of his approach pleases, since the continuum of development never deviates from a common set of first principles.

Admittedly, the example he chose, the eight-queens problem, was an eminently suitable subject for the illustration. The problem itself is essentially either iterative or recursive. (Interestingly, Wirth coded both an iterative and a recursive solution.) In a different kind of program, one with many types of data to be processed, or with discretely different types of processes, we believe that it helps to have such aids as data flow diagrams, hierarchical charts of module trees, lexical data definitions, and the other forms of inspective documentation that have been discussed in this chapter. Also, since his was an individual effort, documentation did not enter into a solution of communication problems.

Nevertheless, Wirth's concept of stepwise refinement remains a disciplined and uninterrupted way of thinking, common to all phases of development, for reaching those milestones of which we have written that light the way of a monotonic decrease of abstraction. This book is about quality assurance, and quality assurance implies control. One does not attempt to control another's cognitive processes. Thus, Wirth's method is not a proper subject for our further amplification. We submit, however, that every software development manager would do well to consider making the source paper required reading for his staff.

In a later paper, Wirth wrote, "In fact, the method of stepwise decomposition and refinement of the programming task automatically leads to GOTO-free programs; the absence of jumps is not the initial aim, but the final outcome of the exercise."[31] Perhaps the essence of structured programming lies somewhere in this statement.

ORDER IN PROGRESS

By degrees the anarchy finds a way into private houses, and ends by getting among the animals and infecting them.

SOCRATES

The separate phases of analysis, design, and code that were introduced in Chapter 3 have now been redefined in terms of software engineering technology and methodology. Still, no matter how carefully the precepts of decomposition and structured programming are followed, no matter how lucidly and thoroughly the developing solution is documented, care must be taken to make certain that the edges of the phases remain distinct. The opportunity to reestimate and reevaluate the planned staffing levels, discussed in some detail earlier, depends on a concrete understanding of precisely where in the development cycle one is. If coding has started before the top-level design has been completed, what credibility can we impart to the estimates for detailed design and coding?

Even where the practices of software engineering are the rule, rather than the exception, the weight of habit presses heavily to telescope, or even invert, the order of the several phases. Programmers, no less than other people, are given to tackling first those problems they understand. This leads to a strong impulse to the bottom-up design and code of the more tractable parts of the program prior to completion of the design task. Rework is inevitable as the iterative design process redefines interfaces. An understandable propensity to understate the effect of changes to the presumed interfaces of previously coded modules creates untoward, expensive, integration problems downstream. This, of course, extends to the tendency to write code prior to detailed design, to start design prior to the definition of the requirements, and, indeed, to any intermediate step within any of the development phases.

There is no more effective way of serving the interests of efficiency and quality than ensuring that software development progresses in a planned, orderly manner.

Beyond establishing natural milestones for refining resource and cost estimates and staffing plans, and providing management with a view of the quantifiable orderly progress of the development project, the division of the effort into sequential tasks has a further important benefit. Since the documentation or code that provides the tangible evidence of the end of each phase is the basis for the next effort, it is marked by sufficient detail to provide the foundation for both of the following:

1. Verifying that it derives directly from the results of the previous phase, and does not introduce new concepts or approaches that have not previously been verified

2. Validating consistency with the constraints and requirements of the problem being solved

Verification and validation are so often said as a single word that one forgets that there is a conceptual difference between them. Both connote traceability to the problem being solved; verification accomplishing this by assuring that the process of solution evolves linearly step-by-step; validation providing the user (or a representative) opportunity to assess the partial solution in terms of needs and resources without concern of how the solution was derived.*

In the absence of verification and validation, program development can, and often does, miss the target; provide a solution, yes, but not specific to the problem for which development is funded. Flagrant examples are machine tool postprocessors optimized for the wrong machine features, or navigation computers requiring more memory than can be provided. Subtler examples are programs that do not lend themselves to contemplated expansion. Verification and validation also assures compliance with relevant planning, documentation, and programming standards. How one goes about performing verification and validation is left for Chapter 9. In the present context, we are concerned simply with preserving the validity of the milestones at which verification and validation occurs.

In brief, the reasons for concern for the integrity of the development phases are several: preservation of the monotonic decomposition methodology, assurance that estimating and planning refinement have firm and visible bases, and verification and validation. It would, of course, be doctrinaire to state that certain critical experiments must not be taken early in the development of a program. If, for example, in a real-time program it was known early on that a hyperbolic function would have to be evaluated somewhere in the program, it would be appropriate to experiment in actual code with various polynomial

---

*It is perhaps inevitable that in some quarters, including various offices within the United States military establishment, these definitions are quite nearly reversed. Given the necessary choice, we have defined the two words along the lines used in the August 1977 draft of the IEEE Computer Society's "Software Engineering Terminology."

approximations to determine the trade-offs between accuracy and execution time. Also, in a program marked by sharp vertical divisions, such as the game discussed in Chapter 3, one can conceive of starting coding in one division while still designing another. This creates some difficulties for management controls, but they are solvable.

In one approach to software development, considerable creativity is required to define significant milestones. This is the concept of top-down programming when it is narrowly defined to encourage sharply asymmetrical development of the hierarchical tree for the purpose of rapidly coding and testing the processes that are believed to be the gist of the problem. This approach, which partly ignores the iteration inherent in the process of structured decomposition and programming, is often referred to as the design-a-little–code-a-little method. It has been successfully used in the chief programmer team method of development. Chief programmer team, despite well-documented[32,33] early successes, has had spotty acceptance, owing to its dependence on a single programmer of singular superiority. (One wonders, given such a programmer, would success be denied any technique used?) Nevertheless, certain of its features, including the design-a-little–code-a-little method, have been more widely adopted. Maintaining control and progress or problem visibility in this environment is no small challenge. We question whether the profits offered are an adequate return for the risks incurred.

Keeping the development phases distinct is no small matter even under the best of circumstances. There must be room for exceptions, for testing some code while most design remains to be performed, for working out selected details while some interfaces remain undefined, for considering certain architectural matters while awaiting completion of the analysis of the problem. Nevertheless, the principle of order and control ought not in the least be compromised. The call is for software management standards, applied not with irrelevant rigidity, but with an understanding of the real issues.

SUMMARY

1. The quality of software must be built into it during the period of its development. This implies a need for software engineering rather than the partly organized, nonsystematic approaches of the past.

2. The development of a systematic solution can take its cue from Dijkstra's "levels of abstraction." Software development can proceed from the most abstract representation of the program (a general concept of what it is to do) to the most specific (working code), with each sequential stage taking the form of a response to the results of the previous step. For the purpose of control, it is wise to define each level in terms of measurable milestones. Up to the start of testing, the tangible outputs from a minimum set of these

milestones consist of a requirements definition specification, top-level design documentation, detailed design documentation and of course, code.

3. The term "structured programming" is usually used to describe the use of a minimum set of straightforward logic constructs to control program flow. We can view the systematic approach as an attack of complexity through structured development, a magnification of the concept of structured programming.

4. If developed using traditional methods, a good software requirements definition, or performance specification, is tedious to generate and tedious to use. It is not surprising that such specifications are often inadequate. Forms of documentation which lend themselves to structured development of the requirements and of immediate use of structure in the ensuing design phase include special requirements languages, data flow diagrams, and data dictionaries.

5. Plans and estimates for the production of software can also follow a course leading from abstraction to specificity. As the program becomes better defined, staffing plans should be updated. This helps to avoid both under-staffing, with concomitant and often irrecoverable schedule slips, and over-staffing, which can easily be counterproductive. The appropriate times to review management plans are at the milestones that make visible the progress of development.

6. A functionally modular program reduces staffing requirements while allowing more persons to work in parallel. It greatly abets software maintenance by reducing the risk that a change made to one part of the program will affect another, seemingly irrelevant, part. It also permits more effective testing.

7. Functional modularity implies independence among the modules. To the extent practicable, a tree structure is highly desired. However, where the goal must be compromised, there are other techniques for minimizing modular interdependence.

8. At the level of detailed design, structured programming will dramatically reduce program complexity and the potential for generating software errors. Although the emphasis has been on the structuring of program control flow, the structuring of data ought not to be neglected.

9. No less than the documentation of the performance specification, committing design concepts to paper can be greatly improved over traditional methods. Among techniques that can largely — and often completely — replace the ubiquitous flowchart, are HIPO and program design languages, the latter being especially desirable since it lends itself to machine-readable form for subsequent computerized analysis.

10. With respect to productivity and quality, compiler languages offer many advantages over assembler languages. Nevertheless, much code continues to be written in the latter form. For many of the applications where assembler language appears mandatory, there are techniques that offer the best of both alternatives.

11. All compiler languages are not alike. Features that abet quality are the inclusion of structured program control forms, the capability of recursion, assertion testing, and data checking based on redundancy.

12. The systematic step-by-step progression from the abstract to the concrete is easily compromised if the several stages are telescoped, for which unfortunate practice software people have exhibited a strong tendency. A technique to inhibit this is to require that no stage be undertaken without *verifying* the results of the preceding effort. The most important contribution that can be made by software quality assurance is found in its role of an independent agent in the verification process.

REFERENCES

1. Barry Boehm, "Software Engineering," *IEEE Transactions on Computers*, Vol. C-25, December 1976, pp. 1226–1241.

2. Edsger W. Dijkstra, "Complexity Controlled by Hierarchical Ordering of Function and Variability," Conference of the NATO Science Committee, Garmisch, Germany, Oct. 1968. Paper reprinted in J. M. Buxton, P. Naur, B. Randell, *Software Engineering: Concepts and Techniques*, Petrocelli/Charter, New York, 1976, pp. 114–116.

3. Glenford Myers, *Software Reliability: Principles and Practices*, Wiley-Interscience, New York, 1976, pp. 75–78.

4. Edsger W. Dijkstra, "The Structure of the 'THE' Multiprogramming System," *CACM*, Vol. 11, May 1968, pp. 341–346.

5. C. Böhm and G. Jacopini, "Flow Diagrams, Turing Machines and Languages with Only Two Formation Rules," *CACM*, Vol. 9, May 1966, pp. 366–371.

6. Carl Davis and Charles Vick, "The Software Development System," *IEEE Transactions on Software Engineering*, Vol. SE-3, January 1977, pp. 69–84.

7. Daniel Teichroew and Ernest A. Hershey III, "PSL/PSA: A Computer-Aided Technique for Structured Documentation and Analysis of Information Processing Systems," *IEEE Transactions on Software Engineering*, Vol. SE-3, January 1977, pp. 41–48.

8. F. E. Allen and J. Cocke, "A Program Data Flow Analysis Procedure," *CACM*, Vol. 19, March 1976, pp. 137–147.

9. Tom DeMarco, *Structured Analysis and System Specifications*, Yourdon, New York, 1978.

10. D. T. Ross and K. E. Schoman, Jr., "Structured Analysis for Requirements Definition," *IEEE Transactions on Software Engineering*, Vol. SE-3, January 1977, pp. 6–15.

11. Frederick P. Brooks, Jr., *The Mythical Man-Month*, Addison-Wesley, Reading, Mass., 1975.

12. Lawrence H. Putnam, "A General Empirical Solution to the Macro Software Sizing and Estimating Problem," *IEEE Transactions on Software Engineering*, Vol. SE-4, July 1978, pp. 345–361.

13. John Gaffney, Jr. and Gilbert Heller, "Macro Variable Software Models for Application to Improved Software Development Management," *Workshop on Quantitative Software Models for Reliability, Complexity, and Cost*, October 1979, IEEE Cat. No. TH0067-9, pp. 63–68.

14. W. P. Stevens, G. J. Myers, and L. L. Constantine, "Structured Design," *IBM Systems Journal*, Vol. 13, 1974, pp. 115–139.

15. Glenford J. Myers, *Composite/Structured Design*, Van Nostrand Reinhold, New York, 1978.

16. Edward Yourdon and Larry Constantine, *Structured Design: Fundamentals of A Discipline of Program and Systems Design*, Prentice-Hall, Englewood Cliffs, N.J., 1979.

17. Clement L. McGowan and John R. Kelly, *Top-Down Structured Programming Techniques*, Petrocelli/Charter, New York, 1975.

18. Edsger W. Dijkstra, "Go To Statement Considered Harmful," *CACM*, Vol. 11, March 1968, pp. 147–148.

19. Donald E. Knuth, "Structured Programming with Go To Statements," *ACM Computing Surveys*, Vol. 6, December 1974, pp. 261–302.

20. C. A. R. Hoare, "Data Reliability," *Proceedings of the 1975 International Conference on Reliable Software*, April 1975, IEEE Cat. No. 75CH0940-7CSR, pp. 528–533.

21. J. F. Stay, "HIPO and Integrated Program Design," *IBM Systems Journal*, Vol. 15, 1976, pp. 143–154.

22. Stephen Caine and E. Kent Gordon, "PDL — A Tool for Software Design," *AFIPS Proceedings of the 1975 National Computer Conference*, Vol. 44, AFIPS Press, 1975, Montvale, N.J., pp. 271–276.

23. Lorna L. Cheng, *Program Design Languages: An Introduction*, ESD-TR-77-324, prepared by the Mitre Corporation for the USAF AFSC Electronic Systems Division, available as AD-A051672 from National Technical Information Service, U.S. Department of Commerce, Washington, 1978.

24. R. W. Floyd, "Assigning Meanings to Programs," *Proceedings of the Symposia in Applied Mathematics*, Vol. 19, American Mathematical Society, Providence, R.I., 1967, pp. 19–32.

25. C. A. R. Hoare, "An Axiomatic Basis for Computer Programming," *CACM*, Vol. 12, October 1969, pp. 576–583.

26. Sidney L. Hantler and James C. King, "An Introduction to Proving the Correctness of Programs," *ACM Computing Surveys*, Vol. 8, September 1976, pp. 331–353.

27. Susanne K. Langer, *Philosophy in A New Key*, Mentor Book, New American Library, New York, 1948, by arrangement with Harvard University Press.

28. R. Holt, D. Wortman, J. Cordy, and D. Crowe, "The EUCLID Language: A Progress Report," *Proceedings 1978 Annual Conference, Association for Computing Machinery*, pp. 111–115.

29. Richard E. Fairley, "ALADDIN: Assembly Language Assertion Driver Debugging Interpreter," *IEEE Transactions on Software Engineering*, Vol. SE-5, July 1979, pp. 426–428.

30. Niklaus Wirth, "Program Development by Stepwise Refinement," *CACM*, Vol. 14, April 1971, pp. 221–227.

31. Niklaus Wirth, "On the Composition of Well-Structured Programs," *ACM Computing Surveys*, Vol. 6, December 1974, pp. 247–259.

32. J. D. Aron, Report given at Conference of the NATO Science Committee, Rome, October 1969. Report printed in J. M. Buxton, P. Naur, and B. Randell, *Software Engineering: Concepts and Techniques*, Petrocelli/Charter, New York, 1976, pp. 188–190.

33. F. T. Baker, "Chief programmer team management of production programming," *IBM Systems Journal*, Vol. 11, 1972, pp. 56–73.

Chapter 6

Configuration Management

The word "configuration" applies to a set of computer software characteristics described in documentation and realized in code. The configuration evolves during development in a series of *baselines,* or formal document and code software definitions. Even as the configuration is developing, it is changing. The configuration of software is an endless story of change. Configuration management is the management of those changes.

It is not uncommon for configuration management to be regarded as a postdevelopment activity. True, as a consequence of the absolute necessity of formal change control to protect the interests of software users, configuration management is most visible during the operation and maintenance part of the software life cycle, but it is an imperative during development also, when the rate of change is at a maximum. The configuration management activities during development differ in several respects from those during the operation and maintenance period; we will cover both.

We usually think of configuration management of software as a form of control necessary for large systems. Actually, even the smallest programs may require configuration management. One has only to think of the first use of microprocessors by the Ajax Medical Instrument company. This application was for a sputum analyzer. Ole Charlie wrote the program. We no longer remember whether he was an electronic engineer trying his hand at the programming of these new devices, microprocessors, or whether he was the first programmer ever hired by Ajax. In either case, he was a one-man programming department.

Ole Charlie did some design on the backs of some proverbial envelopes, wrote the code, debugged it, burned the code into PROMs, got the equipment to work. The envelopes and the program listings, stained with proverbial coffee, were stored in a drawer in Charlie's desk. Also in the desk was a floppy disk containing the source code and the binary program load. This was Charlie's *library*. The same drawer also held the paper tape, punched from the floppy disk, used to operate the machine that "burned" the program into PROMs.

As time passed, more and more enhancements were made to the sputum analyzer, most of them accomplished by adding on to the program. Ole Charlie just kept adding to the material in his desk drawer. Any time a new change is required, Ole Charlie just opens the drawer, moves the bologna sandwich and thermos bottle aside, and pulls out his reference documentation. Last we heard, Ajax had taken out a $0.25 million life insurance policy on Charlie. That's what they figure it will take to reprogram the analyzer if Ole Charlie has to be replaced. As he smilingly told the director of development one day, "Don't you worry none about what's in those programs, I got a top-drawer control system."

We knew of at least one case where the gist of this is true. We know of several cases in the banking industry where only one person knows the current configuration, and he's not telling. We have also seen it in manufacturing. However, most instances of uncertainty of the configuration of software have nothing whatever to do with job security, as the popular euphemism has it. As at Ajax Instruments, it is the result of management standards that accommodate indifferent documentation or laxity in maintaining currency among the documents and with respect to the programs. We have already discussed documentation. In this chapter, we address the problem of maintaining configuration integrity in the face of change.

Apart from documentation, we are also concerned with the accuracy with which we can define programs themselves. The results of development tests are of no use unless the programs tested can be unambiguously traced back to source code. This presents interesting problems when binary patches are employed to get around bugs; when for each module there are several source code files (today's, yesterday's, and last week's) bearing the same name; and when each programmer has his own disk or tape copy of the partially integrated system. After development, with the program in operation at multiple sites, one is exposed to the hazard of local tailoring of the program to unique preferences of style or, more substantively, optimization needs; also, local repairs of latent defects that are not reported back to the point of distribution.

DOCUMENTS AND BASELINES

There are any number of ways of defining the documents that constitute the paper definition of a program. Even within the military, we find considerable divergence from one service branch to another. In noting that we have avoided association with any of these, or with any single industrial standard, the casual observer may conclude that we are consciously attempting to avoid the need to choose favorites. Not so. The documentation that will frame the reference for the discussion of configuration management strategies is the same documentation — with a few additions — that we referred to in the last chapter. That is, we contend that the documentation required at any time for the definition of software is that which forms the basis for further development, validation, or use of the software.

Accordingly, we list some 17 documents or types of documents upon which we can base a discussion of configuration management:

1. Computer program development plan

2. Quality assurance plan

3. Configuration management plan

4. System description specification

5. Software requirements specification

6. Module tree structure

7. Module specifications

8. Data base description

9. Other top-level documentation

10. Module design descriptions

11. Source code listings

12. Integration test plan

13. Qualification and acceptance test plans

14. Test procedures

15. Test reports

16. Load maps

17. User manuals

It must be understood that these are representative, and that, unquestionably, there are other valid ways to divide the sum of the required documentation. The contents of the seventeen are not all self-evident from the titles given. Some brief definitions follow.

The computer program development plan describes how the software will be developed. At a minimum, it establishes the responsibilities for each functional organization taking part in the development, including the control responsibility for each; the standards and conventions (e.g., programming language, documentation methods, module interface rules) that will be followed;

schedule and workforce plans; identification of all formal test sequences; testing methodologies; frequency and content of managerial reports; and planned facility use (e.g., expected hours per week of the local computer facility, hours per week of ROM storage simulators).

The quality assurance plan will be discussed in greater detail in later chapters. For the present, we will summarize it by stating that it will describe the manner in which independent assessment will be made of the fidelity with which other plans are being executed and with which the evolving software will satisfy the system requirements, with emphasis on the techniques to be used for quality reporting and follow-up of corrective actions.

The configuration management plan will define responsibilities for configuration management, auditing and status reporting plans, change authorities and controls, methods that will be employed for library control, a catalog or index of documents and programs, and other matters that will be discussed in this chapter. It is not immediately apparent why this and the two previous plans should be under configuration control. Certainly, of all the documents, there is least need to control these. Nevertheless, since the three are to a considerable extent interrelated, we want to make certain that if one needs to be modified, a formal change process will require examination of the effect of the modification on the other two.

A system description specification is a document, or family of documents, describing the problem that the software is ultimately to solve. This specification is not directed specifically to software, but covers software, hardware, and human operations as well. While it is not required for most computer software applications, there are projects where it is clearly needed. For example, the specification is the top document for the definition of a new computer system, including all system software packages. We would also expect to see such a specification to define the prime requirements for other systems of which software forms but a single element. Instrumentation systems, process control, and telecommunications systems are further examples of the applications for which system specifications are appropriate. We may note that a single systems specification may give rise to several software specifications, as, for example, in a real-time system embedding an array of processors.

Chapter 5 discussed software requirements specifications. The next four items on the list are, of course, the top-level design documentation package. At least two of these will, with near certainty, be revised during the detailed design phase: the module configuration will be expanded into lower hierarchical tiers, and the data base will be given greater detail. Specifications for the added modules may or may not be added to the set produced at the time of top-level design. This is a matter of the level of detail into which the top-level design effort went. The added modules may be of such low hierarchical rank and of such limited scope that the function of each may be completely stated in a set of comment statements inserted at the head of the code.

The description of the design of the individual modules was also covered in

Chapter 5. It may be observed that the sum of the detailed design documentation at the time of software delivery includes these descriptions as well as the refined top-level design documentation. In short, the further detailing of, say, the data base description, moves it from the realm of the top-level design documentation to that of detailed design documentation. After development, this is of small concern, for the maintenance programmers will consider the aggregate of the design documentation as a de facto design specification.

The integration test plan explains how the various modules will be combined into a working whole. It will reference techniques (e.g., bottom-up, top-down), hardware and software resources that will be required, the general sequences in which modules will be combined, and an outline of the test procedures to be used. If there is more than one computer program involved, as in a system employing two or more computers communicating with each other, or a system wherein one program overlays another in the same computer to complete the processing task started by the first, the plan will cover interprogram integration as well. Also, if the software is embedded in hardware, a hardware-software integration plan will be required. For simplicity, we are subsuming all integration test plans under the one title.

We define acceptance tests, if separate from qualification tests, as the test series used to sell software developed under contract. We define qualification tests as the in-plant software validation by the development team. Qualification and acceptance test plans state the purpose of each test in each series, the responsibilities of the various organizations (software development, software quality assurance, etc.), the hardware and software resources required, and an outline of the test procedures that will be used.

Each of the many test procedures, at a minimum, identifies the general test conditions (e.g., for an air traffic control system, radar outages or the number of aircraft being handled), the source(s) of data (stimuli) and the specifics of these data, and the expected results (responses to the stimuli), including the points at which observations are made. The procedures will also cover any postexecution data reduction and analysis that is required.

Test reports may be as simple as signed-off data sheets originally appended to test procedures, or may include observations that were not easily anticipated by the procedures. For example, one could hardly quantify all of the expectations of the tests of the Backgammon and Bridge software discussed in Chapter 3.

Load maps, or link maps, as they are sometimes called, are produced by link-editors to show, as a minimum, the starting address of each of the units (modules, common data areas, and a few other items we have had no need to discuss) constituting a program load. A load map is the only hard copy (readable report) of the composition of an executable program.

Of user manuals, we shall say only that the information included must be sufficient for a person totally unfamiliar with the program, but of appropriate training or other background, to use the software to its full capability.

Thus, for the purpose of establishing a base for a discussion of configuration management practice, do we define software documentation. In one document type or another, one can find the information required to control, plan, develop, maintain, verify, validate, and use software. We shall see that these documents easily lend themselves to inclusion in the baselines about to be introduced.

The earlier, cursory, definition of "baseline," a term we have borrowed from the military, needs amplification. Viewed from a suitable distance, a baseline is the definition, applicable at any given time, of a product. It is subject to both amplification and revision. For software, the baseline, during the early stages of development, is that documentation that defines or describes what the software will be. Later baselines are actual programs and their documentation. We shall define those baselines that are key to the assurance of software quality much as they were recently defined by Bersoff, Henderson, and Siegel,[1] since the baselines they identified were broad enough to embrace systems of both hardware and software. However, to conform with the development phases as described in Chapter 5, we shall split their "design baseline" into a top-level design baseline and a detailed design baseline. With this, we have the following:

1. Functional baseline — The definition of the problem; the basis for agreements between buyer and seller; the description of the product that will be developed.

2. Allocated baseline — The apportionment, to specific hardware and software entities, of the functions that must be performed. For a development effort involving only a single computer program operating within an existing computer, the allocated baseline is the same as the functional baseline. That is, unless it were considered advantageous, for planning purposes, to prepare separate performance requirements definitions for each of the major portions of the program. Doing so implies that each of these portions will henceforth be controlled as a separate item.

3. Top-design baseline — For each software entity, the overall scheme of meeting its requirements.

4. Detailed design baseline — For each software entity, the description of how it will be built.

5. Product baseline — The definition of each software entity at the time of formal test.

6. Operational baseline — The definition of each software entity at any time during its service life.

Any formal change to a baseline represents a new baseline of the same name. The name changes only when the information (including code), applicable to the new name, has been developed.

Before using these new definitions, let us get rid of the pompous term, "software entity." What we are really referring to is a *computer program configuration item*. There is no firm rule for determining what a computer program configuration item should be. In a multiprocessing system, it is reasonable to assign to the program operating in each computer a unique configuration identification. For example, a central data base serving a distributed processing system would be a configuration item separate from the programs resident in the remote processors. Considering the converse, if, in a single computer, we have several independent programs operating in concert, it usually is advisable to consider each a configuration item. Generally, computer program configuration items should not span the boundary between computers or independent programs. They should encompass all functionally related software operating within a single computer. The underlying purpose is to allocate them so that there is correspondence between each configuration item and each unique development plan. A consequence of this is that the computer program development plan, the quality assurance plan, and the configuration management plan may all be modified in the allocated baseline.

It is the description of a computer program configuration item, at any stage in its life cycle, that must be controlled. Several configuration items may constitute the software of a system, but from the time that the performance requirements of any one has been defined, that item is subject to the control of all 17 documents peculiar to it, from baseline 2 through baseline 6.

Given this, we now form Table 6-1 to allocate the 17 documentation types listed earlier to the six baselines. We also include source code files, relocatable code files, and executable program loads (also called *load modules* and *program loads*) in the table.

With the exception of certain planning documents, Table 6-1 illustrates the point that once an item has been baselined,* it remains baselined. Even development test procedures and reports continue to be required during operation and maintenance, partly to provide an audit trail of anomalous behavior (recall Mary's use of old test reports in Chapter 5), and partly to permit repetition of tests after maintenance activities.

> The immortality granted baselined documents and program files reflects the fact that as the program nears the end of development and is becoming better defined, the early definitions remain valid and continue to be useful in helping those, both within and without the development team, to understand the program.

*Admittedly, an egregiously bad verb, but so well entrenched that we take refuge in the shelter of common usage.

TABLE 6-1

Controlled material	Baseline					
	Functional	Allocated	Top design	Detailed design	Product	Operational
Computer program development plan	o—————————————————o					
Quality assurance plan	o—————————————————o					
Configuration management plan	o—————————————————————————o					
System description specification	o—————————————————————————o					
Software requirements specification		o———————————————————————o				
Module tree structure			o———————————————o			
Module specifications			o———————————————o			
Data base description			o———————————————o			
Other top-level documentation			o———————————————o			
Module design descriptions				o———————————o		
Source code listings					o———o	
Integration test plan			o———————o			
Qualification and acceptance test plans		o———————————————o				
Test procedures				o———————————o		
Test reports					o———o	
Load maps					o———o	
User manuals				o———————————o		
Source code					o———o	
Relocatable object code files					o———o	
Executable program load					o———o	

What this really means is that most of the documentation serves a multiplicity of functions:

- Definition of the program to be used in the next development phase

- Definition of the program for verification against the previous definition and validation relative to the first (system description document) definition

- Participation as a unique element in the overall documentation scheme required for postdevelopment maintenance

This is cost effective, while at the same time uncompromising in its satisfaction of the essential needs of development, quality assurance, management, and maintenance. It is cost effective and uncompromising, that is, if all the documents remain consistent with each other and with the code. This is what baselining means. Once baselined, every document must remain under change control until such time (for most documents, code death) that it no longer forms a part of the current baseline.

Beyond those top-level design documents that will change simply to reflect the subsequent development of more detailed information, other changes are inevitable. Even during development we can, with reasonable certainty, expect to see the software requirements specification change. Something will not have been thought out optimally. Later, it will become apparent. Certainly, as design errors are discovered during testing, source code, executable code, and various design documents will be changed. Heraclitus anticipated the software life cycle 2500 years ago when he said, "All is flux, nothing is stationary."

CODE

That changes have been made to documentation can be determined by inspection of the documents. Similarly, although not a simple task, one can, by visual means, check to see that one document is consistent with another. Code is quite another matter. One cannot easily determine that the object code representing a module was, in fact, compiled from a given source code definition of the module. This is no small matter, since during the test process there may at a given time exist several source and binary files bearing the same module name. Nor is there assurance that any is an accurate reflection of the design documentation.

This business gets further complicated during integration. Whether accomplished in a top-down or bottom-up regimen, each time a module or group of modules is added to the system, the system is changed. Figure 6-1 illustrates, in a kind of data flow diagram, the metamorphosis that changes a source file into a testable program.

It is evident that if we wish to know what we tested, we shall have to have module source, module binary, and executable loads under control. As the system is building, this can get most interesting. Consider the introduction of a new module to those previously integrated. If integration is by top-down techniques, the module would earlier have been represented by a stub. How can

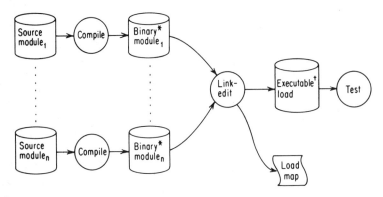

*Also called object module or target module.

†Also called program load.

FIGURE 6-1   Key Points for Code Control.

one differentiate between these two versions of the program load? This is where we first make use of the load map. For the purpose of the link editor, the object module needs to be given a name; presumably based on the same name that it has been referred to in the documentation. Let us then give the module's stub a unique prefix or suffix. By inspection of the load map generated along with the program load, we can determine whether the program was tested with the module or with the stub.

We seem to have solved one part of the code control problem, but appearances have deceived. There is no guarantee that the load map can be correlated with the program load. That is, the program load is located on a disk somewhere — perhaps, if a test is in progress, mounted on a disk drive itself — and the paper the load map is printed on is somewhere else. We must go further. We must give the program load a *version identification*, have that identification incorporated in the load itself (perhaps as a header record), and have the link editor print the version identification at the top of the load map. In turn, this means that we shall have to be able to input the version identification to the link editor at link-edit time.

There is more to code control than the unique identification of program loads. We have also to consider source and object module files. Again, we shall have to adopt an auditable identification scheme, implemented with the assistance of systems software. Specifically, if we uniquely identify source files, not just by module name, but also by version or revision or both, we shall want the compiler to pass this secondary labeling on to the object code.

What we have been calling code control is generally called *library control*, although the term "library," which we have yet to define, will be used in a somewhat narrower sense.* Before going further into the matter of library control, let us reflect on the last few assertions that have been made. In effect, we have contended that library control must be implemented with the help of software tools. We shall return to these in Chapter 8. At this time we will simply assume we have them. This is not to say that tools alone can solve the problem of library control; simply that effective library control cannot be assured without them. Even with appropriate tools, we shall see that there are difficulties. However, *tools are the only way to make the history of code transformations inspectable; the only way to be able to "see" what has been tested.*

Unambiguous labeling of code files, is, in any case, essential. There is no need to dwell on how this can be done, since the number of adequate standards that can be established is virtually unlimited. Frequently, the method employed will be predicated by existing systems software. The scheme we present serves no purpose other than the illustration of the essential parts. Note, however, that we extend it beyond the needs of library control to include control of documents as well. The scheme has four major parts:

PF—ROOTMODULE—VL—RC

PF	Two-letter prefix for indicating type of file or document (e.g., TP for test procedure, SF for source file, RS for requirements specification, ST for stub),
ROOT	Four-letter code for identifying the computer program configuration item
MODULE	Six-letter code for module name, or test (e.g., QUALIF), or, if executable code, some other name
VL	Two-letter code for version level, starting with AA
RC	Two-letter code for revision, starting with AA

It may be noted that for control purposes, it matters little whether a change is to implement a new version or a revision. Thus, distinguishing between the two is mostly a mnemonic useful during development, and may, with little loss, be done away with for the operational baseline.

---

*In some quarters, "library" has not a narrower meaning, but a wider one, including documentation, support software, and tools. We prefer to reserve the term for program material—specifically file-oriented code—reflecting the unique control mechanisms required for code.

We define "version" to reflect capability. During integration, whenever new modules are added, the version code is incremented. For computer program configuration items or for new modules, at the time the operational baseline is formed the version level reverts to the version level of the system description specification. Modules borrowed without modification from earlier programs retain the version level with which they arrived. It is frequently preferable to copy the source file and give it the root identification of the new configuration item in which it will be used.

A *revision* is a change made to a version to improve performance or remove a defect. When part of the operational baseline, all documents have to agree with code in version level, but not necessarily in revision suffix. For example, removal of a defect may reflect an error in code, but not in design. Mostly, revisions work backwards from code or design documentation through documentation of increasing abstraction. This applies to the design baselines, the product baseline, and the operational baseline. Version upgrades normally work in the forward direction; the requirements documents are changed, and the modification then ripples downwards to code.

LIBRARY CONTROL

Given an unambiguous labeling method and the tools to profit from it, it remains to effect the control of code. Imagine a team of programmers during integration. Some modules are still being coded, some are in unit test, others are emerging from unit test to join those previously integrated. Each programmer responsible for one or more modules has a copy of the source file for it; let us assume on disk. She may also have a backup. She may or may not have physical possession of the disk she is working with. During unit test, making changes several times a day, she will, if prudent, create special test files for the source and resulting object files. After each successful test, she is likely to rename the test source file with the proper module name. Alternatively, she may overwrite the old source with new. In either case, she may slip up somewhere in the process and lose correspondence between the active source file and the backup.

The whole business is one of dealing, even as we pointedly do now, with details that seem remote from the programmer's real purposes of producing a satisfactory product. This is fertile ground in which to breed mix-ups. We continue: at the time the programmer and the programmer's supervisor agree that the module is ready for integration, the appropriate source file must be found and concatenated with the other source files in a *library*. The library may be so unstructured as to be no more than a disk bearing individual source files, or it may be of the form of a homogeneous file with indexes to the starting address of each module. The relocatable object code is concatenated to a similar binary library used for building program loads.

At this point the module becomes part of a locally controlled product baseline. Once the system is built, and formal test is ready to be started, the local product baseline will become the real product baseline; that is, subject to external configuration control. In the meantime, control is still necessary, but because changes are being made daily, the formality of control boards cannot be applied.

One likes to think that during integration the entropy, or inherent randomness, of the system is monotonically decreasing. However, chaos is never more than a few "fixes" away. During integration, a module runs amok. The fix turns out to be considerable, and the programmer regresses to the unit test mode to check and debug the revised module. In effect, he is back in the preintegration mode just described, with the possible consequence of his submitting the wrong code set for further integration. Worse, the concurrent existence of several forms of a module is replicated in the large by the possibility of multiple sets of partially integrated code. That is, a change is made to the immature system and the fix is evaluated. To avoid the risk of the change creating more harm than good, the last form of the program is retained. This can be done in a number of ways: multiple libraries, compilation from both source modules and libraries, or perhaps by just retaining the last program load. Whatever the means, there is no lack of opportunity for losing track of what each disk file truly represents.

Enter the *librarian*. Many programming departments have augmented their staffs with nonprogramming personnel who act as intermediaries between the programmers and the code files. Once a code file goes under local control, all changes to it are made by the librarian.* The librarian is also responsible for link-editing program loads used for testing, for distributing and archiving all hard copy (as a minimum, program listings, load maps, and test results), and for creating backup files. A librarian can also be given the task of updating design documentation, based on information provided by programmers. This does not imply that the librarian can assume responsibility for the consistency between code and documentation; the librarian cannot be expected to know that a change is required to any of the documentation unless so told. Nor do we mean to suggest that the librarian may make changes to the master copies of any documentation without change board approval.

Now that the integration process seems to be coming under control, we shall perturb matters once more by introducing the business of *patches*. In a large software system, rather than take the time to recompile and re-link-edit, integration teams frequently get around bugs by substituting new binary instruction sequences for some of those found in the executable load. Binary

---

*After a code file has been placed under control, further changes to the program are usually made first to copies of the file distributed by the librarian. After the modification has been tested, using the copy, the librarian copies the change into the master, where the tests are repeated.

patches may serve purposes other than convenience. For any size system, it may be efficient to use patches to trap certain operations to determine the error underlying an observed fault, or to temporarily force execution around a troublesome area.

The problem created by binary patches is that until they are resolved in source code, the executable code bearing the patches represents an otherwise undefined program. In the long run, the solution is simply to rerun all tests once the source code has been modified to reflect the patches. This, however, does not relieve the problem of correlating the results of various debug runs made with patched programs. It's the familiar problem: if the patches in each test are different, because of entry errors or simple confusion, it is difficult to make sense of the data. This, too, has a solution. Patches should be permitted only if entered into the system from a file of patches. This patch file can be under the librarian's local configuration control.

Although integration places the greatest strain on the buckram of library control, this control mechanism is at its greatest criticality during formal test operations. Then, the authenticity of validation extends no further than the confidence one has in knowing what was tested. We shall see in Chapter 8 where the tools briefly noted earlier, when buttressed by a diligent librarian, will make the composition of tested code auditable.

FIRMWARE

Embedded software often ends up cast into ROMs (read only memory), PROMs (programmable read only memory), or one of the several variants of PROMs. For all but the smallest programs, individual ROMs (we shall use this term to cover all of these devices) do not have the capacity to contain the entire program, with the consequence that the operational program resides in an array of ROMs.

Consider that a program of 3000 sixteen-bit binary locations is to be transferred to a set of identical ROMs, each having 1000 addresses of four bits of storage. Twelve ROMs will be required, and a reasonable way to do it would be as shown in Figure 6-2.

To make certain that each ROM is inserted into the correct place on the assembly (e.g., printed wiring board) that will physically house the program, it is necessary to label each ROM in a fashion that will be consistent with the interconnections of the assembly. In other words, it is necessary to correlate the ROMs with the program load addresses output by the link editor.

The transform from program load binary words to individual ROM bit patterns is performed in a mapping program. A proper mapping program will provide hard copy correlation of the contents of each program load address to addresses within each ROM. This document must be added to those for which configuration control is mandated.

Further, there must be a way of cross-referencing the unique identification marked on each ROM with the ROM references of the hard copy of the transformation map. If this cannot be accomplished by inputting the set of unique identifiers to the mapping program, the cross-reference will have to be made up manually and subsequently maintained under configuration control. There is no other way to make certain that each ROM is properly assembled.

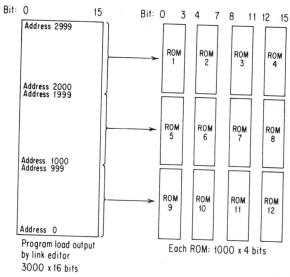

FIGURE 6-2   ROM Mapping.

It is possible to perform the mapping and cross-referencing within the link editor. Given this degree of tooling, all the necessary information will appear on the load map, obviating the need for the additional controlled documents.

THE CONFIGURATION MANAGEMENT PLAN

Predictable software never just happens; it gets planned. Table 6-1 noted, among other plans, that one needs to plan for configuration management. Specifically, what is required is early identification to all interested parties of the documents and program files that will be controlled, when they go under control who controls, and how changes are made and controlled.

Since a configuration management plan must address the specifics of the project to be controlled, it is peculiar to that project. Nevertheless, it should be possible for most of the substance of the plan to be given by reference to a configuration management standard that applies to all software projects undertaken by the development or maintenance organization. For example, the format of software release notices and change notices should be uniform.

Whether by reference or by explicit text, a plan can be expected to cover the following material.

Catalog of Controlled Items

Each document and program file to be controlled must be itemized. Moreover, each should be tied to a specific computer program configuration item, and, if applicable, to a specific program module. This implies that the plan itself is subject to change, since individual modules are not defined at the time the plan is prepared. In a multiprocessor system, even the configuration items may not be known at that time. The catalog should also include provisions for later incorporation of version and revision identifications. To avoid distribution of the entire plan each time the catalog is updated, it may be more convenient to include the catalog as a controlled supplement to the plan.

Control Authority and Responsibility

The role of the configuration manager should be identified, and the individual should be named, at least by position. The plan must also define the authority and constituency of the change control board, the office responsible for release of each controlled item (generically, that is; the catalog does not have to be repeated), and the office responsible for code and other files prior to formal release. The person or persons having physical control of documentation masters and files should be stipulated, and, if possession is transferred, the time of that transfer relative to one of the published milestones. The specific responsibilities of the librarians and any local configuration personnel are also given. As a corollary, operations not permitted to personnel must be stated. For example, if a librarian is used, the plan should state that no programmer may modify a master source file after it is released.

Easily overlooked, but of major importance, are the controlling mechanisms to be used by those responsible for configuration management. For example, the contents and distribution of the configuration manager's reports should be cited.

Change Procedure

During integration, locally controlled code may be changed on demand, at periodic intervals, or a combination of the two. The practice that will be followed must be stated, along with the measures that will be taken to preserve an audit trail of the changes from the baseline and the means whereby the configuration manager will be alerted to potential modification of controlled documentation.

Once formal testing has started, a more formal procedure is called for, involving change requests and the responsibility for initiating them, the convening of the control board, the initiation of change notices, and the authorization of tasks to effect changes. To avoid the costly delays that a formal procedure can entail, allowances must be made to permit quick fixes to be made. As a rule of thumb, if requirements specifications or module specifications don't have to be modified, quick fixes should be permitted. However, the plan must include the manner in which these repairs will be brought to the attention of the configuration manager.

Earlier, we had noted that there are two paths for changes: one brought about by software failures, and the other as a result of modified or augmented requirements. Either can occur during the development period, but failures predominate by a large margin. That margin is reduced, under the best of circumstances even reversed, once the operational baseline is established. Performance change requests are handled somewhat differently from a change to rectify an error. As before, design documentation, source code listings, load maps, and code files are the subject of change. However, now we shall also expect changes to the requirements specification (possibly the system description, as well), test procedures (and possibly test plans, if a major modification), and perhaps the users' manual. For changes to repair an error, cost and schedule estimates may not have been necessary if the repair was small. For changes affecting the requirements specification, they are mandatory regardless of size. The change board must make certain that all cost and schedule input is received from the proper sources.

The precise steps to implement the change procedure, regardless of the source of the change request, the need for the change, or the baseline affected, must be stipulated in the plan.

DISTRIBUTION

The distribution of software to multiple users may seem like a small matter, but it can create problems that affect both the operation and maintenance of programs. This may be true under the best of circumstances, but we shall introduce the problem by considering the worst of circumstances: the distribution of source code. We like to think that source code is something users never need. Certainly, even if proprietary disclosure is not at issue, one likes not to release source code, since there is no assurance that the receiver will maintain configuration control of the code. Yet, programs have been built where tailoring for each operational facility is required at the source code level and by the receiving personnel. An alert software quality assurance person will spot this possibility early in the development period and insist on a better solution. Once source code is modified, there is no assurance that later repairs or enhancements will work with the field-altered code.

As we have hinted, keeping source code in-house does not end the concern for distribution. An inevitable problem occurs when all of the parts of a program system do not apply to all of the users. For example, a large system may include components not needed at all installations. Consider a proprietary digital logic simulation system with built-in libraries of available off-the-shelf integrated circuit packages. A user of only metal-on-silicon logic isn't going to want to pay for the updates to the emitter-coupled-logic library or the transistor-transistor-logic library. If customer satisfaction is to be maintained, it is necessary to make certain that all customers get the updates they are entitled to. Quality assurance should want to see that the configuration control system includes the list of user options.

In this regard it is helpful to have the group of modules comprising an option to be a unique computer program configuration item. We might extend the definitions of module and computer program configuration item to include data bases, or libraries, for this purpose, since — as in the example — they, as well as program units, are likely to be unequally distributed. In any case, considering options as unique configuration items makes the bookkeeping much easier.

The distribution problem gets more complicated when there are several versions, each with options, in the field. Now it is important to keep track of which installation has which version or option configuration. The installations will, of course, from time to time change their software configurations; to add capability, drop capability, reflect a change in the hardware configuration, and so on. Given this common situation, it is clear why we recommend placing installation configuration status under control.

One solution applicable to geographically dispersed distributed systems* is to distribute updates directly from the central data base to the remote processors. In this manner, the distribution can be under the direct control of a data base incorporating the remote configuration status. As always, there is a caveat to which quality should be alerted. Either the distribution format should embody redundancy for error detection, or the new version, when received, should be "read back," to assure its safe passage via telecommunications. Users of new updates are, under the best of circumstances, suspicious of the new code, and are all too quick to blame their own operational errors on a faulty copy of the update. In the excellent but imperfect environment of telecommunications lines, users will profit from some reassurance.

EVOLUTION

During the operation and maintenance period, it is common for concurrent versions of programs to slowly evolve. That is, in time we may expect several

---

*Distributed systems are those in which the processing load is divided among multiple computers, generally operating with a common data base.

operational baselines. We alluded to this in the discussion of distribution, but there is more to coping with the problem than simply placing the installation configurations under control. We have also to consider the multiplicity of documentation and code files that will be created.

Figure 6-3 is a much simplified schema of the materials under configuration control for a newly released program.

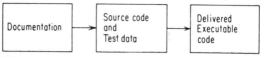

FIGURE 6-3   Initial Release.

Within days, the program is recompiled to operate on computers different from the first. Slight changes in the source code accommodate the unique properties of the compilers peculiar to the different computers. This is shown in Figure 6-4.

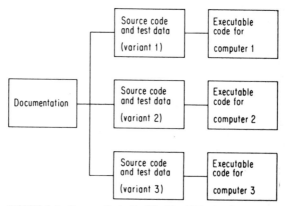

FIGURE 6-4   Source Code Modified for Different Computers.

Some months later, the first enhancement is made available. This is released as a new version, but not to all installations. Perhaps it cost more, or was designed to handle a special peripheral device not common to all installations. It may even be a capability peculiar to certain geographic areas. Whatever the reasons, the new version does not supersede the old. Rather, both continue to be supported. In time, there are other versions, each tailored to different computers, and we have the schema of Figure 6-5.

To make matters worse (we can seem never to leave bad enough alone), each version will be subject to its own revisions. At any moment, we may have version 1, revision 6; version 2, revision 4; and version 3, revision 4. The configuration manager had best make certain that the configuration management plan is well-equipped to unambiguously identify all the material under con-

trol. During the period of operation and maintenance, the configuration manager's job is much more than that of keeping the old configuration catalogs
properly dusted.

One function includes a seat, possibly the presiding position, on the change
board. In the repair of defects, the board has to authorize each repair that will

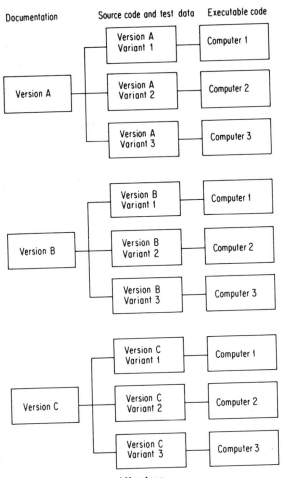

FIGURE 6-5 Concurrent Versions.

be made (it may be that the response to some problem reports is to not fix the
problem, but to modify the documentation), and to determine whether each
repair will be issued as an update or whether several repairs will be "batched"
and released only when the last is ready. Each release, whether to correct one
problem or many, requires incrementing the revision identifier, as in the identification scheme illustrated earlier. Similarly, the change board authorizes

each version. The board also authorizes the retirement of support (including record-keeping) for old versions, although the decision to do so will likely arise from marketing or technical considerations.

The conduct of its affairs requires the change board to assume more of a marketing or cost evaluation (or both) posture during operation and maintenance than during development. It may be appropriate to have somewhat differently constituted boards for control of the operational baseline than for the others.

CONFIGURATION MANAGEMENT AND QUALITY

F. Brooks has an interesting observation about program maintenance. After noting that systems development is a process during which entropy decreases, he goes on to say, "Program maintenance is an entropy-increasing process, and even its most skillful execution only delays the subsidence of the system into unfixable obsolescence."[2] What can hasten this more than a loss of currency of documentation? If quality is to help get the most out of the programming dollar, it must make certain that the configuration of documents and files remains under control.

If quality is to validate the performance of code, either at the product baseline or during the operational baseline, it must be able to trace that code back to source code, design documentation, and requirements documentation.

If quality is to be concerned with user satisfaction, apart from the conspicuous matters of the usability and reliability of code, it must make certain that users receive the correct updates.

Simply put, configuration management, if not vested in the quality organization, should be subject, no less than programming activities, to quality audits. Change to software, at all baselines, is unavoidable. Quality and uncertainty of product are inimical. Configuration management is nothing less than the bounding of that uncertainty in the face of continuous change.

The art of progress is to preserve order amid change and to preserve change amid order.

ALFRED NORTH WHITEHEAD

SUMMARY

1. Configuration management is the management of change, and software seems ever to be changing.

2. A baseline is the current and controlled definition of a program. As the software becomes less abstractly defined, descriptive documentation, and finally code, is added at discrete intervals of time to create new baselines. Updates of existing documentation and code also establish new baselines.

3. It is convenient to think in terms of the functional, allocated, top-design, detailed design, product, and operational baselines. Only the last two involve code. For the most part, documentation required to define each of the pre-code baselines should serve to verify that baseline relative to its predecessor; should serve as the basis of the succeeding effort. In brief, baselines should correlate to the milestones of one's development plan.

4. The control of code itself — whether source code or binary in its several forms — is considerably more difficult than that of documentation, simply because code does not lend itself to inspection. The term "library control" is applied to the management of code so that each form may be unambiguously traced to its predecessor and ultimately to the documentation produced in earlier baselines.

5. Without appropriate software tools, library control is all but impossible.

6. Software that ends up resident in read-only-memory (ROMs and PROMs), also referred to as firmware, presents further problems. These can be solved by extensions to the library control scheme.

7. A configuration management plan should specify maintenance of a catalog of controlled material, the delegation of control authority and responsibility, and a procedure for effecting changes.

8. Software distributed to many installations, and software that evolves into a large set of variants, present unique problems in configuration management during the operation and maintenance phase. These, too, are solvable.

REFERENCES

1. E. Bersoff, V. Henderson, and S. Siegel, "Software Configuration Management: A. Tutorial," *Computer,* IEEE Computer Society magazine, Vol. 12, No. 1, January 1979.

2. Frederick P. Brooks, Jr. *The Mythical Man-Month,* Addison-Wesley, Reading, Mass., 1975, p. 123.

Chapter 7

Testing

You are a programmer, and you have just finished generating the code for the task assigned to you, and now you want to prove that it works. Right? Right in the sense that this is a fairly factual representation of real life, but wrong if you expect testing to be a *productive* means of making a program more correct. The primary goal of testing ought not be the demonstration of the correctness of a program:

> The goal of testing ought to be the uncovering of defects within the program.

Defects it will surely have; perhaps 50 per 1000 lines of untested code. We have dwelled sufficiently in earlier pages on the ease with which faults can be built into the fabric of a program. In this chapter we deal with the methodology of exposing those faults so that they can be corrected. It may seem obvious, especially to members of the quality community, that testing should be an activity planned and designed to detect as many defects and areas of weakness as possible. Yet, if left entirely to those who build software, tests will tend to find a minimum of problems. We do not mean to suggest that software developers wish to conceal their mistakes. One must, however, recognize that to a formidable extent, software is the product of its builders' cognitive processes. It would be unnatural if we did not inwardly feel that the logic of our thinking was inherently correct. Programmers are commonly surprised each time they find a bug. They may not be surprised that a software failure occurred, but on finally locating the source of the problem, they are filled with wonderment over how they "could have been so stupid." The answer, of course, is that software gives them plenty of opportunity, but that fact is more easily accepted at an intellectual level than at an emotional one.

Beyond considerations of the nature of our noble species, there are other reasons why programmers, testing their own programs, look to the pudding for proof rather than for lumps. Some, having lived with the same program for days, weeks, or longer, in their impatience to get on to new things are disposed to make quick work of testing. We might note that the opposite is also true: there are programmers who will try to be as thorough as possible out of fear that they will be recalled to the program upon the future occurrence of a failure.

Perhaps the most significant reason that programmers, if left entirely to their own resources, are less likely than outsiders to find their own errors, is that they know the design of their programs. How can they not design tests that are influenced by their knowledge of the design of the program? The consequence is that their tests tend to demonstrate the fidelity with which the code implements the design, at the expense of finding flaws in the design itself. As we shall soon see, there is also an important place for tests designed with full awareness of the details of the program structure. For the present, we are content to establish the case that this place is not occupied by all testing activities.

None of this is to suggest that testers who had no part in the development of a program are assured of finding all the defects within it. We do, however, expect that for a fixed number of test hours they will find more faults than the developers will. The sum of this matter is not, as it may appear, that we recommend that newborn code be ripped from the embrace of its creator. Rather, we argue that the most productive testing process is one carried out by a team comprising both development people and outsiders (read quality personnel), all of whom have assigned roles in each of the phases of testing.

As we develop a test schema, we should bear in mind that regardless of the number of bugs that have been exposed during testing, there remains no proof that none lie hidden. Tests find defects, but do not prove the absence of defects. The measure of a well-designed test is the number of flaws it can find.

TESTABILITY

The design of a test case is not the only ingredient contributing to the productivity of a test. The program being tested can also influence the quality of the test. We will, for the moment, assume that test cases are based on the operational environment for which the program has been developed. Given this, one may reasonably expect that the responses of the program to test stimuli will be partitioned in a manner that reflects the structure of the program. For example, in an inventory control system, a transaction reporting the receipt of supplies should be processed in that part of the program that is concerned with additions to inventory; it should be ignored in code associated exclusively with withdrawals. Thus, one need not check the response at all "test points" (i.e., key processing nodes, such as module entry points), but only at certain predetermined ones. What this implies is the attribute of functional modularity built into the program.

Functional modularity is but one of the four examples of characterstics of testable programs found in the IEEE Computer Society's definition of "testable." The others allude to the facility with which diagnostics may be invoked, the inclusion of code for the evaluation of invariants,* and annotation of evaluation criteria placed in the source code at the points at which measurements are made. The following is the definition these examples support:

> **A software product is testable to the extent that it facilitates the establishment of verification criteria and supports evaluation of its performance.**[1]

No one will quarrel with the intent of this definition. Certainly it deals with software features and attributes that improve the productivity of the test process. However, once the code has been written the definition is not especially useful to the development of test methodologies. A definition that relates to the specifics of the transformations of data is of greater interest; one that we shall explore.

Interestingly, the cited characteristic of modularity supports an entirely different definition of testability. This one views the program structure as a set of processing nodes with interconnecting paths. S. N. Mohanty[2] defines the testability (T_{ij}) of the node N_{ij} (the jth node at the ith hierarchical abstraction level) as

$$T_{ij} = A_{ij} \times P_{ij}$$

where A_{ij}, the *accessibility* of the node, is a measure of the number of nodes that have to be traversed, starting from the departure point, to reach N_{ij}, and P_{ij} is the probability of successful execution of the node. That is, considering

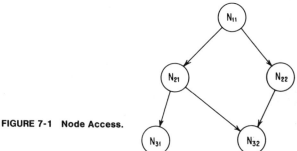

FIGURE 7-1 Node Access.

the structure as a directed graph, as in Figure 7-1, we have accessibility of any given node as the iterative function of the accessibility of the nodes separating it from the root of the graph.

The accessibility of N_{11} is, by definition, 1. The accessibility of N_{21} is the product of its likelihood of being selected (in this case, one-half) and the prob-

*See the discussion of verification aids in Chapter 5.

ability of the successful execution of N_{11}. The accessibility of N_{31} depends in a similar manner on N_{21}, while that of N_{32} depends on N_{21} and N_{22}.

Thus, testability is a function of the ability to reach a node based on the states created by the test stimuli, the success of other execution processes, and the success with which the node performs its processes. Mohanty goes on to use T_{ij} in the definitions of the testability of logical paths and the entire logical structure. For our purposes, it is sufficient to infer from these concepts that the more defect-ridden a program is or the more involuted its structure, the harder it will be to probe its vital organs.

Both of these definitions of testability imply knowledge of the structure of the program. As we noted at the beginning of this chapter, the design of a test by one knowledgeable of the design of the program, leads to verification of the code with respect to the design, but without regard to design faults. Extrapolating, too much knowledge of any level of the program (detailed design, overall structure, even the role of one program in a system of programs) may be damaging to the verification of that level.

At the other extreme, we have the tests of software "black boxes." The black box is tested against its requirements definition without regard to its construction. Unfortunately, such end-to-end tests (pour some data into the figurative input port and inspect the response at the output port) can encompass only a tiny portion of the total transformation space. In Chapter 4, we used a disarmingly simple directed graph to model the astronomical number of discrete states that a program can assume. Black-box testing is no more than the evaluation of the generation of a statistically insignificant number of those states.

If neither extreme seems to offer the testing productivity we are looking for, where does that leave us? The answer is that we are left somewhere in the middle, but not necessarily in a static position. As we shall see, certain test objectives will favor the one extreme, while others will tend to the opposite direction. We call the span between (and including) the two extremes the *strategic test space*. A properly conceived sequence of test phases will, in the aggregate, encompass the full span.

NODES AND PATHS

One thing is clear. A program cannot be said to have been properly tested until all the code has been executed. A single successful execution of a segment does not, of course, prove the segment is free of defects; the segment may work properly with certain groups of other segments, but not with all. We may find it convenient to think of the problem as one of interfaces, but this is simplistic, since interfaces are implemented in the very code segments being exercised.

Similarly, changing our focus from code segments to program paths, we should want to make certain that, in the very least, the path between each pair of nodes, as in Figure 7-1, is executed before we are finished testing. Let us define the path between any two nodes as an *atomic path*. If all of these are executed, certitude also will have been gained that all of the nodes have been tested. In brief, we shall have executed all the segments while trying out the program control mechanisms.

We can now go a step further, and concatenate the atomic paths into path sequences. Thus, labeling the atomic path from N_{ij} to N_{kl} as L_{ijkl} (Mohanty's convention), we see the path from N_{11} to N_{31} in Figure 7-1 as $L_{1121} + L_{2131}$, and the path from N_{11} to N_{32} as $L_{1121} + L_{2132} \cup L_{1122} + L_{2232}$. Even at this point, one can sense from these expressions an ill wind gathering to drive us on to the shores of futility. As one continues, the number of terms builds rapidly, and in short order one realizes that to go on in this vein is to attempt, in a bottom-up fashion, to grapple with the astronomical total number of end-to-end paths. Where then, does one stop?

In an unstructured program, one might as well stop before starting. In a structured program, however, one can take advantage of the single-entry–single-exit, or closed-form, constraints and find many obvious terminal node pairs that bound sufficiently modest range to permit thorough testing in this manner. The directed graph of Figure 7-2 has five unique paths from N_{11} to N_{51}.

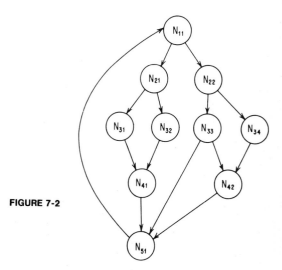

FIGURE 7-2

They are easy to identify, and can be exercised by suitable test data to switch the conditional branches at N_{11}, N_{21}, N_{22}, and N_{33}. However, we have enclosed the model in a loop, the path from N_{51} to N_{11}. If the loop is executed n times, the number of paths that can be executed is really 5^n. It is as though the five obvious paths were concatenated in n ways. For example, if the first time through the execution sequence, the course is N_{11}, N_{21}, N_{31}, N_{41}, and N_{51}, and the second iteration invokes the path N_{11}, N_{22}, N_{33}, N_{42}, N_{51}, then in the two passes through the model a new path has been created: N_{11}, N_{21}, N_{31}, N_{41}, N_{51}, N_{11}, N_{22}, N_{33}, N_{42}, N_{51}.

This illustrates the intuitive understanding that within a closed structure of the size typical for a single module, 100 percent path testing may be possible, but not to the extent that it can include all of the virtual paths created by looping.

In a general way, the expectations and limitations of path testing can be summarized using the three categories of implementation defects devised by J. Goodenough and S. Gerhart.[3] These categories are missing control flow paths, inappropriate path selection, and inappropriate or missing action. Missing control paths cannot be tested because they are not there to be tested. Yet, their absence can cause software failures. An example is the path around a division node taken when the test for a nonzero divisor fails. If the test had never been programmed, the path around the node does not exist.

Of their second category, Goodenough and Gerhart cite, as an example, incorrect or inadequate branch conditions. One might exercise all the paths, but some of the paths will be taken under the wrong conditions.

The third category is the one that yields the profit. Adding two numbers instead of multiplying them, passing the wrong data from one module to another, and failing to initialize data are several of the many kinds of defects that will be caught in path testing.

Thus, as a fundamental test method, the deliberate execution of sequences of atomic paths is seen as a productive technique at the "knowledge-of-the-program" end of the strategic test space. Mohanty's concepts, which are intended to lead to determination of the tests required to test all paths, are useful background to understanding the problem of reaching all paths, a problem made manageable by modest module size and structured programming.

Before leaving the matter of nodes and branches, we point out one curiosity. It is quite possible, indeed not uncommon, to include in a program paths that are impossible to reach. Module Alpha, before passing control to module Bravo, checks to see if some error condition (e.g., a negative file pointer) exists. If so, it calls not Bravo, but an error routine. Module Bravo, however, also checks the same error condition. It does so because its programmer wanted assurance that the module would not cause some kind of catastrophic failure if it were passed a meaningless pointer. In tests involving both Alpha and Bravo, the path paved in Bravo to rescue the system from a negative pointer will never be taken, and so will never be tested. This is analogous to the example given in Chapter 3 of harmless coding errors that will never be caught by testing. Harmless, that is, until a subsequent change to the program exposes the path to execution. In general, it is not unusual to have program paths that, to be accessed, require an impossible set of conditions.

STRESS AND BOUNDARY TESTS

Tests that attempt to assess the operational limits of a program are independent of path tests, and may be found anywhere within the strategic test space, but generally closer to the black-box end. Boundary tests determine the operational limits with respect to predictable environments. For example, if file space is limited, but may be shared in any manner among several individual files, one can test various high volume combinations of input to determine which, if any, will cause the file to reach its limits. Some years ago one of the authors had designed a program system to provide solutions to a problem generically known as the traveling salesman problem.* The algorithm used was an iterative one, in which chains of various "cities and routes" were created as interim solutions. There was no presumptive way of knowing how long any chain might get, but it was clear that if one, or two, or maybe three chains grew to sufficient size, they would prevent other chains from "maturing" in the iterative process. Only by tinkering with various combinations of "cities and towns" did we learn the earmarks of a data set that could cause the program to generate correct, but suboptimal answers. This was subsequently documented and offered as a caveat to the adventurous users of the program.

Another boundary test is the measure of the average time it will take for a time-sharing system to respond to a carriage return command, given 25 active terminals, 50 terminals, 75 terminals, and so forth. In brief, boundary tests are used to calibrate the performance envelope of a software system.

The tests of individual parts of a system may also include exercise at the possible limits. For example, modules performing mathematical operations would be exposed to data at the minimum and maximum magnitudes, and at any uniquely sensitive points between them. However, these boundary tests are conducted to expose inadequate design or faulty code, rather than to explore performance.

The distinction between stress and boundary tests, while not great, is recognizable to the quality manager. As we define them, stress tests are analogous to destructive physical tests. To test the tensile strength of fishing line, one subjects the line to increasing stress until it finally parts. Similarly, to determine the rate of traffic a message switching system can bear before the wait queues fill up, one gradually increases the rate of data input. The number of aircraft an air traffic control system can handle without falling behind real time is determined by gradually increasing the number of tracked targets. Another example is the exploration of the job mix a virtual system can handle

---

*So named because it seeks the shortest route interconnecting a number of independent nodes. It has been used to solve such diverse problems as multistage rocket trajectory optimizations and critical path project control. We know of no application actually dealing with traveling salesmen, but then we know of no case where the equally classic 0/1 knapsack problem was ever encountered on the Appalachian or Pacific Crest trails.

before so much time is spent in moving pages into real memory from virtual that no useful work gets done.

Frequently, stress and boundary tests result in a "breaking point" well below one's expectations. This may be a symptom of a defect in code, design, or even specified requirements. It occurs when a combination of paths is executed for the first time. In this sense, the tests have had the effect of testing against postulated operational environments, the tests that dominate the middle and black-box end of the strategic test space.

Stress and boundary tests have several similarities to the environmental testing performed on hardware. Although we expect that failures will occur, these tests are not specifically directed to the exposure of outright defects. Rather, they are designed to define performance in given environmental conditions. Only if the performance falls below acceptable limits when confronted with a quantified environment as stipulated in the requirements definition, can one properly speak of a defect. Since the definition of such environments is usually difficult, these tests are easily overlooked by those who attack the testing activity as no more than either a search for defects or a proof of performance. This is wrong. In time, a user, not told of the program's environmental limitations, will report the program's inadequacies. Although stress and boundary tests don't apply to all software, when they do it should be quality's responsibility to see to it that they are performed.

STRATEGY

The overriding purpose of testing is to find interior defects so that they can be corrected; secondarily, to determine the operational limitations of software. For other than the smaller programs which are not our concern, this requires a set of approaches covering the strategic test space. We have already seen that the knowledge-of-the-code end of that space can be occupied by path testing. The other extreme lends itself to stress and boundary tests. The middle ground is occupied by exposure to presumed operational environments. What is required is an overall strategy, spanning the strategic test space, quite as deliberate in its methodology as was the systematic development on which analysis, design, and code were based.

Indeed, even as the systematic strategy of Chapter 5 was based on levels of abstraction, we return to that concept in this chapter. We do so, however, with one major variation. In Chapter 5, we worked our way from the most abstract definition of the software to the most specific. Here, the opposite course will be followed. We shall start with the unit tests of each module at the most specific (only here we consider "specific" to refer to knowledge of the code) end of the strategic test space, and work our way up to the black-box test of the finished article for the basis of acceptance.

In a general way, Figure 7-3 summarizes this concept. The process from system design to code is mirrored by the progression of tests that, at each stage, validate their design and code counterparts.

We must admit that in dividing the entire test process into these four categories, the last two were somewhat arbitrarily selected. One might, for example, break out a separate test of hardware-software integration, where that

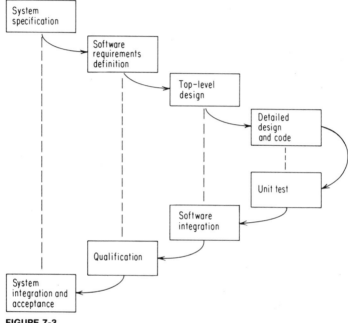

FIGURE 7-3

applies. One can also define, for a system of multiple computer program configuration items, a test of the success of their integration. We could also define acceptance tests or certification tests. To serve the purposes of illustration, we settled on those categories that generically encompass all test activity and subsume any classifications we left out.

Unit and integration testing have been previously defined. Qualification testing is the formal test phase, conducted in a controlled environment, of the program's ability to meet its stipulated performance specification. It is also a process of measuring the limitations and constraints of the program. System testing culminates in the test of the conformance of the program — and other programs and hardware with which it will operate — to the requirements for the system. It too may include, but at the systems level, acceptance criteria and the measurement of limitations and constraints.

Before tackling the tactics appropriate to each of the test series, we shall want to consider further the fundamental strategies that, reflecting a monotonic increase of abstraction, will predicate those tactics.

It is obvious that at each stage we want to expose as many defects as possible; the total number of defects found is the sum of those found at each stage. There is, however, a second, only slightly less obvious reason for wanting to maximize the number of bugs found in each test series. The longer a defect remains in the system, the more expensive it is to remove it. A bug exposed in unit testing is, by definition, known to be in the module under test. If initially discovered during integration, then before it can be squashed it must first be isolated to one of the modules (not necessarily the one just introduced to the system) forming the partial program. If found during the later tests, it must be isolated to somewhere in a system of still greater scope. Moreover, access to individual nodes becomes more restricted as test time passes, further limiting the effectiveness of diagnostic procedures. Finally, down to a point close to the end of all testing, the number of persons whose work may be held up by the search for a fault, or who may be directly involved in the search party, also increases.

Thus, the tactics that are formulated must be based not on the number of defects found per unit of time or unit of work-hours, but on a measure of effectiveness that incorporates both the success in exposing defects and the failure of leaving some still uncovered. Specifically, we can measure the efficacy of testing as

$$E = \frac{D_f}{D_f + D_r} \times 100$$

where D_f = defects found
D_r = defects remaining after the test

Assume that a program initially harboring 400 defects was exposed to the four formally defined test phases of Figure 7-3. Let us hypothesize that for each phase $E = 50$. We can then tabulate the results of each test phase:

	E	D_f	D_r
Unit test	50	200	200
Integration	50	100	100
Qualification	50	50	50
System	50	25	25

The overall efficacy is

$$\frac{375}{400} \times 100 = 93.75$$

Assume, however, that we change the emphasis of our methods to improve the efficacy of the earlier stages at the expense of the later ones. That is, we shall be willing to spend more in time and tools for unit and integration tests than for qualification and system tests. Based on this strategy, we shall assign $E_{unit} = 70$, $E_{integration} = 70$, $E_{qualification} = 30$, and $E_{system} = 30$. The tabulated results show some improvement:

	E	**D_f**	**D_r**
Unit test	70	280	120
Integration	70	84	36
Qualification	30	11	25
System	30	8	17

The overall efficacy is

$$\frac{383}{400} \times 100 = 95.75$$

The net number of defects remaining in the program has been reduced from 25 to 17, for a total improvement of 32 percent. Unfortunately, this analysis is hypothetical at best. One does not really have the latitude, nor does one usually have adequate quantified experience, to choose tactics and tools that will provide the precise efficacy for each test phase one expects. Nevertheless, there are three valid conclusions we can draw from this analysis:

1. The efficacy of one's test techniques must be measured and used as a basis for quality improvement.

2. The emphasis of the early tests should be entirely on the exposure of defects. Not until the later tests should performance be a consideration.

3. It is unthinkable to cut short unit and integration testing to meet a previously established schedule.

Table 7-1 summarizes the issues, thus far explored, that form the basis for test strategy. The table also includes a topic not yet developed: the increasing role of quality as one progresses through the sequence of tests. Weights from 1 (lightest) to 4 are assigned to the several key factors as they apply to each of the four basic test phases. The weighting is a relative matter; the differences in the applicability of an item from phase to phase are greater for some items than for others.

TABLE 7-1

	Unit test	Integra- tion	Qualifi- cation	System test
Knowledge of the contents of the program	4	3	2	1
Efficacy of path testing	4	3	2	1
Efficacy of stress and boundary testing	1	2	3	4
Testing with diagnostic input	4	3	2	1
Testing with typical operational input	1	2	3	4
Emphasis on defect removal	4	3	2	1
Emphasis on performance	1	2	3	4
Extent of quality's participation	1	2	3	4

UNIT TEST

The series of tests that constitute unit test (or module test) are directed to the discovery of faults within each module. These faults can either be failure of the code to reflect the design or failure of the code and design to satisfy the module's specified requirements. If the module is a utility routine and has modules subordinate to it, unit test of the top-most module of the set (the one we would think of as the utility routine) would include testing of the entire set.*

Unit testing is very much part of module development. In fact, the IEEE definition[1] of the software life cycle includes module code and test as a single phase, chronologically situated between "design" and "test." From the point of view of both the programmer and management, this makes good sense. In our definition of the life cycle, starting back in Chapter 3, grouping unit test with

*There is just enough of a contradiction in terms here to offend the semantically minded reader, who might prefer to think of the test of the ensemble as a test series separate from unit test. The distinction is more pedantic than substantive, since the disciplines under which the utility is assembled remain those of unit testing.

other testing, rather than with the coding activity, permits a somewhat more cohesive exposition of test strategy. Nevertheless, it remains that the coding of a module is not truly complete until the module has been debugged.

This carries the implication that unit test should be mostly an informal process. The formality that attaches is the proof that the module has been properly exercised. From this one can too easily conclude that the greater part of unit testing is based on the programmer's informal test runs, and that the module test procedure need only demonstrate compliance with the module's requirements specification.

Indeed, the module test procedure should include a validation test, but more is required. Table 7-1 assigns to unit test the most productive use of path testing, and path testing of segments of code limited in size is a most effective way of discovering defects. Thus, we would expect that a unit test procedure would include test cases for the execution of specific control paths and correlation of these cases with the code or with design documentation.

Table 7-1 also indicates that unit test is more likely to profit from contrived input than that distilled, or adapted to a given module, from operational input. Consider the software for a radar tracking system. One of the modules, Polcar, converts target position in polar coordinates (range, azimuth angle, and elevation angle) to cartesian coordinates (x,y,z). It is not pertinent to the test of Polcar that the input test data be derived from data synthesized to include the effects of encoder granularity, jitter, and other operational phenomena. What is required is that the input for the tests encompass all limit conditions (e.g., angles at multiples of 90°, magnitudes of range, x, y, and z from zero to the maximum, data sets that create algebraic singularities) applicable to the module, even if some of the conditions are considered to have no probability of occurrence in the operational environment. This may sound like an excuse for overdesign, but rigorous testing of this kind provides a degree of tolerance to errors made during the top-level design, later to be manifested as interface failures. For modules like Polcar, this testing also produces error calibration data in the boundary zones, one place where exploratory boundary testing *is* appropriate at the module level.

Diagnostic input, rather than data that seems related to the system requirements, is also the most certain way to force execution of all paths. One cares not why a path is executed, simply that it is taken. One of the disadvantages of pure top-down testing, wherein unit test is conducted with the module operating *in loco* in the evolving system, is that such input may be difficult to synthesize. Consider a module, at some hierarchical remove from the input modules of a system, that takes a given path based upon two variables, g and η.

Figure 7-4 depicts the branch to the path in question as a node within the module. The two variables that force the branch are each doubly transformed from four input data. Moreover, the transformations are not necessarily the result of straightforward algebraic operations. That is, the functions in each node might be conditional propositions. For example, the function $\mathcal{H}$ (c,f) might be

If c has occurred and f has not

    Then $g = 1$

    Else $g = 0$

Producing the required g and η from the eight input variables, as one must do if the module is tested *in loco* with the modules hierarchically above it, is far more demanding than simply setting the variables as desired for a test of

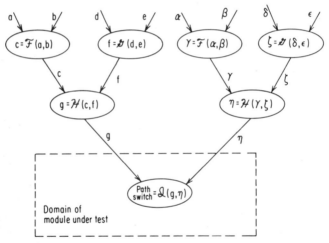

FIGURE 7-4   Transformation of Input Data to Test Stimuli.

the module in isolation. This, of course, is simply another way of saying that program nodes (including the path selection decision points) are most testable when within an isolated module.

Parenthetically, we note that of all the paths most likely to go unexercised, none are so likely to be ignored as those associated with error handling. Programmers are fairly dutiful about putting in traps for certain errors (e.g., checking pointers before using them to make certain they are within range, or checking for zero divisors), especially when they know that the ones they missed will be picked up by quality at the design review, but they are not equally diligent about testing them. "What the hell, it's never going to be used anyway." Also, the fact that an error is trapped is no assurance that corrective action can be taken. We recall one programmer whose code contained a trap for an illegal data condition, but whose escape route, if the prohibited condition arose, was simply to come to a program halt. The comment he placed before the halt instruction was "Drop back 10 yards and punt."

Proving Correctness

Testing is not the only way to discover faults. One can also attempt to prove correctness. In Chapter 5 we discussed, under the topic of languages, assertion tests. Positing and evaluating assertions of the relationships among variables is a powerful mechanism for the checkout of a program and can lead to a proof of the program's correctness.

Apart from the use of software tools, it is possible to abstractly (but not infallibly) prove correctness. Proofs that assertions are implied by previous assertions (going back to the input assertion) and the transformations between them, derive from theorem-proving techniques based on a formal method commonly referred to as the predicate calculus. While this approach is, in the least, intriguing, its application is extremely tedious for all but the smallest modules. Thus, although the concept of proving correctness is compellingly attractive, it has not yet, nor will it, replace the need for testing.

There are further limitations. One may prove the code correct with respect to its specification, but is the specification itself correct? Unit testing does not attempt to validate module specifications, but recognition of specification errors is a not infrequent by-product of unit testing. In an entirely different problem, we find that the compiler that implements the programming language may have eccentricities that the assertions cannot take into account.

Finally, a proof implies deductive reasoning based on applying rules of inference to appropriate axioms of the program and its environment. The FOR statement in PASCAL permits a process to be repeated a fixed number of times. In forming the grade average of the upper half of the graduating class, the FOR statement would be used to sum the grades of the students from the midpoint to the top, assuming they were listed in grade-point order. Quite deliberately, PASCAL was designed to forbid modifying the iteration interval within the body of a loop, since to do so would preclude an axiomatic rule to explain the FOR statement.[4] Developing programs with axiomatic proofs as a goal is hardly the rule, however, and for most programs it is exceedingly difficult to formulate inclusive axioms. Lacking these, we are left with the proof of correctness of assertions, but no proof that the assertions prove correctness of the program.

Thus, proofs and tests are alike in that neither can eliminate the possibility of potential software failures. It is better to consider each to be supportive of the other in the production of reliable software. In particular, until more is known of the defect-finding efficiency of correctness proofs, we would tend not to base a validation plan on their use except for unusually critical program sequences, such as the kernel of the file privacy mechanism of a multiprogramming system. Readers who are interested in the approach will find a good treatment of it by J. D. Ullman.[5]

Similar to proof-of-correctness is the concept of symbolic execution. Here, "a program is 'symbolically' executed for a set of *classes* of inputs."[6] For example, a routine to add two numbers would not be given an infinite set of number pairs, but the symbols "*a*" and "*b*." The step-by-step analysis (admittedly, not too many steps in this one) follows the transformations of the input symbols. The final result should be "*a* + *b*." Matters get more complicated when control flow is a function of input data. Here one must establish an input class for each control path, requiring analyses not unlike those involved in proof-of-correctness.

Symbolic execution has difficulty in dealing with other practical considerations, such as using variables derived from input for the indexing of data arrays or accounting for round-off errors. Problems of this kind — which are not easily coped with by proof-of-correctness, either — coupled with the lack of data on the efficiency of defect finding, tend to preclude the application of the technique from standard quality assurance programs at this time.

Static Analysis

Another technique to augment testing's exposure of faults is static analysis. This is really a collective term to describe a number of related techniques that attempt to root out structural and semantic defects. The targets for these analyses include both design data and code. To a large degree, the techniques lend themselves to tooling, thus providing cost effectivity.

Interestingly, compilers and link editors have been performing some of these analyses for years, but rarely have the results been incorporated into a validation scheme that ensures corrective action. Typical output data generated by static analysis include the following:

- The number of each type of source statement used (an input for certain types of software models — see Part 5)

- Cross-references for operands

- The presumed use of operands (input data, table index, etc.)

- Cross-reference of called module entry points

- Unused variables

- Mismatched module interfaces

- Inconsistent use of common data areas

- Uninitialized variables

It will be noted that several of these are global in nature. That is, they apply not to unit testing but to integration testing. One would want to apply appropriate static analysis at both the module level and the computer program configuration item level.

The use of static analysis prior to actual test can reduce the time it takes to track down the cause of test failures. Moreover, it is reasonable to expect that static analysis will expose some defects that will slip by execution tests; not because it is intrinsically more thorough, but because it attacks latent faults from a different quarter. In a published experiment, static analysis was responsible for the detection of 16 percent of the errors seeded* in a large program. Path testing caught 25 percent of the errors.[7] An overview of static analysis can be found in an article by R. Fairley.[8]

Code Inspection

One of the more attractive techniques for finding defects at the module level is the actual detailed inspection of the code itself. Just as requirements definitions and the various design documents can be inspected for consistency and accuracy, so can code. As is the case with correctness proofs, symbolic execution, and static analysis, code inspection is not a substitute for actual exercise of code, but a means of exposing faults that might otherwise go undetected. Significantly, the defects found by code inspection, as by the other supplementary methods, are removed more easily.

It is important to distinguish between code inspection, code walk-throughs, and code audits. Code audits are conducted to determine the fidelity with which coding standards have been adhered to. Code audits are concerned with such matters as comments and banners, the labeling of instructions and operands, the location of declaration statements, and so forth. Walk-throughs are rather like show and tell. The programmer explains the code to a group of peers, and all attempt to find flaws. Usually, the group isn't content to simply identify problems, it also attempts to solve them. Thus, of the time spent by the group, only part is for defect exposure. Walk-throughs are informal, in keeping with the goal of not letting the programmer of the code feel the need for defensiveness.

---

*One way to improve the accuracy with which defect exposure techniques are evaluated is to employ them in a known environment. Instead of using them on a program that needs debugging, one takes a program that has been providing failure-free performance for some time, deliberately infests it with bugs, and awaits the testers' report of bugs found. Seeding has also been used in new software prior to test. The object here is to measure the ratio of seeded bugs found to those still in hiding. Applying this ratio to unseeded defects that were found should, presumably, yield the number of real defects left in the program. This technique works well for state fisheries using tagged stock and random retrieval patterns to estimate fresh-water fish populations. Its success in software has been spotty.

Code inspections, by contrast, are more formal, although in no sense conducted as adversary proceedings. Defects that are found are noted in a log for subsequent corrective action. The members of the inspection team are not the homogeneous group found at walk-throughs, but individuals with separate roles on the project (design, test, code, etc.). Check lists are used to make certain that all branches and interfaces have been explored, and that no potential source of defects has been overlooked. For example, has the team checked for provisions for remedial action for buffer overflows? For inadvertent extensions of common data areas?

The result of this organized approach is that code inspections may be expected to find more errors than actual execution. Gannon's experiment[7] also included tooled path testing and inspection. Of two error categories (computational and logic), path testing found the greater number of errors. Of the other five categories (input-output, data handling, interface, data definition, and data base), inspection unearthed the greater number. Of even greater importance, in all seven categories the average time to find and correct an error was less for inspection than for path testing. Net increases of productivity have also been reported by M. E. Fagan, whose experiment showed a savings of 94 hours per 1000 lines of code.[9]

As attractive as code inspection appears, one must remember that in no way does it replace tests of a module's execution; it augments them. Also, all members of the inspection team must be fluent in the programming language. It would be difficult to productively implement in a small programming shop working with several assembly languages. Further, code inspection would fail utterly if design documentation is less than thorough, explicit, and current; all of which it should be in any case. We simply mean that if one is starting a software quality assurance activity, code inspection is not the place to do it.

Quality's Contribution

Table 7-1 indicates that quality is less involved with unit test than with other test phases, but less is still a lot. Quality must review the plans and procedures to make certain that they will yield a good harvest of defects; that they are not contrived to prove correctness. If formal correctness proofs are employed, they should be performed or checked by quality, since quality represents an independent auditor less likely to be influenced by knowledge of what was intended. Static analysis is compellingly analogous to inspection activities in which quality has a long tradition of cost-effectivity. Quality, as the totally objective auditor, should be represented on every code inspection team. While quality need not—indeed, should not—be present during most of the actual testing, it should witness execution of test cases cited in the formal test procedures to affirm operation in accordance with the procedures and to authenticate data.

INTEGRATION TESTS

In Chapter 4 we discussed bottom-up, top-down, and modified top-down testing. We have defined modified top-down testing as top-down integration, starting with the top module of the system, of modules that have previously been unit tested outside the system. It is this method that frames our discussion of integration testing, since it accommodates access, in unit test, to the inside of modules for path execution, while (1) offering the top-down advantages of emphasizing the exercise of the weightiest control functions, and (2) accelerating the availability of the operational input mechanisms for driver stimuli.

Integration is the test of the interfaces between the modules. The speed with which it can be accomplished is directly related to the care with which design (especially top-level design) and unit test have been planned and performed. Thus, we find in integration the first cost savings realized from the verification process. Under the best of circumstances, integration will take about as long as all of unit test; under old-fashioned development methodologies, it will require multiples of the work-hours used in unit test.

The objective of integration is exposure of interface defects. Superficially, this suggests that only the linkages between modules need be examined for the source of failures. In reality, the faults are often buried within the modules' internal operations. No design is perfect; no unit test 100 percent effective. Nevertheless, the tests are directed to the manner in which the parts of a computer program configuration item operate with each other. The order with which modules are joined to the evolving system must be planned with the thought that the new paths created at each step will be sufficiently well-defined to permit the design of appropriate test cases. As a predicate for establishing integration tactics, this seems ingenuous until one considers iterations that encompass a group of modules. The ability to exercise more than a few paths with a given test case is often impaired by missing modules. In Figure 7-5 we have module Bravo subordinate to Alpha, and Charlie and Delta subordinate to Alpha.

Depending on Bravo's response to being invoked by Alpha, Alpha may again transfer control to Bravo. Further, Bravo, depending upon its interim computations, may call either Charlie or Delta. In each of the lowest three modules we symbolically indicate three processing paths. Each time Alpha invokes Bravo, the potential exists for implementing any of 18 paths. In our example, we postulate an iterative process in which the determination of whether or not another iteration will be taken is a function of the paths traversed within the model. In short, Alpha, Bravo, and Charlie constitute a loop.

Although we do not expect nearly the density of path testing in integration that strategy assigns to unit test, certain multimodule paths must be executed if the interfaces are to be properly exercised. In Figure 7-5, the stubs for Charlie and Delta might have to be quite ambitious if Bravo's marriage to Alpha is to be properly consummated. Barring other constraints, it would be productive to add Charlie and Delta to the system directly after Bravo has been integrated. Thus, we find that integration often takes vertical forms, rather than proceding one hierarchical tier after another, as the term "top-down" might seem to indicate.

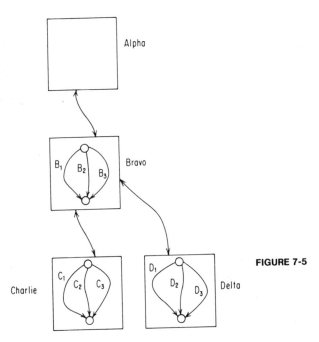

FIGURE 7-5

On the other hand, in Figure 7-6 we have Echo calling Fox or Gulf iteratively, with the internal path taken by the subordinate module a possible consequence of the last call to its sibling. All three are really in one loop. In the absence of other constraints, it looks as though it would make good sense to integrate Gulf directly after Fox (or vice versa) before adding the module(s) subordinate to Fox to the system. In other words, we have a horizontal integration scheme.

As we had said in Chapter 4, to simplify the implementation of test cases and to get the system working in an operational mode as quickly as possible, we also want the modules that interface with the outside world integrated early.

A fourth general consideration is to link-edit the utilities into the system early. They will be used by many of the other modules, and moreover, can be worked into the system on a noninterfering basis.

Summarizing, there are a number of issues to be considered in determining the order in which modules join the system. If not settled by careful planning, productivity or thoroughness or both will suffer. If not documented in a test plan, the careful planning will be wasted.

In addition to outlining the integration paths that will be taken, the test plan must also state the environment for integration, with emphasis on any hardware or software resources that will be required. This is especially critical for real-time programs, where, if the computer program configuration item is to be tested in a maximally controlled environment, the online hardware must be represented by surrogates of one form or another. Not infrequently, this calls for the development or purchase of new equipment, software tools, or both. Since these may be long lead time items, it is important that the test plan be prepared early in program development. The final plan should be available at about the time the top-level design is ready for review.

The plan will also outline the procedures that must be developed for each stage of integration. The procedures themselves must start by identifying the purpose of the test. "This test is to check the integration of module Alpha" is an inadequate definition of purpose; "The test will exercise Alpha's capability of locating delinquent accounts in the hold file, given no delinquencies, all delinquencies, and random delinquencies" is considerably better. The procedures also specify the input stimuli and their point of application, as well as the expected results and their point of observation. Other information required

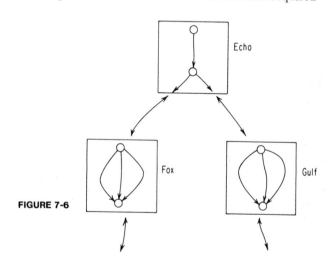

FIGURE 7-6

to assure the productivity and repeatability of the test will also be included as appropriate.

What should not be in the procedures are type and qualification of personnel, order of switches that must be energized, and other information appropriate to factory inspection procedures. Incredibly, we have seen specifications for the preparation of software test procedures that call for this very information.

The procedures, as well as the test plan, should be reviewed in terms of verification of the computer program configuration item top-level design. The wise reviewer will focus attention on the capability of the test designs to flush out defects. For the reasons given at the start of this chapter, the designs may unconsciously be biased in favor of demonstrating correct behavior.

Quality will want to be on hand during integration to certify the authenticity of the data collected, the adherence to library control practices, and, of course, the fidelity with which the procedures are being followed. It is not, however, feasible to turn the conduct of integration testing over to an independent test team. Although the tests must demonstrate that the design of the program has been satisfied, the prime purpose is the exposure of faults. A good set of test designs will find faults, and the development team must be available to further isolate and repair them. It is not uncommon to spend a large portion of the integration time in devising and executing diagnostic tests, beyond those for which procedures were prepared, to chase down the cause of failures.

In short, integration is still an integral part of development, and the role of quality must be restricted to auditing, not controlling.

To assert that integration belongs to the development team is not the same as saying that the module designers must be the testers. Separate integration teams are frequently used, especially for large systems. Their constituency, however, is drawn from the development group.

The sum of the tests used in integration will cover the entire strategic test space. Some module-to-module path testing with forcing functions will have been performed; there will have been execution with representative operational input requiring the modules to work together in various logical configurations, and some of these will border on stress and boundary tests. Quality will have reviewed the integration plans and procedures, monitored the tests to confirm conformance to the procedures and to library control standards, and certified the data. As we noted in the discussion of unit testing, certain static analyses may also have been conducted, most suitably by quality, at the configuration item level.

At the conclusion of integration, ownership of the program is transferred to an independent validation team. This means that the tests will no longer be controlled (they may still be conducted) by the developers, but by others.

QUALIFICATION

The "others" selected to control the qualification tests are those responsible for the internal acceptance of designs and manufactured goods; namely, quality. Qualification is the in-plant validation of software products by quality. Successful conclusion of this phase means that an independent program is certified for use, a single configuration item in a distributed system is ready to be integrated with other software, or a program for an embedded application is ready to be integrated with its associated hardware.

Qualification tests of independent software developed under contract may also serve as tests for product acceptance by the customer. This is not of any great importance, other than that the plans and procedures may have to be accepted by the customer, who may also want to witness the tests. Qualification testing, in any case, should result in the demonstration, under a formal regimen, of the capability of the program to meet its stipulated requirements.

By the time qualification testing is reached, the emphasis will have begun to shift from the search for defects to the proof of performance. Nevertheless, even here defects will most likely be found. The design of the tests should be scrutinized to make certain that the opportunity to uncover defects is not wasted. The defects one most expects to find are those of the program's non-conformity with the computer program configuration item requirements specification. To be sure, the top-level design was verified against the specification, and integration testing demonstrated compliance of the code with the top-level design. Still, this does not assure us that the code and the specification conform. Syllogisms have their place, but this is not one of them. We have differences of interpretation to contend with, not to mention human errors by both the implementers and the verifiers. Thus, the procedures are reviewed in relation to the specification only, and not to design documentation.

It is at qualification time that the interior workings of the program are, at last, of little interest. This is bottom line testing: does the product do what it is supposed to do, and how well? Qualification must include a sufficient variety of discrete combinations of representative operational input, and over the full operational range, to provide confidence in the structural integrity of the software. Moreover, the input must include invalid data or combinations of data to try to defeat the (now invisible) error handling mechanisms of the software.

For many programs, the number of input combinations is so great that it is impossible to presumptively determine an input space representative of the program's full capabilities. The only feasible solution is to include the use of random input: "live" pulses from a sweeping pulse generator to simulate radar returns, social security numbers generated by a random function generator, and so on. These, of course, would be used only after tests have been performed with predetermined conditions to measure the salient performance characteristics.

Since we expect to find some failures during qualification, a mechanism is required to repeat previous tests after a fault has surfaced and been repaired. The efficiency with which these *regression* tests are performed can be greatly improved if the input for each test case can be stored. If random input is used, this implies capturing the random data on disk or tape. In turn, this means that, ideally, even "live" data for embedded software should be derived from computer driven sources. In other words, we should want the pulse generator simulating random radar returns to be triggered by a computer programmed with the appropriate algorithms or with the capacity to retrieve stored data. For programs having a variety of input ports (literally or figuratively), a fairly elaborate test fixture is required to synchronize the several data sources to ensure repeatability and the capability of correctly interpreting failure modes. It is possible that the test bed required will have to be so complex that it is economically unfeasible. This is a decision quality will have to make with the aid of the development community.

Considering the many options, as well as imperatives, that bear upon the planning of qualification, it is clear that quality must, in conjunction with the development personnel, plan the tests early in the life cycle of the program.

We continue: if it is possible to use computers to assure the repeatability of input data, why not use them to capture and store the configuration item's responses? Again, there may be limits to the feasibility of this. If the response must be observed on an oscilloscope, not much can be done unless a high speed optical digitizer is available. Still, the output of most computer programs is computer readable, and if both output and input can be stored for later use, it is possible to partly automate regression testing, to run a test case a second (or nth time) and compare the results with those that were previously obtained and, on analysis, proven correct.

However it is achieved, it is absolutely essential that the procedures for qualification ensure repeatability and that regression testing be performed. If it is at all possible, regression testing should be automated.

To some extent, qualification tests may be viewed as stress testing of the success of integration. That is, one can use qualification to see if the metaphoric glue of integration holds under limiting conditions. Actually, the stress tests are directed to measurable performance, and not specifically to the manner in which earlier interface problems were resolved. Still, if faults are discovered as a result of stress tests, there is a good likelihood that they will be traceable to the overall design, wherein the interfaces were initially defined, or to modifications of that design made during integration testing. Thus, in diagnosing failure causes during qualification, it is helpful to be able to regress to integration tests as well as earlier qualification tests. Comparison of the program's behavior during the tests may provide a much-needed clue to the hidden defect.

Acceptance Criteria

One of the thorniest problems attending software quality is the establishment of the basis for accepting or rejecting a program. It is not sufficient to simply state that the program must be proven to be in conformance to its specification. Certainly, a program that processes an alphabetically ordered file of names to print mailing labels in order of zip code can be demonstrated to do its thing, given a suitable sample input file and a pair of tireless eyes to observe the output. And surely a navigation computer can be demonstrated to produce a position fix within the stipulated tolerance and within the maximum elapsed time. We can even test the mailing list program's capability to handle the maximum specified input file. We can test the navigation program at the four corners of the "rectangle" formed by the minimum and maximum longitudes and latitudes over which it was specified to operate.

However, we have seen that it is impossible to explicitly qualify for all operational conditions. It is implicit, but not otherwise specified, that the mailing list program operate even when Wm. Zygote's zip code is the highest numbered code in the input file. Yet, it is possible that the program contains a flaw that shows up only when the last input name is also the last that should be output. And if the test designer anticipated that, did he also anticipate testing to see if all goes well when Abner Aaronson's name is associated with the lowest zip code? Was the performance specification thorough enough to specify both an odd number of input records and an even number? Probably not; this is an implicit requirement for a sorting program, and, interestingly, a surprisingly frequent source of error. Similarly, the navigation program specification cannot include enumeration of every potential combination of raw measurement input that produces a position fix within the stipulated geographic bounds. Yet, some of these may produce results out of tolerance with respect to accuracy or execution time.

Simply put, acceptance must be based not only on the capability of performing the nominal functions within stipulated error limits at a few fixed points, but under as wide a diversity of circumstances as we can conceive, and then some. In short, we are back to random input, from which, in complex programs, we can be quite certain failures will occur. From this, we can now work toward including in acceptance criteria a requirement for evidence from which inference can be drawn that the number of defects remaining at the conclusion of the tests does not exceed a specified limit.

We are not suggesting that defects uncovered should be reburied; except under pathological conditions they should be repaired immediately upon being found. However, the number found during testing with random stimuli should be a clue to the number that remain. Without getting mathematical about it (that we leave for Part 5), it is reasonable to expect that the buggier a program is, the more bugs we'll find.

Still, it would be simplistic to state that "Testing with random input shall continue for n run-time hours. Each failure shall be repaired before resuming test. If more than f failures occur when n hours are reached, the program shall be rejected." Imagine, if you will, the reaction of the 30 bright, eager men and women of the development team (not to mention the already unnerved configuration manager and the worrywarts of software quality assurance) when the program is adjudged unacceptable because the maximum number of allowed failures was exceeded—even though all occurred during the first 10 of the stipulated 50 hours test duration.

In Chapter 3 we illustrated the typical decay of the rate of failure discoveries, given random input. This suggests that time between failures, or the rate at which the time between failures increases, might be a more valid criterion. Indeed, rather than specify n hours as a rigidly defined test time, it makes more sense to state "Testing with random input shall continue for at least n hours of run time, and until the time between successive failures exceeds t hours for at least three successive failures, at which time the program, having previously passed the specific performance tests of Part A, shall be accepted."

In fact, one can go further. If the data exhibit an adequate fit to a predetermined reliability model of the kind discussed in Part 5, one can compute the software equivalent of mean time to failure (MTTF) or other statistical inferences and base acceptance on that.* In any event, criteria based on the rate of failure rather than the number of failures will avoid nonacceptance of a potentially usable program in favor of delaying acceptance until reliability has been demonstrated, a solution that serves the interests of development, quality, management, and the user. Note the analogy to a reliability growth test where the maturity of the design with regard to reliability is demonstrated when the rate of growth equals a specified goal.

Qualification and Proof of Usability

To a large extent, qualification establishes the usability of software. At least, it affirms the usability to the same level of success that the specification for the software anticipated the operational use of the program. However, specifications, even in the best of all worlds, are not detailed enough to cover every operating circumstances to which software is exposed. This was the reason for the tests with random input. Moreover, specifications are never prescient. The actual environment for operation may differ from that visualized at requirements time.

A friend of ours recently took the oath for the New Jersey bar. When the judge administering the oath said "Repeat after me: I swear, or affirm, that ... ," our friend was the only one of the new lawyers to say either "I swear" or "I affirm." All the others repeated "I swear or affirm." Similarly, we recall a program that engaged the factory worker user in a long dialogue, in which, to initialize the program, the user was told to "Reply yes or no to each of the following." It took a bit to train a few of the users not to type "Yes or no" to each of the questions. Apparently, these workers were sufficiently transfixed

---

*This is deliberate waffling. We hesitate to use the term "MTTF" without interpreting its meaning within this context. More, in Part 5.

by the forbidding omniscience of the monster to fear offending it by anything other than the answer they thought it wanted. Thus do the best laid plans of civil libertarians and system architects gang awry.

Of a graver nature, many programs have lacked the flexibility to handle all the problems one would expect them capable of. A program that successfully solved the problem of routing the interconnections of 10-in by 8-in printed wiring boards was baffled by boards with aspect ratios greater than 2:1. The program had been specified to route the boards then in use, and no one, including the programmers, thought to test it under other circumstances.

A real-time program operating with a radar system worked marvellously in the laboratory, but was discovered to overload intermittently in a real environment. The problem was isolated to the noise filtering algorithm. It handled the specified noise spectrum successfully, but the customer's specification did not accurately reflect the physical world.

The full measure of usability cannot be taken during qualification; only evaluation, as we termed it in Chapter 3, can answer that. Basically, qualification validates only up to the response to the question "Does the program satisfy its specified requirements?" The balance of validation, the test of the specification, is what evaluation is really about.

SYSTEMS TESTS

If the computer program configuration item that has emerged from its qualification tests is one of several designed to operate in concert, or is embedded in a hardware system, or both, it will be exercised in yet one more series of tests. This does not necessarily mean that the configuration item has never before communicated with one or more of its siblings or with operational hardware. Although we have defined both integration and qualification as testing of the isolated configuration item, on occasion these stages will include operation with other programs or with end-product instrumentation.

These possibilities had not been examined earlier because, ideally, we should like to have confidence in the configuration item prior to the test of its execution in the more complex system environment. This is analogous to performing unit tests of modules prior to incorporating them into the still evolving configuration item. Attempting to test the coordinated operation of freshly minted programs, or the operation of new software and new hardware, can be dismayingly slow. A test fails: is the problem in configuration item Alpha or configuration item Bravo, in the software or in the hardware?

As much as we may prefer to merge only qualified programs with other programs or with hardware, our desire is not always attainable. Not infrequently, a program may be so inextricably bound to some of the hardware in which it is embedded that the capability of simulating that hardware with software or simpler test hardware is too limited to be of any real use. To some extent, we may view the simulation of other elements of the system as system level stubs and drivers. Some real-time input can be synthesized with adequate realism, and some hardware responses can be creditably dubbed, but real interaction is very difficult at best.

The extent to which it is difficult to test software is an inverse measure of the success with which the system design, not just that of each computer program configuration item, was the product of a functional modular decomposition. The more independence among the elements of a system, the simpler will be the functional interfaces.

Still, even in a well-designed system, there may be circumstances that warrant some early multi-configuration item or software-hardware testing. Thus, that part of systems testing that is really systems integration testing may be less a distinct test phase than an ongoing operation that threads its way through the previously defined integration and (especially) qualification stages.

System level integration (or whatever remains of it following configuration item qualification) is conducted within the same managerial disciplines as the integration of a program. Early plans are required, and procedures must be approved prior to testing. The test cases are directed to the satisfaction of the system design, or more accurately, to expose defects in the system design, much as program integration was directed to the configuration item top-level design. Thus, the pretest documentation is reviewed in terms of verification of that overall design of which the program is but one black box. Quality's role during the actual tests is that of auditing; the system designers are usually the "owners" of the system elements, and it is their function to actually operate the system and track down the source of each problem. Several systems producers, especially those who develop large systems, have found that a separate integration team is the most productive way of welding the elements of a system into a unified whole.

Acceptance

Thus far we have addressed only integration of a system. Qualification (or as it is more frequently called in this context, acceptance) of the system is the final formally defined test phase in the preoperational life of software. As one might expect, the management aspects of configuration item qualification apply equally to system acceptance: independent testers validate against approved procedures, regression testing is necessary if software (or hardware) changes are made during the tests, and, after all specific performance aspects of the system specification have been satisfied, testing with abundant random stimuli is the preferred basis for acceptance or rejection criteria.

There are a few unique aspects to the acceptance testing of embedded software that we should touch upon. For one, embedded software is frequently charged with the task of intermittently testing the operation of its associated hardware. This is not very different from ordinary peripheral diagnostic procedures, except that the tests are interleaved with the primary operational functions, rather than being performed in an offline mode. The specifics of these integrity tests are not generally given in the system specification. Thus, the validation of the capability, accomplished by forcing hardware failures or degradation, will usually be with respect to the software requirements definition.

We are also concerned with the storage of embedded programs. If, in the operational configuration the program is to be stored in semiconductor ROM or PROM devices, one would expect it to be acceptance tested using this operational memory. Heretofore, more easily modified memory was no problem, since the discovery of multiple defects was anticipated, with consequent alterations of the program presumed. However, execution of real-time programs with anything other than the operational configuration is not a totally valid test. In particular, program storage substituting for ROM or PROM may operate with different fetch time characteristics, affecting the rate at which the software can process data. Unfortunately, unless erasable, the semiconductor devices with which acceptance testing is started must be considered expendable; at least one repairable software failure is bound to occur. A possible solution is a rigorous certification of the ability of a substitute memory to accurately emulate the final storage medium. Such certification might have to take into account wiring lengths, interference, and other electrical matters for situations involving very high speed access. Even here, however, some testing with the operational memory will still be required to validate the mapping into ROM or PROM.

Finally, as was discussed earlier, the stimuli and observed results of hardware-software tests are not all easily converted to machine readability or machine generation. Automated regression testing and analysis is not always practicable.

Testing During Operation and Maintenance

Automated regression tests are especially useful for operation and maintenance. After the repair of a defect during the operation and maintenance period, it is necessary to repeat the tests used to establish the operability of the program. These, of course, are used only after the execution of tests to confirm the success of the bug-squashing effort. One of the peculiarities of software is that following a repair, its state, rather than being restored to the factory-fresh condition, is one that has not previously existed. Thus, quality, before pronouncing the new revision ready for use, must make certain that new bugs weren't introduced.

We have the same problem with modifications made to enhance operation or to adapt the program to a new environment. Here, however, the old "factory tests" may no longer fully apply. Thus, planning is required to define the new set of tests that will prove the operability of the program.

For embedded software we remain concerned with the continued ability to simulate an outside world environment and the capture of test results. The elaborate test bed prepared earlier has either to be maintained during operation and maintenance or be capable of being assembled anew. This is an expensive proposition, and must be reckoned early in the determination of cost of support throughout the life cycle.

It should be clear that to one extent or another any of the other test phases described in this chapter may apply to operation and maintenance. We note, however, that for minor revisions, affected modules most frequently are unit tested *in loco*, rather than as isolated programs, to obviate the need for special driver programs. This does not represent a compromise of the quality solution, since we are not here concerned with the integration of many untried modules.

THE LAST TEST

When has software undergone its last test? A program, having survived the unit test of its parts, integration testing, qualification testing, and perhaps systems integration and acceptance, may be thought to be fully tested at delivery. As the reader is now tired of hearing, this is not tantamount to a statement that the program is delivered free of bugs. Thus, we have more tests conducted during operation and maintenance — the tests performed after each repair.

Yet all these tests are but a fraction of the total number that will be run on the program. Given the astronomical number of discrete states that are inherent in the structure of software, every execution of a program is potentially a unique one; in a sense, is a new test. The last test that is performed is the last execution of the program prior to code death. Only then does software quality assurance bundle its records and send them off to the archives.

SUMMARY

1. The primary goal of testing should not be the demonstration of correct performance but the exposure of hidden defects. The tendency exists for a programmer to design tests of his own code that are directed toward proving correct performance.

2. While still in the design stage, we may view a program's testability in terms of its functional modularity and other matters independent of the structure of the code. At the code level, testability is a measure of the accessibility of the nodes of the program to the application of test stimuli.

3. Testing should take place over the entire "strategic test space," that conceptual software gymnasium that has the program exercised by tests designed with knowledge of the code at one end and by the evaluation of the performance of the software "black box" at the other.

4. Testing with knowledge of the code should emphasize the testing of individual paths and nodes. This is most appropriate for unit level and integration testing.

5. As testing progresses toward the black-box extreme, emphasis can shift to the use of postulated operational input. It is also important to determine the stress limits of software (stress testing) and the performance envelope within specification tolerances (boundary tests).

6. Somewhat arbitrarily, the test process can be divided into four sequential stages: unit test, integration, qualification, and systems test. These four, in addition to exposing defects, serve to validate the detailed design and code, top-level design, software requirements definition, and system specification, respectively. Essentially, this creates a backwards trace of the development through the levels of abstraction of Chapter 5.

7. The longer a defect remains in the system, the more expensive it is to remove it. This reinforces the need to emphasize defect exposure in the earlier test stages.

8. It is generally easier to apply test stimuli to exercise specific nodes and paths within modules when the modules are tested in isolation.

9. Beyond the usual test techniques, other methods of detecting faults are formal correctness proofs, static analysis, and code inspection.

10. In its validation of the top-level design, integration takes on the form of the testing of module interfaces. Integration should be performed in accordance with approved plans and procedures, even though the tests fundamentally remain development tests.

11. Qualification should be under the control of quality. Defects will be found even at this stage. Since these are formal tests, regression testing is necessary to prove that rework has not created additional problems.

12. Acceptance is a thorny issue. In addition to testing at specified performance points, the software should be subjected to many test cases comprising random input.

13. To the extent possible, embedded software should be tested separately prior to being integrated with systems hardware. The difficulties of diagnosing problems associated with new hardware and new software can be partly

alleviated by independent testing. Acceptance of embedded software, however, is implicit in the system acceptance process.

14. It is essential that test procedures be sufficiently comprehensive and detailed to be repeatable. This is necessary not only for regression testing prior to delivery, but also after maintenance activities, to make certain that presumably unaffected functions were in fact not altered.

REFERENCES

1. R. Posten and M. Hecht (eds.), "Software Engineering Terminology" (Draft), IEEE Computer Society, Technical Committee on Software Engineering, Subcommittee on Software Engineering Standards, March 1978.

2. Siba N. Mohanty, "Models and Measurements for Quality Assessment of Software," *ACM Computing Surveys*, Vol. 11, No. 3, September 1979, pp. 251–275.

3. John Goodenough and Susan Gerhart, "Toward a Theory of Test Data Selection," *1975 International Conference on Reliable Software*, IEEE Cat. No. 75CH0940-7CSR, pp. 493–510.

4. Ralph London, "A View of Program Verification," *1975 International Conference on Reliable Software*, IEEE Cat. No. 75CH0940-7CSR, pp. 534–545.

5. J. D. Ullman, *Fundamental Concepts of Programming Systems*, Addison-Wesley, Reading, Mass., 1976, pp. 299–316.

6. James King, "Symbolic Execution and Program Testing," *CACM*, Vol. 19, No. 7, July 1976, pp. 385–394.

7. Carolyn Gannon, "Error Detection Using Path Testing and Static Analysis," *Computer*, IEEE Computer Society Magazine, Vol. 12, No. 8, August 1979, pp. 26–31.

8. Richard Fairley, "Tutorial: Static Analysis and Dynamic Testing of Computer Software," *Computer*, IEEE Computer Society magazine, Vol. 11, No. 4, April 1978, pp. 14–23.

9. M. E. Fagan, "Design and Code Inspection to Reduce Errors in Program Development," *IBM System Journal*, Vol. 15, No. 3, 1976, pp. 182–211.

Chapter 8
Tools

It is necessary to shorten a 10-ft plank by 2 ft. Two approaches to accomplishing the task immediately present themselves. In the first of these, we call upon the strongest person on the payroll to break the plank with a sharp blow of the hand. The second solution requires an expenditure of capital for the purchase of a wood saw. Also, it temporarily reduces our available workforce while one of our workers is engaged in the process of acquiring the saw. Do we hesitate in electing the second method? Never. Decisive managers that we are, we immediately dispatch someone to get the proper tool.

Even transcending considerations of workman's compensation, we recognize that while the karate chop will do the job, our experience, or imagination, tells us that the break will leave jagged edges that must be filed smooth before the piece can be used. Finding the thought of unnecessary rework repugnant, we accept the tooled solution without further contemplation of the alternative.

For reasons that are not at all clear to the authors, similar rationales for software tools are not always given the benefit of the managerial considerations given handsaws. In the end, software quality assurance's interest in software development and maintenance tools focuses on their effectiveness in reducing rework. To one extent or another, each of the tool classes that will be discussed helps to improve the quality of software products. Not only do tools lessen the amount of rework required after delivery, they also reduce rework during development. The net result is that tools improve productivity.

Actually, most of the tools employed today are oriented toward the improvement of productivity, with quality considerations a casual by-product. Recall the primitive monitor of Chapter 3 that made Carol's workday so much more efficient. It did so in a direct way by relieving her of time-consuming procedures. Indirectly, it further contributed to Carol's productivity by performing operations that are error-prone if executed by people.

Among the tools we have previously introduced that are predominently code-productive, as the expression has it, are the following:

Operating systems

Assemblers

Compilers

Interpreters

Link editors

In this chapter we wish to concentrate on tools that have a direct influence on quality. Thus, we shall not discuss tools, of which the above list is but a subset, that are principally code-productive, except that we shall find new, quality-oriented extensions of link editors. However, just as code-productive tools also enhance software quality, most quality-oriented tools also have a secondary effect on the improvement of productivity. This fact should not be overlooked at the time an investment in such tools is under consideration. As we describe the classes of tools, where applicable we shall draw attention to those features especially suited to economic justification having nothing to do with reducing rework.

One cannot discuss individual tools or classes of tools without first identifying them. This would seem to be a simple enough process. However, there exists a kind of symbiosis in quality tools that tends to muddle attempts at creating a sensible taxonomy. For example, a highly useful asset is a tool that automatically generates sets of input data for exercising a program in accordance with a presumed operational environment. It can, and does, stand apart from other automated aids in improving test coverage. Another invaluable tool that can comfortably stand alone is the program that analyzes the results of a test, flagging any anomalies that may have occurred. We should want to clearly identify both of these as potential candidates for one's tool kit. If, however, one goes a step further and combines the two, the basis for automated regression testing becomes apparent. The effectiveness of tools for regression testing is far more than that of the sum of the two principal constituents. Clearly, we want regression aids to occupy a prominent part in our taxonomy.

One could, of course, define only the most basic of tools, leaving out the tool sets that make so much sense as ensembles. This is tantamount to suggesting that mechanical assemblers be provided with a separate ratchet wrench for each hex nut currently used in the company's products, rather than a set consisting of a ratchet handle and a dozen removable sockets.

At the other extreme, a taxonomy can be devised in which ensembles, such as regression systems, totally subsume their parts, some of which can be completely justified on their own. In addition to the implicit suggestion that the parts have no value as independent tools, this approach also runs into trouble when each of two ensembles comprises, among other components, the same major tool.

We have taken a middle course. In some cases we have identified classes of tools of very narrow scope, while other of the classes we name comprise a variety of individual tools, including some also classified separately. If this sounds like waffling, which it most assuredly is, the motive is defensible: the classes found in our taxonomy span those attainable by the small programming shop of modest budget and needs to those that should be considered for the development of large programming systems. The reader looking for a fine-grained treatment would do well to read Don Reifer's excellent 1979 paper,[1] in which he defines 32 tools (although in a few cases he, too, combines some closely related tools in composite categories). The other extreme is found in the very thoughtful paper by C. V. Ramamoorthy and S. F. Ho on automated evaluation systems.[2]

TOOLS AND THEIR APPLICATIONS

The codification scheme that we have gone to indecent lengths to justify is depicted in Table 8-1. This table also indicates the principal application or applications for each tool or class of tools. "Analysis and design," the first of these applications, requires no explanation. "Configuration management and library control" applies throughout the life cycle. Under "coding and code analysis," we include tools that are instrumental in permitting the writing of code that is less error-prone, as well as tools that process written code in an attempt to uncover defects. The heading "active fault finding" refers to actual code execution toward the knowledge-of-the-code end of the strategic test space, as described in Chapter 7. Where a tool is noted as applicable to this activity, it is understood to be either an aid to the running of the test or a means of improving the efficacy of the test. The last application, "performance measurement," is similar, but applies to those tests conducted toward the code-hidden-from-the-tester end of the strategic test space.

With that, we can now look at each of these classes of tools in the light of their contributions to the production of quality software.

Basic Diagnostics

The earliest diagnostic aids that were developed belong to the family of break-point, snapshot, dump, and trace. Each serves the purpose of providing narrow visibility of the execution history of a program. They are generally invoked as assembler or compiler directives; that is, commands inserted in the source file prior to assembly or compilation.

Breakpoint is merely the device wherein execution is halted at a predetermined value of the program counter, often to invoke one of the other diagnos-

TABLE 8-1

Tool class	Analysis and design	Configuration management/Library Control	Coding and code analysis	Active fault finding	Performance measurement
			Application		
Basic diagnostics				X	
Change tracker		X			
Comparator		X			
Definition and design processor	X				
Dynamic analysis				X	
Emulator and simulator	X			X	X
Flowcharter		X			
Global cross-reference mapper		X		X	
Host system		X	X	X	X
Librarian		X			
Link editor		X		X	X
Postprocessors				X	X
Preprocessors			X	X	
Regression test system				X	X
Software development workbooks	X	X	X		
Standards analyser			X		
Static analysis			X		
System performance monitor					X
Test case generator				X	X

tics. It may serve no greater purpose than permitting the tester to inspect a visual display of the contents of one of the registers, or it may be used to trigger hard-copy output of all or part of memory *(dump)*. Breakpoint can also be implemented in such a way that execution resumes after the diagnostic has completed its operation.

Dump, which was just defined, is often regarded as the "last resort" in tracking down the source of a problem. It provides as complete a picture as one wants of the contents of memory (and usually the machine registers as well) at the time execution stopped. Reading page after page of densely formatted octal or hexadecimal numbers is not one's favorite way of discovering what went wrong, but sometimes it is the only way.

Snapshot is similar to dump, except that it provides a record of narrowly defined areas of memory and does not require a program halt in the usual sense. Snapshot facilities often include formatting of output data into something more readable than octal or hexadecimal numbers. *Trace* is similar to snapshot, except that it provides a recurring output of generic operations (e.g., computations associated with conditional branches) rather than specific data items.

That we have included these basic diagnostic tools in this collection is not to imply that they are to be considered in the same class as the more powerful testing tools that dominate Table 8-1. These basic tools do not fill the more difficult role of causing a fault to manifest itself as a failure, but that of helping to locate elusive faults when a failure has occurred.

Change Tracker

A source code file may go through a number of changes in its lifetime. It is most helpful to have an audit trail of these changes, especially once the program has been placed under configuration control. A change tracker can be developed to provide as little information as the date of each change and the identification of the person making the change, or can output not only this information but a record of the change itself. The information is stored in a file retrievable at any time.

Most modern operating systems include *file managers* to keep track of where files are located, to concatenate files, to add new files, to delete unused files, and so on. A change tracker can be implemented as a modification to a file manager. If one is using an independent editor (no file manager) for interactive source code entry and modification, the editor can be expanded to include the capability of building the audit trail directly behind the statement (usually END) that tells the compiler that there are no further source statements to be processed.

Comparator

The simplest of the library control tools is the *comparator*. At the source code level, it reads two files of what are purported to be the same program, and, in source record format, lists any differences between the two.

Even as simple a tool as a comparator is not immune from the problems that can attend computer software. The first comparator we ever built was not endowed with sufficient ability to handle the problem of a record's having been added to or deleted from one file but not the other. With the comparator unable to recognize that following the interfile discrepancy, both files were identical, but skewed by one record; the result was pages of useless output that (slightly rearranged) looked like this:

Record No.	File 1	File 2
.	.	.
.	.	.
.	.	.
16	IF(Q(I).GT.X) CALL ALPHA	DO 6 I = 1,N
17	IF(Q(I).LT.Y) CALL BETA	IF(Q(I).GT.X) CALL ALPHA
18	Z = X/Q(I) + Q(I)/Y	IF(Q(I).LT.Y) CALL BETA
19	L = IFIX(X)MOD(I)	Z = X/Q(I) + Q(I)/Y
.	.	.
.	.	.
.	.	.

The moral to this anecdote is that software tools should be developed under the same quality disciplines as any other programs. This oversight, which caused users to eschew use of the tool until the problem was corrected, would probably have been caught at a requirements definition review.

Comparators are also useful for determining any differences between object code files, or indeed any pair of files. When used to compare files of test results, a comparator forms part of a regression test system.

Definition and Design Processor

With this class of programs, we introduce more complex software tools. Most generally, this class processes software requirements or design descriptions prepared in machine-readable form, especially the requirements language and design language forms noted in Chapter 5. To one degree or another, the outputs of these processors encompass the tracing of requirements from initial stipulation to design to source code.

One still-evolving system that covers the full range is Gypsy. As reported in late 1978,[3] Gypsy, designed as either a formal specification language or a program language, is used most effectively as a verifiable program description language. The verifiability, rooted in generalized axioms, incorporates — among other techniques — the use of assertions in the specification source file. To check consistency between actual and formal parameters in routine calls, Gypsy incorporates strong data typing.

Specification and design languages can, of course, be defined and used whether or not analysis tools are provided. However, their virtue of being machine readable makes the use of tools to extract information compellingly attractive. In Chapter 5 we used the U.S. Army's Requirements Statement Language (RSL) an an example. RSL statements, stored in a sophisticated system of files called a relational data base, are operated on by a set of support tools named "requirements engineering and validation system" (REVS). From the data base, REVS extracts information for consistency checks, improper sequences of processing steps, and conflicting uses of system information. REVS also includes an automated simulation generator and execution package to help analyze the dynamic interactions of the individual requirements as they had been specified.[4]

One of the best known tools for analyzing specified requirements is the Problem Statement Analyzer (PSA) designed by the University of Michigan's ISDOS Project to operate on specifications prepared in their Problem Statement Language (PSL). PSA, which is described in reference,[5] provides a variety of reports. Among them are the structure report, which presents the hierarchies either in the form of a node list or in graphical representation; data structure reports showing the contents of data objects (e.g., input items) down to the level of individual elements; the data derivation report, which shows the flow of data from one process to another; and reports of system dynamics — events, conditions, and time intervals. Reports of the modification of the PSL data base are automatically produced at each change made to the data base.

In the design stage, one is continually concerned with maintaining consonance among the parts of the system. Modular decomposition, while reducing the complexity of detailed design tasks, creates a complexity of interfaces. As we noted in Chapter 7, integration testing may be regarded chiefly as the test of those interfaces. Tools that can check the consistency of the defined interfaces are of prime interest. A production tool devised specifically for this purpose was described by B. Boehm et al. as early as 1975.[6] The Design Assertion Consistency Checker (DACC) was developed by TRW to process assertions made of the inputs and outputs of the various parts of a software system design, for the purpose of finding inconsistencies of range, number of data items, data type, and other interface definitions.

An intriguing and well-publicized design system is IBM's APLGOL, designed to support interactive, structured, top-down development of microprocessor applications. "APLGOL 2 is a hybrid language with an 'outer syntax' (ALGOL-like) which contains structures that control the flow of the 'inner syntax' (APL)."[7] The tool kit (XREF) is a set of APL functions applied to the analysis of the APL code generated by the executable design language and by translated decision tables. The reports generated include a hierarchical flow representation of the design of the system, showing the static calling sequences of all system functions, and an interface control document that lists the data interfaces and each function's calls of other functions.

As a final example of this powerful class of tools, we cite the processor for the widely known Program Design Language (PDL) of Caine, Farber, and Gordon, Inc.[8] The reports produced by the PDL processor contain: a description of the body of the design, consisting of flow segments and text segments; a reference tree showing how the segment references are nested; and a cross-reference listing that gives the page and line number at which each segment is referenced.

From these examples, it is clear that the reports produced by analyzers of machine readable requirements and design specifications can provide much of the information needed for a thorough verification of the products of the requirements and design phases.

Dynamic Analysis

Tools for dynamic analysis and static analysis are the ones closest to the heart of software quality, as they are involved directly with the operational software product. Static analysis tools operate upon target programs. That is, the programs being analyzed are not themselves executed. In dynamic analysis, the target program is instrumented to provide a history of its operation.

We can introduce the basic concepts of dynamic analysis by considering a rudimentary example. Assume that a program occupies the first n locations of memory. Let us zero n contiguous locations of a disk file, or, if space permits, of unused computer memory. We shall, by one means or another, trap the program counter such a way that at the execution of each instruction we can write a binary 1 into the disk location equivalent to the contents of the program counter. At the conclusion of an execution of the target program, we run another program to print the beginning and ending addresses of each block of the disk file containing sequential binary 1s. These are the addresses that were executed. Using the load map produced by the link editor and the relative address hard copy output of the compiler, we can determine precisely which branches were and were not executed. If the goal of a series of tests is to execute all branches at least once, this is how we can validate that the goal was met.

More generally, tools for dynamic analysis are either supervisory programs, hardware probes located in the circuitry of the target processor, or software probes inserted in the target program, or any combination of the above, used to provide various statistics on what the program did and how it did it. The information thus gathered is useful for measuring the thoroughness of the test, determining which program segments were executed the most, analyzing the time taken by certain operations, and tracing the values assumed by selected variables during execution.

Most of the tools are in the forms of software probes used to instrument the target program. Thus, we can include the insertion of statements for assertion testing, as discussed in Chapter 5, under the category of dynamic analysis. A software probe may be as simple as the execution mapping example with which we started, a more revealing set of counters used to record the number of times individual instructions were executed, or as complex as the capability of global assertions of the minimum and maximum values of designated variables. The more complex systems of software probes are often instrumented as procedures incorporated in the supervisory software under which the test is performed. These are frequently called *software monitors.* Located in the supervisory software, they have access to data that will also permit their recording processor idle time, the sequence in which modules are called, the execution time of the operation of each module when invoked, I/O channel utilization, and the like. *System performance monitors,* another tool class we shall discuss, are similar, but designed to focus on the performance of the computing system rather than an individual program.

Hardware monitors can also provide this kind of information. A 1977 report by the U.S. Army Test and Evaluation Command makes the interesting observation that "Since the Hardware Monitor does not in any way load the target system, it is well adopted for use with real time systems."[9]

Dynamic analysis is perhaps best identified with path testing or branch testing (much the same thing; branches determine paths), although, as we have already seen, this is but one of the capabilities that fall under this class of tools. In Chapter 7 we had referred to Carolyn Gannon's experiments with path testing and static analysis. The path testing that she reported on was actually conducted using a tool developed by General Research Corporation, providing both static and dynamic path analysis capabilities. Gannon did not report the percentage of branch coverage realized through use of the analyzer, but 90 percent is not unusual for those who have used path testing tools.

A good account of the way in which branch testing tools can be used is given by Holthouse and Hatch.[10] The test analyzer they used was typical in that it provided both a summary report showing the overall percentage of branch coverage of each module, in terms of the possible outcomes of each decision point, and a detailed report on the testing of the individual branch outcomes. The summary report was used to direct the testers' attention to those modules that, using branch testing as the criterion, were inadequately tested. Going to the detailed report, they determined the set of branch outcomes that would improve the coverage, and then fashioned test cases to force these results. The new tests were run, and the cycle repeated, until they had reached a level of coverage considered sufficient.

Using tools much more complex than the simple unary flags with which we started the discussion of dynamic analysis, one can provide branch testing statistics and other data, as well, at the source language level. A good example of this is General Electric's TPL/F system, developed for FORTRAN source programs.[11] Since the structure of the program is much more evident in source language than in object code, interpretation of the results of the test is much easier. It is also simpler to design test cases that directly address the branching decisions of the program.

TPL/F is but one of several tool systems based on FORTRAN. Although FORTRAN seems to be a favorite target for the instrumentation of source code dynamic analyzers, the commercial computing world is not ignored. Reifer and Trattner[12] refer to an analyzer developed by the Capex Corporation to monitor the execution of COBOL source programs. The analyzer generates a histogram of source statement utilization and an estimate of the execution times of source statements.

The power of dynamic analysis tools will take a quantum jump upwards when the tool systems routinely include the capability of automatically instrumenting the target program with probes. Developed by Richard Fairley under sponsorship of the National Science Foundation, an experimental system for ALGOL 60 programs has two major components: one to build a data base containing a syntactic model of the structure of the source target program and some history of its prior execution; and a second, operating interactively, to interrogate the data base and display various reports of the program's behavior. A preprocessor performs a static analysis of the target source code and automatically inserts procedure calls in the program to collect execution data.[13]

Semiautomatic insertion of assertion testing probes, including global assertions, is a feature of McDonnell Douglas's PET system for FORTRAN programs. The assertions are initially established as comments in the source program, later to be instrumented as assertion probes by a preprocessor. PET, described by Stucki and Foshee,[14] is not so much a tool as an evaluation system. In addition to assertion testing, it provides statistics on statement execution counts and control transfers, minimum-maximum range information for each assignment* and DO-loop control parameter, and the first and last values applying to each assignment statement. The monitoring of variable ranges is broad enough to include data arrays and the indexes that locate elements of those arrays.

The value to quality of dynamic analysis tools is evident. It is worth noting, however, that the use of these in helping to optimize programs for execution time, determining a minimum but sufficient set of test cases, providing test documentation, reducing test preparation time, and determining the faults that underlie failures, make their use cost-effective as well.

---

*Assignment is the operation implied by an " = " sign.

Emulator and Simulator

Both of these names mean much the same thing: the use of one system to behave like another. Consider a program developed for a microprocessor devoid of the usual peripheral devices (printer, disk drive, etc.) and powerful operating system of a complete computing system. The lack of these data processing amenities greatly reduces the effectiveness of testing and debugging operations and eliminates the possibility of using most of the software tools for testing described in this chapter.

The problem is solved if one can make a conventionally endowed (host) computer system behave like the naked (target) microprocessor; that is, execute the instructions written for it. Thus, emulation or simulation.

Although, as used in the sense of one computer mimicking a second, the two words describe the same function, many prefer to reserve the term "emulation" for techniques incorporating hardware or microcode in addition to software. For brevity, we shall use the term "simulator" to mean imitators of any construction.

While simulators are used for any type of program where the target processor is ill-suited for development processes, the use of a simulator for embedded applications is especially productive. For one thing, it is possible to start testing and debugging the software while awaiting completion of the prototype hardware. (Yes, it has happened that coding was completed prior to the availability of hardware.) To be sure, the thoroughness with which this can be carried out is a function of the ability of the simulator to accommodate virtual outside world drivers and stubs. However, even at the module level, critical algorithms can be evaluated well in advance of hardware availability.

The other major benefit of the use of simulation for the test of embedded software lies in its capability of avoiding the marriage of totally untried software and new hardware. This was discussed at some length in Chapter 7.

For a simulator to provide useful tests of embedded software, it must be able to provide a measure of simulated execution time, either pseudo-elapsed time or a running count of instruction cycles executed. This immediately raises the question of how much slower simulation is than execution on the target machine. The answer is that it is much slower, especially if the simulator is pure software, requiring dissection of each target instruction and substitution of instructions in the host machine's own language. Z. Jelinski[15] reports that the range of slow-down factors can reach 1000, although the ITT Avionics Division has achieved factors well under 100 with target instruction times as little as a microsecond.

Outside World Simulator   Thus far, we have discussed only the simulation of computers. For testing a program operating in its native (target) processor, simulation can be useful as a representation of the outside world. Here, the simulator can be located either in the same processor, in which case it is not unlike a test driver, or can operate in a second computer, connected to the target computer through the normal input-output mechanisms. The use of a simulator in this sense can, once again, permit software tests to proceed without the availability of new hardware; moreover, without availability of the information environment in which the hardware operates. Thus, one can fashion a laboratory test of software designed to operate in space orbit, or of one of a family of processors in a distributed system. Ultimately, of course, for programs such as those destined for space flight, more elaborate test beds are required to test the integrated system of hardware and software.

Modeling   There is yet one other sense to the use of the word simulation: the construction of programs used to model the effects of a postulated environment for investigating the dimensions of a problem, or the effects of algorithmic processes on responsive targets. An example is a program that can be configured (if not written for the express purpose of the study) to produce the inherent and interactive delays of an air traffic control system. With simulated random aircraft movements applied to the model, investigators can determine saturation modes. Two familiar modeling programs in wide use are GPSS for simulating discrete processes, such as our example, and CSMP for simulating continuous processes, as those defined by a system of differential equations. Programs as these are used during the analysis and design phases of software development to help determine the performance required of software and the effectiveness of the algorithms designed in response to the requirements.

Flowcharter

Although scarcely one of the more important tools, programs that can draw a flowchart from source code are one of the most widely used. The output of these programs will generally be found on line printers, with rows and columns of ordinary print characters forming the outline of the flowchart symbols.

When originally introduced around 1970, flowcharters were touted as a means of automatically providing program documentation. This is indicative of the spirit of the times, when design documentation was produced after the fact, and not as the basis for code writing. As a tool to be used at the current time, we see its use primarily as a means of providing flowchart documentation when contractually required, but not otherwise used for design representation. For example, if one uses PDL to express detailed design, but one's customer insists on deliverable flowcharts, a flowcharter is a cheap way of providing the deliverable data without compromising a superior internal standard. The one problem that may arise is that the customer will not only demand deliverable flowcharts, but will also specify graphic standards as well and will not be amenable to having them changed.

Reifer suggests another use of flowcharters, more attuned to the needs of software quality assurance. He notes that flowcharts generated from the "as-built" code can be compared to flowcharts provided at design time "to show discrepancies and illuminate differences."[1] Although we have no experience with this application, we expect that some problems would be presented in attempting to correlate two sets of flowcharts of differing graphic techniques and layouts.

Among the commercially available, language-dependent flowcharters are Autoflow and Flowgen.

Global Cross-Reference Mapper

In a large program one often needs to know what data get used where, what programs are required for the execution of another, and so forth. Much of this is given by compilers. For example, a compiler will usually provide readable output of *externals*, the names of software elements referenced in a program but not defined within it. In many languages, if one writes

A = ARCTAN (Y,X)

and ARCTAN has not been declared within the body of the procedure, the compiler assumes it is a function that will exist somewhere in the system at link time. At compile time, it is regarded as an external to be resolved at link time, and is listed as such.

The compiler output, however, is generally restricted to a single module, and, moreover, does not provide all of the information that might help expose an inconsistency or help diagnose a fault. One would really like to have the line number, by module, of each operand in a system, the name of the modules using each macro- and subprogram, the names of the data that are transformed within each module, the places where data are originated, and the identification of data that are never used. A mapping program giving all or part of this information is a relatively inexpensive, but well-used tool. It can also serve as the stepping-stone to a more ambitious static analysis system.

Host Systems

Host systems support the development of software for other (target) processors. At the simplest level, they provide the capabilities of data entry, editing, cross-assembly, and cross-compilation of target source code; link editing to produce target program loads; and, perhaps, the capability of some of the other tools described herein — most notably, simulation. The use of the host system provides developers with the peripheral devices and support software that their target processors may lack. The principal application is the development of software for microprocessors.

Going one giant step further, a host system may also provide test control of the target processor itself, and, if the target processor is embedded in a larger system, the signal or information environment for the exercise of the integrated system. Figure 8-1 schematically depicts such a system.

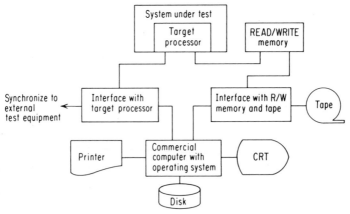

FIGURE 8-1 Host Systems with Online Target Processor Control.

The host computer is at the bottom of the diagram, surrounded by several typical peripheral devices useful for software development: a disk drive, a line printer, and an interactive CRT terminal. This minimum capability is sufficient for the program preparation functions described at the beginning of this section.

At the top of Figure 8-1, we see the system under test, including its embedded processor (or set of processors). For the control of the system and the outside world test environment, an interface is provided (at left of the figure). Let us assume that in the operational state, the system under test will have its program(s) stored in ROM or PROM. Since we expect many changes to be made to the software during test, it is patently uneconomical, and time-consuming as well, to actually execute out of ROM. Consequently, after link editing, the program load is down-loaded to a conventional read-write (R/W) memory, through an appropriate interface device.

The moment finally comes when all testing is completed, save for the last stages of acceptance testing, which will be conducted with the program stored in its operational medium (ROM), and it is time to firm up the program. The program is now down-loaded, not to the R/W memory, but to a tape unit in which the binary patterns will be stored for the manufacture of ROM masks or for the burn-in of PROMs.

Thus, we have a complete development station, one that may be expanded in its software complement to include other of the tools of this chapter: breakpoint-dump-snapshot-trace, simulation, dynamic and static analysis, and library control tools.

Variations of this scheme can take many forms. An interesting one is IBM's hierarchical system for microprocessor support. The system incorporating APLGOL (see Kemerer[7]) uses an IBM System/1 minicomputer to communicate directly with the target processor and a mainframe System/370 computer for assembly and link-editing. The interactive terminals are connected to the S/1 machine. Thus, it becomes the central interface for all activities. The S/1 computer is operated under an event driven executive system, enabling it to operate in an interrupt mode with the target processor, while the S/370 operates under virtual machine software for the hosting of major support software packages.

A very different type of development station is the well-known Programmer's Workbench (PWB). As originally conceived by Bell Telephone Laboratories, PWB was to provide tool support, not for microprocessors, but for IBM S/370 and Univac 1110 mainframe computers. PWB, operating on less powerful DEC PDP-11 machines, provided the development environment for production systems destined to operate on the mainframes. As described by Evan Ivie,[16] apart from convenience and operational efficiency, it was also recognized that a development station independent of the target processors would allow the provision of a single set of tools for less money. Other advantages that were considered included the use of PWB as a solution to the problem of unavailability of the production processor; freedom to choose, as target systems, computers poorly equipped for the purposes of development; and the suitability of an independent system for the testing of applications for the servicing of communications terminals. At this writing, PWB has been used in many installations outside the AT&T system.

The PWB tool kit includes a number of those discussed elsewhere in this section.

To many, host systems have become the sine qua non of microprocessor software development. This has been recognized by the manufacturers of microprocessors, many of whom now produce hardware-software development systems that their customers may purchase.

Librarian

In Chapter 6 we introduced the librarian as a person; a keeper of the records and an intermediary between programmers and programs. The librarian on which we now focus is a software tool. Although neither librarian has much to do with paste and overdue fines, the function of the software version has the greater commonality with the librarian normally found between ceiling-high bookcases. In particular, it is a finder of materials or a source for reference.

Less anthropomorphically, as a finder, a librarian tool is a data retrieval system. Consider the flood of documentation and program files that constitute the baseline of a program. Given the unique identifier of a program unit — computer program configuration item or module — the librarian will retrieve the status of every associated document and program file. The more prim librarian will also report on any inconsistencies among these of versions or revisions or whatever update notation scheme is in use. The information that can be retrieved is limited only to what the human librarian puts in. Unfortunately, so is the accuracy; the need for auditing does not go away.

The opportunity for error is somewhat diminished when the concatenation of individual files into program libraries, as performed under protocols required by compilers and link editors, is vested in the librarian. This ensures that the version and revision suffixes of the elements of libraries will be the same as those reported. These functions, of course, are normally handled by a file manager, as we noted in the discussion of change trackers. Thus, what is really suggested is a system merging the functions of file manager and librarian, with either being the surviving entity in name and operating protocol. Going this far, which really isn't very far at all, it is but a small step further to incorporate the change tracker in the same system.

Link Editor

Defined back in Chapter 2 as a tool designed to bind together the various parts of a program, the link editor can be endowed with additional capabilities to ensure unambiguous traceability of code files. This was noted briefly in Chapter 6. The enhancements that we shall discuss are simple enough to be within the reach of even the smallest programming shop, affording one of the highest returns on investment among tools.

Let us again define the problem. A program load comprises a set of relocatable modules. One needs to know if each of these is the module as currently defined, or an older variant that has, in any of a number of possible ways, been mixed in with an otherwise current set. Currency is denoted by the appropriate suffix or suffixes appended to the module name.

Solution: The compiler outputs the source identification, including suffix, in the header record of the relocatable object file it produces. The link editor is constrained to accept, as the definition of the program it is to output, a list of modules appearing in a *link file*. This list will, of course, include the current suffixes. The link editor then examines each relocatable object file or global data module named in the link file to see if its identification suffix agrees with that in the link file. If not, it outputs diagnostic messages rather than a program load.

This scheme, or a variant of it, is the basis for using a link editor as the final library control check, a check made at the moment of truth, as it were. A modest refinement would have the currency suffix of the program, itself, coded at the head of the link file and output at the top of the load map. This is useful in the maintenance of the test audit trail.

If the program is going to end up in multiple ROMs or PROMs, the link editor is the obvious tool in which to accomplish the mapping from a composite load to a load segmented into portions for each of the semiconductor memories. We say "obvious," because the mapping must be preserved as part of the traceability from ROM or PROM back to source code. If accomplished within the link editor, this information can be printed along with the load map, also required for traceability, thus providing—in a single document—traceability from ROM or PROM address to relocatable module address. Indeed, with one further refinement, the ROM or PROM address can even be output in direct terms of module addresses.

Figure 8-2 depicts such a load map. The starting address of each module in

LOAD MAP	PROGRAM AJAX AG DD		SEP 16 1980
			Page 2
MODULE	PROGRAM ADDRESS (HEX)	ROM	ROM ADDRESS (HEX)
AJAXA001B4	138A	X12	0014
AJAXA001B5	151C	X12	01A4
		X13	0000
AJAXA002A1	1774	X13	01FC
		X14	0000
AJAXA002B1	17EC	X14	0004
AJAXA002B2	19D4	X14	

FIGURE 8-2 Load Map with ROM Mapping.

the conventionally linked program load is printed in the second column. The identification of the ROM and the address within the ROM housing the module's first instruction are found in the last two columns. In Figure 8-2, we see that module AJAX A001B5 starts in ROM X12, uses the balance of the remaining locations of X12, and continues with ROM X13.

Postprocessors

In general, a postprocessor is any program that completes the job started by another. For example, in machine-tool processing, a program is provided to accept the machinist's description of a required milling process and output a sequence of general milling machine commands. A postprocessor now inputs that sequence and outputs a transformation of it specially tailored to the Mammoth Mill-Machine Mfg. Model M1000.

For the milling of computer software, we look to postprocessors to reduce data collected during tests, and perhaps also to analyze them in terms of the expectations of the test. In the simplest of cases, consider a 16-bit navigation computer programmed to accept sensor input and transform it into latitude and longitude. The program is tested with a number of random input data sets, and the computed positions are collected on disk along with the random input. A 32-bit computer now reads the disk; computes its own solutions, using slower, but more precise methods; compares them with the responses of the target processor; and computes the mean, worst case, and the variance of the differences between the two sets of solutions.

As just described, the postprocessor is the program that really completes the test of the target software. However, such a program is necessarily peculiar to specific projects and must be regarded not as a constituent of a general tool kit, but as we regard a custom tool for the production or testing of a single product. Usually, the postprocessors that sacrifice the productivity gained by specificity in favor of more versatile utility are the report generators found in dynamic analysis systems and the comparators used in regression testing systems for the comparison of current test results with those previously achieved.

Preprocessors

In the sense that postprocessors are sometimes required to complete a computational sequence, preprocessors are frequently employed to condition data in preparation for the main computational business. The most common of these are programs to translate one file format to another (as when customer data, received in the customer's format, is to be processed by a computational center's standard programs), programs used to format, for subsequent processing, digitalized data collected from a sensor system, programs used to validate input data, and the like.

The use of a static analyzer (yet to be discussed) to infer software structural characteristics in preparation for dynamic analysis is also an example of preprocessing.

The most common quality-oriented use of preprocessors in software development and maintenance is that related to language processing. For a variety of reasons, the availability of compilers (e.g., PASCAL) that support structured programming is denied to many programming groups. However, for the languages that can be locally compiled, it may be possible to define syntactical extensions containing the structured forms. It remains for programs written in these language supersets to be translated to the compilable forms. For example, neither COBOL nor FORTRAN (except as amended by MIL-STD-1753) can compile the set of Böhm-Jacopini constructs, treated so prominently in Chapter

5. A preprocessor such as RATFOR,[17] however, allows the programmer to couch his control flow in the form of IF-(implied THEN)-ELSE, WHILE, REPEAT-UNTIL, and sequence. The output of the preprocessor is the source program translated into a file of standard FORTRAN source statements.

To our knowledge, no structured preprocessor language handles the structuring of data. One must also expect that efficiency suffers to the extent of the time taken to preprocess before compiling. In brief, use of a structured language preprocessor is a compromise; a compiler for a structured language is always to be preferred.

Regression Test System

We have previously defined regression testing as the repetition of tests performed at an earlier time. Regression tests are performed after program changes are made during any formal test phase. Regression tests are also performed after changes are made during the period of operation and maintenance to minimize the risk that a modification has introduced a new bug into the system.

The time consumed in regression tests can be considerable. One must get the old procedures, and, if machine-readable, the old test input, run the tests, and compare the new results with the old. If, however, one has the input test data available on disk or tape, the further ability to capture the output on disk or tape, and a comparator to compare the new results with the old, then one also has the principal ingredients of a totally automated regression system. All that remains is the connective tissue to set up each test by naming the appropriate files, initializing and invoking the target program, and, at the conclusion of the test, calling up the comparator to evaluate the results with respect to the archival norm.

"All that remains" may be quite a bit. What has just been described is an operating system with run-time supervisors, a versatile data base structure, and an efficient human-machine communications system. Moreover, as described, the system works only when all machine input and output is machine readable. Still, one can accept less than the whole loaf, in any variety of compromises, while realizing considerable profit. Also, the machine readability of input may be achievable, in the sense of assured repeatability, by programmable stimuli driven by saved data files, as described in Chapter 7. We note that saved data files are not the only way of controlling programmable input devices. One can also energize them by programs producing drive input on the fly.

If one cares to add further automation to the system, one can also generate test input in a repeatable fashion by using a *test case generator*, yet to be discussed. As will be seen in a few pages, there can be considerable overlap between the more elaborate test case generators and regression systems.

Thus, whatever the obstacles, there are any number of measures that can be taken toward attaining the goal of automated regression testing. The value to the validation process, especially that applying to large software systems, is obvious.

Software Development Workbooks

Thus far, we have focused our attention on tools in the form of software or — to a much lesser extent — hardware. It is time to introduce a paper tool, one requiring no capital investment, yet serving the interests of both productivity and quality.

Software development workbooks are collections of all of the documentation attending the design and test of individual modules. At the lower hierarchical levels, it is probably inefficient to maintain a workbook for each module. For relatively small programs, a workbook would apply to each module at the division level, as we defined it in Chapter 3. For larger programs, a workbook is appropriate for each module appearing on the hierarchical chart developed in the top-level design activity. In the organization that assigns one person to perform module design, code, and unit test, the workbook is the reference for the requirements laid upon that person, and the record of work to date in meeting those requirements. In short, regardless of program size, workbooks generally apply to programmers on a one-to-one basis, but uniquely related to specific parts of the complete computer program.

Exactly what it is that goes into a workbook will depend upon the specifics of the development methodology. Generally, however, one would expect to find the specified requirements for the module as the first entry, perhaps accompanied by the computer program configuration item data base design and any other global information required to design the module. Later, the workbook will contain the module design documentation, followed by a record of deficiencies — with room to fill in corrective actions — resulting from the module design review. Next comes the latest compilation listing of the code. This, in turn, may be followed by the results of static analysis (to be discussed shortly), a code inspection report, or any other defect-finding procedure that took place between the completion of code and the start of testing.

The workbook should also include the unit test procedure, as well as any interim test results the programmer feels will be useful. Eventually, of course, the last set of results conforming to the procedure will be inserted. The information thereafter relates to changes: changes in the design made during module development, changes to any of the material as a result of integration, qualification, or system level tests, and changes resulting from modified requirements. This is not intended to be the repository for the change audit trail. Rather, it is a road map to refresh the programmer's memory of which roads were traveled and why.

As a tool for improving productivity, the workbook acts as an instrument for promoting efficiency. As a quality tool, the workbook provides an auditable record that information for prompting changes and corrections has been disseminated to the person involved. Further, the workbook can be checked against the configuration control records to make certain that the latter include a record of all the changes made since the last baseline was established.

Workbooks of this kind exist under a variety of names. For example: Unit Development Folder (TRW), Software Engineering Notebook (CSC),[18] and Software Development Notebook (GE).[19]

Standards Analyzer

This is one of the less impressive tools in that it has little direct bearing on software quality. Nevertheless, it can reduce the cost of assuring quality standards. Software development departments generally establish code standards to improve the readability of code. These standards are usually applied to such items as indentation schemes, the naming of operands, the placement and format of comments and banners, placement of nonexecutable statements (e.g., declarations), and the like.

Code standards are important; they will save effort again and again during operation and maintenance; even earlier if code inspection is practiced. However, if one establishes standards, then one has to enforce them. This can be done manually, at no small expense of time, or by a program designed to seek and list violations of the standards.

Static Analysis

Tools that perform static analyses of computer programs are programs that probe the structure and syntactical characteristics of previously untested software. The target programs do not, of course, have to be untested, but overall efficiency is gained by performing the static analysis first. The input data to the static analyzer is the source code of the target program. Thus, static analysis tools are language dependent.

Earlier, we had noted the use of static analyzers as preprocessors for certain dynamic analyzers, performing the role of automatically instrumenting the target code for dynamic testing. Generally, however, static analysis is an independent activity, justifying its cost by its exposure of structural and semantic defects.

In addition to finding outright faults, static analysis can also detect certain failure-prone constructions. The use of a variable for a data index without prior testing of its range is a potential for failure. Even if the decision is made not to incorporate a check in the program, a record of these suspicious findings may be of help in locating faults responsible for failures found in stress tests.

Ramamoorthy and Ho[2] classify static analysis tools into the separate categories of code analysis, program structure checks, module interface checks, and event sequence checks. Viewed this way, it can be seen that some of these analyses can be performed by compilers, link editors, global cross-reference mappers, and even standards analyzers. However, most of the desired information yields only to tools specifically designed for the purpose.

In particular, it is in the exposure of clearcut defects that static analysis most pays off. Among the defects that may slip past a compiler but get caught by a static analyzer are the following:

- Unused variables (indicative of a fault likely elsewhere in the code)

- Module interfaces mismatched in terms of the number and type of arguments

- Inconsistent use of global data (one module uses a datum as a file index; a second module uses it as an exponent)

- Uninitialized variables

- Infinite loops

- Code that cannot be executed

- Mismatched parameter lists (e.g., an output data list inconsistent with an output format statement)

- Improperly nested loops

Beyond suspicious practices and defect finding, static analysis can produce other output of value:

- Use, by count, of specific types of source statements and number of variables, as used, for example, in the prediction of error-prone modules

- Cross-reference of operands and module entry points

- Tabulated output of how data appear to be used, for confirming that these uses were the intended ones (e.g., that JSUB is, indeed, meant to be an index to a datum in an array)

- Graphic depiction of loop structures, including nesting of loops and lists of the operands within the range of each loop

In Chapter 7 we noted that defects found by static analysis can generally be removed more rapidly than those found by actual test. The reason for this is that testing, unless conducted with the probes of dynamic analysis, reveals failures, not faults. We speak of testing, especially toward the knowledge-of-the-code end of the strategic test space, as a series of exercises in exposing defects. It does so, but not directly. What is observed is a failure; the cause is not immediately known but must be diagnosed. Static analysis, however, reveals not failures, but faults that have the potential for creating failures. Thus, static analysis not only offers the possibility of finding some defects that may elude a finite testing sequence, but by laundering the program of many of its defects, can significantly reduce the time expended during the test phase on fault diagnosis.

Static analysis is, of course, never used as a substitute for actual execution of target code. Static analysis cannot form numerical assignments to variable subscripts or indexes, hence cannot determine which of the elements of an array or list is the subject of an operation. Nor can static analysis predict the paths that will be taken as a consequence of any input data set. What these analysis tools do provide is the exposure of a significant number of defects, and a great deal of information about the hidden structure of a program in its as-built condition.

In addition to Reifer[1] and Ramamoorthy and Ho,[2] other material on static analysis — under which term we have included static interface checking and structure analysis — can be found in Gannon[20] and Fairley.[13]

System Performance Monitor

This is a catchall term for programs, integrated into the operating system of a computer, that provide various statistics regarding the performance of the computer system. To software quality, the usefulness of such monitors is realized if an objective of the target program is efficiency of utilization of system resources, a condition that arises whenever the target program is an element of the supervisory software of the system.

For example, in a virtual operating system, evaluation of the system should include knowledge of the performance of algorithms for resource allocation, identification of performance bottlenecks, measurements of profiles of the system loading and paging rates, and an understanding of the effect of the system software strategies on individual programs.

System performance monitors are tools developed to gather this information. Using run-time instrumentation similar to that used in dynamic testing, as well as access to system tables, software procedures collect statistics on percent CPU utilization, percent storage utilization, queue lengths, paging rates, snapshots of status, traces of user terminal transactions, and so forth. Data collection is generally instigated by timed interrupts, thus permitting specific data to be gathered at predetermined intervals. A description of the tools developed for the measurement of the performance of IBM's S/370 Virtual Machine Facility (VM/370) provides interesting reading.[21]

Test Case Generator

Under the subject of regression test systems, we alluded to tools designed to produce test input data. In one manner of implementation, data files are preloaded with sets of input data generated from machine readable, highly formalized test procedures. Test case generators capable of interpreting iterative procedures can produce large amounts of data from relatively short procedures. All test procedures are not inherently iterative, so this feature is not always of great use. Consider, however, an air traffic control system. For testing, one wants the flight paths of a number of aircraft to be generated. Each of these can be developed iteratively, given an initial position at a specific moment of relative time and stipulated orthogonal velocities.

Test case generators of this kind are much like simulator programs. The salient differences lie in their greater generality, the externally applied and inspectable procedure, and — if the output does go into a file and not directly into the target system — the accompanying program that will read the data file in a time-keyed manner.

If it is possible to develop test input on the basis of test scenarios, it should also be possible, except for certain stress and boundary tests, to determine the expected results at various points of observation. Implementation of the capability of handling expectations, input in a manner similar to that provided for test stimuli, is another feature of test case generators.

In knowledge-of-the-code tests, a more powerful test case generator can be implemented as part of an automatic test system, such as that described by Panzel,[11] and previously noted under the topic of dynamic analysis. Here, target source code and a formalized procedure are both input to the TPL/F test procedure processor. Stimuli are generated, the test is run, and a report of the results is generated. This is also an example of a test case generator useful for diagnosing problems. Having access to the contents of the program, the system allows the procedure to directly reference any variable in the target program; moreover, to specify execution of specific program segments. These capabilities are not attained without giving up something; repeating an earlier comment, systems that operate at the source code level are necessarily language dependent, a limitation that may be significant in many programming shops.

TOOL KITS

As we had forewarned in the discussion of the taxonomy of tools, there is considerable overlap among the tool classes we selected as our classification scheme. Although our rationale was the desire to present the flavor of tooling at levels of interest appropriate to both the small programming shop and the large software factory, the classification serves yet another purpose. By segregating some of the tools that may be elements of one or more larger tool sets, we also mapped alternative routes to maximally tooled development environments. For example, the class of test case generators can grow into dynamic analysis systems or regression test systems or both.

The development of a system of tools, then, can be an evolutionary process, and one wants to take care that sufficient planning is performed to ensure that the interfaces between tools are defined early enough to avoid redundant tool acquisition. Tool planning should be a continuous process, marked by periodic meetings of representatives of software development, quality, configuration management, and maintenance to ensure that plans for further stocking of the tool kit are consonant with the specific needs of all the functions. If in a currently primitive tool environment, it is best to proceed somewhat slowly. Experience gained with newly introduced tools can be used to good advantage in refining the definition of the larger tool systems yet to be acquired. In any case, it is important that the tool interfaces be well defined with respect to the common data bases on which they will operate and the design and test environment in which they will be used. It is all too easy to progress in too many directions at once, resulting in redundancy and in tools difficult to use. The ultimate danger is in a software consummation of Thoreau's remark, "Men have become tools of their tools."

What is considered a full tool kit? In a report commenting on the Department of Defense's Pebbleman, a postulated development environment for the DOD's language ADA, Peter Elzer noted that a virtual storage area of some 200,000 to 300,000 words seems appropriate.[22] This is one measure of adequacy, but Elzer was writing within the context of a hypothetical ADA software world. What of the software factory supporting several languages? What of the programming shop developing and maintaining production systems of modest size or embedded software for consumer appliances? For these latter facilities, tools totaling 20,000 to 30,000 words may be the maximum the budget can bear. Software tooling should be approached as any other investment for manufacture: an economic analysis should be made of the benefits to be realized (including the cost of rework) versus the cost of acquisition.

We have used the term "software factory" several times without bothering with a definition; nor shall we define it now. Similarly, we shall use the phrase "software cottage industry" without definition, save to say that it typifies the milieu of software development up to the 1970s; indeed much of it today. In a large sense, the thrust of this book reflects a historical mission of quality assurance: the replacement of inefficient cottage methods with those appropriate to mechanized factories. If, as paleontologists would have us believe, the use of tools is one of the characteristics distinguishing early human beings from apes, we have a basis for grasping the difference between a software factory and a software cottage industry.

SUMMARY

1. As there are tools for the production of hardware, so are there tools for the production of software, and for the same reasons: productivity and quality.

2. Quality-oriented software tools also have a favorable effect on productivity. This fact should not be overlooked when considering a tool investment.

3. Table 8-1 summarizes the tool or tool categories applicable to software quality.

4. Few software development facilities are as tooled as they can be.

REFERENCES

1. Don Reifer, "Software Quality Assurance Tools and Techniques," *Proceedings NSIA Software Conference*, Buena Park, Calif., February 1979, pp. 47–90.

2. C. V. Ramamoorthy and Siu-Bun F. Ho, "Testing Large Software with Automated Software Evaluation Systems," *IEEE Transactions on Software Engineering*, Vol. SE-1, No. 1, March 1975, pp. 46–58.

3. D. Good, R. Cohen, L. Hunter, "A Report on the Development of Gypsy," *Proceedings 1978 Annual Conference*, Association for Computing Machinery, pp. 116–122.

4. C. Davis and C. Vick, "The Software Development System," *IEEE Transactions on Software Engineering*, Vol. SE-3, No. 1, January 1977, pp. 69–84.

5. D. Teichroew and E. A. Hershey III, *Computer Aided Structured Documentation and Analysis of Information Processing System Requirements*, ISDOS Project, Department of Industrial and Operations Engineering, University of Michigan, prepared for presentation at SHARE XLVII, 1976.

6. B. Boehm, R. McClean, and D. Urfig, "Some Experience with Automated Aids to the Design of Large-Scale Reliable Software," *IEEE Transactions on Software Engineering*, Vol. SE-1, March 1975, pp. 125–133.

7. N. J. Kemerer, *A Development Method for Microprocessor Systems/Software*, IBM No. 780TP0048, IBM Federal Systems Division, Oswego, New York, 1978.

8. Stephen Caine and E. Kent Gordon, "PDL — A Tool for Software Design," *Proceedings of the 1975 National Computer Conference*, AFIPS, Montvale, N.J., 1975, pp. 168–173.

9. J. Gary Nelson, *Testing Subcommittee Input Report to Study: Software Testing Policies and Procedures*, Technical Report SY-2-77, Headquarters, U.S. Army Test and Evaluation Command, February 1977.

10. Mark Holthouse and Mark Hatch, "Experience with Automated Testing Analysis," *Computer*, IEEE Computer Society magazine, Vol. 12, No. 8, August 1979, pp. 33–36.

11. David Panzel, "Automated Software Test Drivers," *Computer,* IEEE Computer Society magazine, Vol. 10, No. 4, April 1978, pp. 44–50.

12. D. J. Reifer and S. Trattner, "A Glossary for Software Tools and Techniques," *Computer,* IEEE Computer Society magazine, Vol. 9, No. 7, July 1977, pp. 52–60.

13. Richard E. Fairley, "Tutorial: Static Analysis and Dynamic Testing of Computer Software," *Computer,* IEEE Computer Society magazine, Vol. 10, No. 4, April 1978, pp. 14–23.

14. L. Stucki and G. Foshee, "New Assertion Concepts for Self-Metric Software Validation," *1975 International Conference on Reliable Software,* IEEE Cat. No. 75CHO940-7CSR, pp. 59–71.

15. Z. Jelinski, "Configuration Management and Software Development Techniques," *Defense Systems Management Review,* Vol. 2, No. 3, Summer 1979, Defense Systems Management College, Ft. Belvoir, Va., pp. 74–87.

16. Evan Ivie, "The Programmer's Workbench — A Machine for Software Development," *CACM,* Vol. 20, No. 10, October 1977, pp. 746–753.

17. B. Kernighan and P. Plauger, *Software Tools,* Addison-Wesley, Reading, Mass., Copyright 1976 by Bell Telephone Laboratories, Inc., and Yourdon Inc.

18. Kurt Fischer, "A Methodology for Developing Quality Software," *Thirty-Third Annual Technical Conference Transactions,* American Society for Quality Control, 1979, pp. 364–371.

19. John McKissick, Jr., and Robert Price, "The Software Development Notebook — A Proven Technique," *Proceedings 1979 Annual Reliability and Maintainability Symposium,* IEEE Cat. No. 79CH1429-OR, pp. 168–173.

20. Carolyn Gannon, "Error Detection Using Path Testing and Static Analysis," *Computer,* IEEE Computer Society magazine, Vol. 12, No. 8, August 1979, pp. 26–31.

21. P. H. Callaway, "Performance Measurement Tools for VM/370," *IBM Systems Journal,* Vol. 14, No. 2, 1975, pp. 134–160.

22. Peter Elzer, *Some Observations Concerning Existing Software Environments,* distributed by Defense Advanced Research Projects Agency, Arlington, Va., May 1979.

Chapter 9

The Quality
Program

In the mid-1970s, we ran into a longtime associate at a technical conference held in a distant city. After the usual amenities, which, in a desperate attempt at recalling names, included mutual and badly disguised glances at the other chap's conference badge, we were asked what we were doing so many miles from home. We explained that we were scheduled to present a tutorial on computer software quality control.

"What kind of quality?"

"Computer software," we answered.

"You mean programs and that kind of stuff?"

"Yes."

"How did you get into that?"

"Well," one of us pontificated, "More and more of our products are being built with computers in them, and the quality of the product is no better than the quality of the programs driving the computers."

"Maybe so," he countered, "But what in hell do you do, look at the holes in paper tapes to see if they are cut all the way through? From this you're going to make a living?"

After his last guffaw, we, of course, seized upon this as an opportunity to give the tutorial a dry run before a skeptical audience, but we didn't get very far. He really was not very interested.

The 1970s attitude of many quality managers, we suspect, had been that software quality assurance was something they would just as soon see go away. It involved new practices, dealing with new people, learning new forms of communication. But then, this was mirrored by the feeling prevalent among many software managers. Some went further: "I don't need quality in my hair all the time, and besides, they can't do anything for me."

If, indeed, the software quality assurance role were at the level of inspecting the quality of the holes punched in paper tape, their feelings would have been totally justified. But the scope of software quality assurance activities is painted on a far broader canvas, one that stretches from the conceptual stage of new software all the way to code death. The interests served by these activities include those of software users, upper management, and even the software community.

THE ROLE OF QUALITY

The key to the contributions of software quality assurance is found in the historical distance between quality and the production of goods or supply of services. Quality's role is that of monitoring adherance to standards, and any compromise of established performance, methods, or acceptance criteria is viewed by quality as just that. Quality is also a keeper of records and a user of these records in the search of ways to improve performance. In this vein, we note that rarely has the software community been able to record defect histories in a manner that would permit them to use past problems for the profit of the present. This, despite the fact that roughly half of all software activity is spent in the search for and correction of defects. The independent position of quality has also made it the traditional ombudsman of the user of goods and services, and the instrument of management for the unbiased validation of conformity to specified performance.

Since this chapter is devoted to how software quality assurance continues the quality role into the world of computer software, we should like first to provide a neat, pithy, definition of software quality assurance. We see, however, three facets so distinct that each bears its own definition.

A Management Tool for Control and Visibility

There are any number of ways in which the managers of software development and maintenance report the status of their work to management: periodic reports of progress, of expenditure of labor hours or dollars, and of problems; budget forecasts; reports of cost-to-complete; and the like. But what is management to make of a report that "The overall design of the program is now complete," if the overall design has not been verified to be consonant with the requirements laid upon the program, or if it reflects an internal complexity twice that envisioned at the time the project was planned? How much more useful a report from software quality assurance that "The overall design has been verified, with six deficiencies noted. Development estimates it will take two weeks to correct these. Also, the division between the accounting, optimizing, and archival sections appears needlessly muddled and a potential source of integration difficulty. Software has agreed to look at this again to see if a more straightforward approach can be worked out."

In the absence of objective evaluation, the first hint that a development project is in trouble usually occurs at some point after the start of testing; under the worst of practices, after the user gets the program. Reviews of the requirements definition and design material can provide this kind of information — may even permit correction at the source — long before testing has started.

Management has learned to be wary of software development projects. In some instances, management has sought reassurance by requiring the development people to report status in a tedious battery of reports, all at frequent intervals. This is not only time-consuming, it may also be counterproductive if it diverts software management from its job of managing software development or maintenance. Not infrequently, the reports are produced in a cursory manner, reflecting the software managers' own sets of priorities. If, in theory, the reports might have been useful, in practice they are unreliable. We can understand management's fear that its current projects might join the history of cost, schedule, or performance disasters, but a baffling set of overlapping reports is not a solution, but a reaction. This method of foreseeing the future course of the project is little more reliable than that of sacrificing a goat and calling in the neighborhood oracle to examine the smoldering entrails.

If software quality assurance did nothing more than provide a better window for management to gain early awareness of impending problems, it would justify its existence. As it turns out, software quality assurance does much more.

A Representative of the User Community

Those who develop and maintain computer programs are seldom the users of the programs. There are two kinds of users: those who are awaiting the completion of new software or software modifications and those who receive previously used software.* Each group has its own problems.

Potential users who have contracted for the development or modification of software for their unique application have much the same concerns as the management of the people executing the contract. Quite often, the buyers are heavily dependent on the readiness of the software at some stipulated date. If that date becomes doubtful, they need as much advance notice as possible. If there are performance versus schedule trade-offs that can be made, it is easier for such users to discuss these matters knowing that the traditional in-plant representative of the customer, quality, is party to the decision-making process. Such customers are also pleased to know that the performance of the software will have been independently validated.

Indeed, users of any new software are learning that independent validation is of inestimable value to them. No user, including employees of the same company as the software producers, enjoys being the first to find a software problem. The honor of being the problem's first casualty carries with it hours

---

*Other than the antique and art markets, we know of no other business where the secondhand product is preferred to the new.

of trying to determine how the software was misused and, later, the indecision about whether the problem may possibly be in the software rather than its application. Beyond attempting to reduce the number of defects that delivered software will contain, one of the jobs of software quality assurance is to minimize the number of first encounters with new problems by getting the word out to all users once the matter has been reported and investigated.

Those who have just received their issue of existing programs are also supported by software quality assurance. The personnel of a computer facility about to convert to a new operating system will want to know that the operating system has been designed to be maintainable; that the investment the facility makes in programs that will run under the system will reap a return for many years. Software quality assurance's concern for maintainability profits no one so much as the users.

The usability of software, as experienced by those who are most affected, is also a concern of software quality assurance. Just as quality gathers feedback from the users of services (when was the last time you filled out one of those little cards found in every hotel room?), software quality assurance makes it its business to find out how the recipients of software judge the product. Is the documentation adequate? Does the software do what was expected? Have any installation difficulties been experienced? If support was requested was it prompt and helpful? Are there any modifications that would improve the program's utility?

The image of a software producer may be the image of software quality assurance.

An Approach to Improving Productivity, Reliability, Maintainability

The first definition of software quality assurance stressed management visibility. An effective quality program, paradoxically, reduces much of the need for visibility by preventing problems from occurring and by helping to solve many of those that do occur before it becomes necessary to bring them to the attention of management. This is the essence of software quality assurance: preventing problems from occurring, removing defects, contributing to the usability and maintainability of software, and, through analysis of defect histories, improving the production rate of *deliverable* code.

Chapters 5 through 8 explained the forces that shape the quality of software. The adoption of practices and techniques in the development of software is mostly the responsibility of the development community rather than quality. Quality may encourage structured programming (to use but one example), but it is development that has the responsibility for determining its own standards, and management that approves them. The more these standards reflect "the quality solution," the easier will be quality's task. Indeed, it is really incorrect to state, as we just did, that quality may encourage quality-oriented practices: it is quality's responsibility to do so. For example, if, in a review of the resources estimated for the testing of a program, it is seen that an untoward amount of computer time is required, quality should suggest consideration of the use of code inspection or analysis or test tools (assuming these had not been planned). This is an example of direct support by quality to improve productivity and reliability. Parenthetically, it is also an example of why a maximally effective software quality assurance function must maintain currency in relevant developments in the field of software engineering.

In any case, whatever the standards, it is quality's job to make certain they are adhered to. Standards are established in the interests of productivity, performance acceptability, predictability, and control. Standards are inherently confining, and from time to time there will arise pressure to compromise them, usually at the times they are most needed. Independent control abets software quality by acting to restrain such lapses.

The word "reliability," which we just used, is one that many people have found difficult to relate to computer software. Their problem has its origins in our first introduction to the word, when we heard it used in the context of the wearing out of material things. Yet, what is it that we mean when we say of our aging automobile that it is becoming unreliable? We mean simply that it can no longer be depended on to perform as we expect it should. Would it have been any more reliable had it failed frequently when new, as software is more apt to do?

Martin Shooman, one of the pioneers in the modeling of software reliability (see Part 5), has modified a definition of J. Hesse to provide this: "Software reliability is defined as the probability that a given software program operates for some time period, without an external software error, on the machine for which it was designed given that it is used within design limits."[1] This definition, a suitable basis for the quantification of reliability, expresses the nub of the matter. In a tutorial given at the 1979 Annual Reliability and Maintainability Symposium, Myron Lipow listed attributes of software that lead to reliability. These are accuracy, robustness, consistency, completeness, and self-containedness. Three of these bear some explanation. By "robustness," Lipow referred to the ability of the program to continue performing despite some violations of the assumptions in the specification; that is, not "bombing out" from invalid data or operating circumstances. "Self-containedness" was Lipow's word for software's performance of all of its implicit functions; for example, doing its own error checking. Lipow's definition of "consistency" emphasizes traceability of code to requirements.

A software quality assurance program must contribute to the building in of these attributes in the development of computer software, and to their retention during the years of software maintenance. Once again, the forms of software quality assurance's contributions are its encouragement of quality practices and its insistence that standards be respected. Beyond these, by independently validating software, software quality assurance provides an assessment of Lipow's attributes as realized in the operational software product.

BASICS OF THE SOFTWARE QUALITY ASSURANCE PROGRAM

In the tripartite definition of software quality assurance, we loosely alluded to its role in verification and validation, quality improvement, and education. These, in fact, form the basis of a software quality assurance program. Each will be discussed in detail in this chapter. As a group, they must address the specifics of each software effort to which they will be applied. Moreover, it will be to little purpose if software quality assurance is conducted in a casual manner, meshing intermittently and unpredictably with the development or maintenance effort.

No; software quality assurance must be planned, with each specified task related to a development or maintenance activity. In turn, this means that before there can be software quality assurance, there must be a computer program development plan, which applies to both initial development and major modifications, and in many cases a computer program operational support plan.* Indeed, insistence on these plans being drafted well before development or postdevelopment maintenance begins, is the first quality assurance activity applicable to any software project. Much of the verification and validation part of software quality assurance thereafter will be ensuring adherence to the plans. The computer program development plan had been briefly described in Chapter 6. It simply states the steps required to get from here to there and the methods that will be followed in each step. For the most part, an operational support plan is a configuration plan for operation and maintenance, emphasizing the initiation of change requests, but also identifying the functions responsible for performing each type of software maintenance. For any software organization, the substance of most of either plan should be a set of references to the organization's standards. The balance of the plans represent tailoring these standards to the specifics of the project.

Given a development plan or an operational support plan, a software quality assurance plan can describe how quality assurance will support the software effort: what reviews and audits will take place and when, what the disposition of reviews and audits will be, which tests will be conducted under the control of quality and how they will be conducted, how the correction of discrepancies will be assured, and what the criteria are for quality assurance's acceptance of the product. These few words are all that are required to define the scope of a software quality assurance plan. There are any number of ways in which the plan may be written, but we have included in Part 4 guidelines for the preparation of such plans. Format, however, is not our immediate concern. It is the

---

*Computer program development plan is military terminology. Computer program operational support plan nearly is.

set of activities defined in the plan that commands our interest. That is, a standard for a software quality assurance plan can only define the scope of software quality assurance; it cannot specify the the particulars of the plan itself.

> No one quality plan can suffice for all types of software, all software-producing types of business, all development and maintenance environments, or all management organizations.

The plan appropriate for the development of a 500-Kbyte operating system will be far different from that prepared for a program to operate an electronic scoreboard. The one will follow a development plan geared to a number of unique software components, a set of requirements that will be reviewed by a number of organizations that will want changes made while the software is still being designed, and a many-faceted testing program; the other will track a development plan based on a single program, a fairly stable requirements definition, and a test plan fashioned to accommodate the vagaries associated with hardware-software integration. Nevertheless, despite the impracticality of defining a common plan for both software examples, the fundamentals of software quality assurance that govern the one apply also to the other.

Quality Standards

Before dealing further with the basics of software quality assurance, we should pause to reflect on one of the many differences between hardware quality assurance and software quality assurance. Hardware quality assurance is mostly concerned with the capability of a design to meet performance and reliability standards and with the accuracy with which designs get copied (fabricated). It is the latter that is most often, if too narrowly, identified with the term "quality control." It is also that aspect of quality that most easily lends itself to quantifiable standards. If 0.3 percent of the ball bearings inspected are permitted to be out of round by one micron or less, then one has no question about what ought to be done with a batch of balls 2 percent of which have flat spots. Unfortunately, these standards do not apply to computer software. The capability of copying software designs is trivial. The quality of software is the quality of the design. If quality finds software to be ridden with defects, it means that quality did not perform its function of preventing defects. Finding defects after the fact is hardly worthless — at least it prevents a bad product from plaguing users — but it is not what software quality assurance is all about. We cannot overemphasize that quality assurance is the inspection of a process, not of the end product.

Although the removal and analysis of defects is an important function of quality assurance, it is the prevention of defects that demands most of its attention. Unfortunately, prevention does not easily accommodate numerical standards. In an attempt to emulate the statistical standards of traditional quality, spokespersons for the still new field of software quality assurance have fashioned complicated systems of measures based on the various attributes of software quality. These systems attach numerical weights to the number of GOTO statements, module sizes, thoroughness of documentation (subjective, at best), sophistication of tooling that was used (equally subjective), and the like.* The various weights are then to be algebraically combined, by one formula or another, into some sort of figure of merit. Precisely what one is to do with this number, once calculated, is no clearer than the rest. Certainly, one would never consider refusing to accept a software product on so artificial a basis.

There is no escaping the inevitable fact that numerology is not a substitute for the understanding and industry that are required to make software quality assurance work. Other than product acceptance based partly on the rate of defect discovery, as we discussed in Chapter 7, and defect measurements used as the foundation for quality improvement programs, quantifiable standards are of little help to the software quality assurance inspector. The inspector will simply have to do the job the hard way.

VERIFICATION AND VALIDATION

The gist of verification and validation was stated in the last pages of Chapter 5. Software quality assurance verifies that each new phase of development proceeds on the basis of the work performed in the preceding phase and in consonance with the requirements laid upon the software or, if applicable, the system of which it is a part. What this means is not so much that we are concerned with the new phase as we are with inspecting the output of the preceding phase to determine whether it can serve as the basis for the next stage. This requires, in the early stages, inspection of tangible products of work — specifications, design documentation, and code. Later in the development period, software quality assurance concentrates on the planning of tests and the evaluation of test results against requirements. At all times, software quality assurance is concerned with configuration control.

> If not quite synonymous with software quality assurance, the term verification and validation is the shibboleth that identifies its user's concern for the ultimate usefulness of the software product and the control of the process that produced it. Its place within the tradition of quality assurance is that of a system of progressive in-process inspections.

As an inevitable by-product of these inspections, reviews, and audits, software quality assurance satisfies its function of assuring an orderly sequence of development events. As we noted in Chapter 5, the tendency to telescope the

---

*These measures, for reasons unknown to the authors and not traceable by them, are universally called "metrics."

various steps required to produce a computer program is possibly the greatest single cause of software problems, including those of costs, schedule, reliability, maintainability, and usability. Thus, the fundamental software quality assurance doctrine: *A software quality assurance program must include the provision that work may proceed only with the concurrence of software quality assurance, as based on the review of previous work.*

As a practical matter, schedules being as tight as they nearly always are, one recognizes that some overlap of work phases should be permitted; indeed, can be harmlessly accommodated. Even before the requirements definition is passed on to them, the designers will have some feeling for the problem at hand and can begin to think about appropriate designs for program control. They may even want to look at the approaches to dealing with critical programming problems, if any. Similarly, to determine, say, the execution load of critical loops or the accuracy of certain numerical techniques, some detailed design may be appropriate before the top-level design is complete. In short, a software quality assurance program cannot be doctrinaire about the time separation of the stages of software development, must not become a bureaucratic impediment to the efficient development of software. However, as a way of effecting the principle stated above:

> Each stage of program development should be funded separately, with no more than 20 percent of the funds for each phase allocated without software quality assurance approval.

Defects and Their Prevention

There are any number of ways in which defects can creep into a program. We list a sampling:

Concept Errors

Selected computer(s) inadequate for the task

Inadequate number of or speed of peripherals

Use of computer too general — amount of set-up for each application inappropriate

Use of computer too specific — with small amount of additional effort, a better return on investment can be realized

Errors in Requirements Definition

Accuracies specified do not conform to need

Data environment inadequately described

Erroneous interface definitions

Training of users poorly considered

Initial system state not considered

Functions to be performed are vague

Errors in Top-Level Design

Requirements incorrectly understood

Data base not compatible with data environment

Modular decomposition reflects high intermodular dependency

Major algorithms not evaluated for accuracy or speed

Control structure inexpansible

Control structure ignores processing priorities

Incorrect interface protocols

No validity checks for input data

Errors in Detailed Design

Failure to convert data formats

Incorrect logic in implementing algorithms

No consideration given to effects of round-off or truncation

Indexes not checked for validity

Logic permits infinite loops

Incorrectly understood module specifications

Violations of data base rules

Errors in Code

Confusion of addressing schemes

Undefined loop terminations

Input-output arguments incorrectly defined

Improper use of registers

Undefined variables

Violation of language rules

Violation of programming standards

Errors in Data Entry

Wrong key struck

Character transpositions

Records repeated or omitted

Records not delimited

These are, of course, but a few of the errors possible in each phase. What we wish to illustrate is the variety of errors that can be caught at each step. Removing errors before they can be propagated to create problems in later stages is a major weapon of software quality assurance in its program of preventing errors. The cost of delaying detection until a later phase is no small matter. For example, the failure to use a computer adequate for the job at hand may not be detected until detailed design (perhaps not until qualification tests!) if not caught during the preliminary analysis and concept. If so, all the work subsequent to the preliminary effort may have to be partially scrapped. This may sound too dramatic to be real, but it has actually happened a number of times. Thus it goes: the longer an error remains undetected, the more mischief it creates.

In 1976 Boehm summarized experience at IBM, GTE, and TRW on the relative cost of correcting errors.[2] Normalizing the cost to correct to that of the coding phase, his graph showed the following relative factors:

Requirements phase	.1 to .3
Design	.3 to .6
Code	1
Development test	1.3 to 4
Acceptance test	4 to 6
Operation	4 to 100

Numbers such as these dictate the basis on which all reviews must be designed: they must be conducted with the primary purpose of exposing defects. Actual savings resulting from design inspections and code inspections were published by Fagan, also in 1976. His data, based on a control sample designed by four programmers and coded by seven, showed that the savings per 1000 source statements (excluding comment statements) were 94 programmer-hours for design inspections and 51 hours for code inspections.[3]

Thus, reviews not only assure orderly software development, but are instrumental in the timely removal of defects. One may regard the review process much as we did testing: although the outcome of a review is expected to be an increase in one's confidence that all is proceeding properly, the attitude of software quality assurance should be governed by the premise that the purpose of each review is the exposure of errors.

Reviews

As we have said, the review cycle that is implemented must follow the development plan. Using the phases of development that we have defined and continued to use for illustration, we can visualize the review process in the waterfall chart of Figure 9-1.

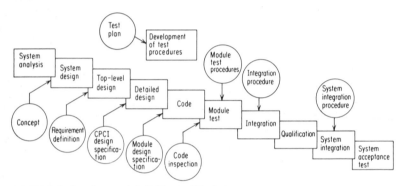

FIGURE 9-1 Development Activities and Reviews.

Each of the reviews is indicated by a circle. The material reviewed is named within each circle. The activity gated by the successful conclusion of each review is at the receiving end of the arrow extending from the review circle. Note that we do not show a review of the test procedures for qualification and systems acceptance. These procedures should be drafted with the participation of software quality assurance, rather than being reviewed after the fact. Also we do not name the material reviewed following the system analysis stage. The tangible output is too diverse to attempt to describe it before the fact. One expects, however, that there will be memorandums, listings produced by computer simulations, or other readable output from the analyses that can frame the form of the review.

A few other notes before we address the reviews of Figure 9-1: from Chapters 3 and 5, it should be clear that each of the lower set of reviews is of material generated in the phase directly above the review. Also, for independent programs, the phases of systems analysis, systems integration, and systems acceptance do not apply; moreover, systems design becomes no more than the preparation of the software requirements definition. We should also note that code inspections are not mandatory in the sense of the other reviews—although productive, they are not inextricably tied in with quality control, since errors produced in coding have no opportunity to be propagated as further sources of error, and since, unlike the material inspected at other reviews, code can be directly tested.

Since Figure 9-1 is intended to depict the relation of reviews to development and modification activities, it does not show software quality assurance's review of the configuration management plan or its configuration management audits throughout the period. We shall return to these later.

Review of System Concept   Although this review can seldom be structured on the basis of formal documents, software quality assurance should have questions similar to the following.

What was used as the basis for understanding user needs: specifications, reports, discussions, other?

On the choice of the computer system architecture (assuming it was made this early), have alternative configurations (federated, distributed, monolithic, array processors) been considered?

If a specific processor(s) has been selected, has consideration been given to both hardware and available support software? Will capital acquisitions of hardware and software be needed?

Has alarming for system failures been considered?

Have critical elements of the concept been identified? Has the handling of these been validated by simulation or analysis?

Does the concept embody software maintenance consistent with the capabilities of those who will perform the maintenance? For example, if parameters tailored to each installation are to be stored in a PROM, do the organizations that will do the tailoring have the training and equipment to prepare new PROMs?

Has someone started on the preparation of a computer program development plan? A configuration management plan?

Does it appear that the software effort can be undertaken by the present staff? If not, is the required rate of staff growth consistent with recruiting experience?

We do not expect that the above questions apply to all software, nor that they are complete in the sense of representing all projects. Even more than in the subsequent phases, attached to the preliminary system design there is a great diversity in the issues that are relevant to any given software application. The nub of the matter is simply this: the adequacy of the planning, the attention paid to the end use of the program, and the investigation of the feasibility of the approach.

Requirements Definition The review is based on the specification for the subject software. Software quality assurance should satisfy itself that the items below have been properly addressed.

Hardware resources (including available memory) have been defined.

Response time has been defined. Minimum reserves of memory, processor load, and I/O channels have been stipulated.

Interfaces to the software have been adequately defined. These include external hardware, other software, and operator interactions. Specifics of data (format, range, scale, source, sink) and software linkages should be documented. For real-time software, the rate at which data will arrive must be specified. (Quite often this can only be done in terms of statistical estimators.)

All functions required by the user and by the system design are accounted for. Key algorithms have been identified. Frequency of computations associated with each function have been stipulated if the program is to operate in real time.

External globals and constants* have been specified.

Required accuracy is documented.

The initial system state is provided, as well as any initialization operations required of the software to satisfy external requirements.

Self-test or diagnostics for external hardware have been specified.

Taken as a whole, these items frame the substance of a review that can answer the question, "Have the requirements for the software and the environment in which it will operate been specified in a manner consistent with the use to which the software will be employed?"

Top-Level Design Documentation In essence, this documentation should describe the "grand design" of the software. There are a number of ways the elements of the design may be apportioned among the various documents. They may even be bound as a single document. Whatever means are used, in the aggregate, the documentation should be reviewed with a number of questions in mind.

---

*The need for specifying external constants may not be obvious, but we can recall an early space tracking program in which five different constants for the radius of the Earth were used — all of them wrong.

If not stipulated earlier, has the programming language that will be used been identified?

Will global constants be expressed in terms of parameters? For example, will the design lead to code of the form AREA = 3.14159 *R** 2 or of the much preferred form AREA = PI* R** 2?

Does the data base specify the structure of tables, and to the extent possible at this time, the format, range, and scale of table entries?

Has the hierarchical structure been defined to the point where the scope of each identified module is narrowed to a set of specific operations? (Note that many of these will be further decomposed during detailed design.)

Does the modular decomposition reflect intermodular independence?

Have the requirements of each module been specified to a level of detail sufficient to permit detailed design to begin?

Have all of the requirements of the software specification been addressed? Are the specified data rates, accuracies, response times, and the like, reflected in the design?

Is the program control system clearly outlined? Does it, or a separate I/O scheme, avoid potential snags caused by defective external devices?* Does the control system trap infinite loops?* Is it expansible? If applicable, is the control system compatible with asynchronous input?

Is there a memory budget allocating estimated storage requirements for each module? Does it leave adequate reserve?

Is there an execution load budget by module or transmodule function? If the latter, is it fine-grained enough to be credible? Does it leave adequate reserve?

Are any unique programming conventions, tools, or techniques anticipated that are not covered by the computer program development plan?

Will it be necessary to acquire any additional software or hardware resources to carry out further development consistent with this design? If so, have they been specified in sufficient detail to permit their acquisition to proceed?

Does the design predicate any constraints or limitations beyond those found in the specification? Are they compatible with the end use and the systems specification?

*These are examples of questions reflecting an anticipation of failure mode effects.

Have validity checks been stipulated? Can corrective action be taken by the module that traps the error? (If not, modularity has been compromised.)

Summarizing, software quality assurance's concerns are to verify that the software specification will be met, the course of further development is well-charted, the software structure reflects an attack on complexity, and the design conforms to the intended application.

Detailed Design These are mostly reviews of module designs, but also include updates of the top-level design documentation. In the latter case, the updates will come to the attention of software quality assurance through its representative on the change control board. Such updates, other than outright changes in the design, are generally in the form of the addition of more detail to the global data base design. These may be reviewed informally in regard to their responsiveness to the software specification. The reviews of the design of those modules identified in the top-level design documentation form the bulk of the detailed design reviews, and in these software quality assurance will have to address several areas.

If applicable, is the hierarchy of submodules defined? Is the function and interface with other submodules of each of these specified? (Recursively, all other items of the module design review may apply to these submodules, except that we would expect no further detail if the design of the submodule is entirely predicated by its specification of performance, a not uncommon circumstance for modules of fewer than 20 or 40 statements.)

Assuming the programming standards call for structured programming, does the detailed design conform to the precepts of structure?

Is the design detailed to the point where each design quantum (flowchart symbol, PDL statement, or whatever) clearly indicates the scope of the code that will implement it?

Have any numerical techniques (e.g., polynomial approximations) been analyzed for accuracy and range? Are they consistent with module specification? With end purpose of software?

Has critical timing, if any, been analyzed? If a module execution load budget applies, are the timing estimates consistent with it?

Have the memory requirements been estimated? (This should be reflected as a change in the budget prepared in the top-level design effort.)

Has each of the functions that were defined in the module specification been addressed?

Does the module design imply previously unstipulated limitations or constraints? Are they acceptable in regard to the user's needs?

Are corrective actions for potentially invalid conditions (e.g., dividing by zero, or the "noise" remaining after the subtraction of two similar values) reasonable in regard to minimizing the effect of system or input failures?

By definition, a successful module design review provides confidence that the planned construction of the module will permit it to fulfill its assigned place in the overall design and that it is ready to be coded.

Code Inspection   In Chapter 7 we discussed code inspection not as a review, but as a supplement to the unit test. It is, in fact, a formally structured review, no less than the others, and software quality assurance should be prepared to look for specific potential modes of failure as well as loss of traceability.

Are there any violations of programming standards?

Are there any deviations from the detailed design documentation?

Are the entry and exit interfaces consistent with other modules and the overall design?

Is there any unreachable code?

Are there any undefined variables?

Are pointers and index variables checked for validity prior to use? If not, is the rationale for ignoring the test acceptable?

Do labels match those in the design documentation?

If the code is in assembly language, is the use of registers consistent with the overall design?

As we have indicated, one can conduct a software quality assurance program without code inspections. Nevertheless, for the reasons given in Chapter 7, the practice is well-regarded.

Test Plan   The computer program development plan should identify the scope of each test plan that will be prepared. One can include all the tests in a single plan, or one can have a separate plan for each type of test. However they are organized, test plans should be prepared early in the development phase and reviewed in time to permit procedures to be prepared and additional test resources procured or developed.

Regardless of the type of test being planned, certain aspects of the planning document should command software quality assurance's interest.

> Are all elements of hardware and support software that are implicit in the plan clearly identified? Are any yet to be acquired, and if so, are there suitable specifications for acquisition (including in-plant development)?

> Will simulation or emulation be used for any of the testing? In an embedded system, will end-product hardware be required prior to systems integration? If so, what is its scheduled availability?

> For software and systems integration, have the sequences of events (integration paths) been identified?

> Are the test procedures that will implement the plan outlined to the point where it is clear they will support demonstration of software adequacy and completeness?

> Have support personnel, other than those representing software and quality, been identified? How has their availability been established?

> Should the further use of tools be considered as an alternative cost-effective approach to defect removal?

These questions apply also to software quality assurance in its participation (ideally, leadership) in the planning for qualification and acceptance testing. The primary concerns are that each test be planned to make effective use of that portion of the strategic test space allocated to it and that all necessary software, hardware, and worker resources will be available when needed.

Test Procedures   The procedures, initially identified in the test plans, govern the conduct of the tests themselves. Procedures assume the availability of all resources and personnel identified in the plans, and stipulate the way they will be used. Reverting back to Figure 7-3, from the chapter on testing, we see a sequence of tests that represents a gradual progression from the knowledge-of-the-code end of the strategic test space to black-box testing. The extent to which procedures are formal should reflect this. Through software integration, the tests are conducted within the environment of development. Although it may be efficient to stipulate all test conditions,* it is mandatory to provide the

---

*These test procedures should, in any case, indicate the manner in which execution of interior control paths and correlation with code and design documentation will be verified. In the absence of tools that report the paths taken, the procedures may have to spell out the branches that will be exercised and the input for reaching them.

specifics for those that demonstrate compliance of module code with module specifications and integrated code with top-level design. In general, one looks for the following in the review of the procedures:

- Unit test will validate module design and code

- Integration will validate top-level design

- Qualification will validate the program relative to the software specification

- System integration will validate the system design

- System acceptance will validate the program relative to the system specification

Beyond these general guidelines, each validation test should be sufficiently explicit in the definition of input stimuli (where it comes from, what it is, where it is applied) to assure repeatability, and sufficiently explicit in the definition of expected results to permit auditing.

The procedure should also name any data reduction procedures that will be followed.

Since software quality assurance is party to the preparation of the procedures used for qualification and acceptance, it is not really correct to state that software qualify assurance reviews these procedures by the above guidelines. Rather, it uses them in drafting the procedures.

Configuration Management Reviews and Audits   If software quality assurance does not have the responsibility for configuration management, it must review the configuration management plan to make certain that there will be no ambiguity surrounding the code that actually is exercised or any question of the currency of the documentation that serves as the reference for validation. The basis for establishing certitude in these matters was discussed in Chapter 6 and will not be repeated here.

Beyond the establishment of a reasonable plan, software quality assurance needs to assure itself that the plan is being followed. This means that the configuration records must be audited at frequent intervals. The process of following a change order to the software requirements through to the last of the affected detailed documents yields quite simply to inspection. However, library control and the change route that initiates in testing and works backwards to design — and maybe even requirements — is another matter.

Library control can be spot-checked using the library control tools discussed in Chapter 8. During integration, such spot checks should be made at least weekly. Half that rate would seem adequate during the later tests.

To determine if test-derived code modifications that affect documentation are properly documented in the form of change requests, thus assuring that the documents will be changed, one must examine changes made to the source code files. This is impractical to do for all changes, so once again spot checks must be relied on.

Discrepancies in library control can create mischief very quickly. In short order the system can degenerate into utter chaos. If the motion picture industry ever runs out of natural phenomona for its disaster epics, it would do well to consider a script based on a large software project that has lost control of its library. Thus, although it may be practicable to permit substantial delays in taking corrective action for defects found in other reviews, problems exposed by configuration management audits must be rectified immediately.

> Software quality assurance must have the authority to freeze all code, even at the expense of halting test activity, if deemed necessary to get the libraries straightened out.

Parenthetically, we note that to take such draconian action also implies that either the frequency of the audits was inadequate, or that the personnel charged with taking corrective action performed irresponsibly.

Review Formats

Reviews may be conducted in a variety of ways. However, other than the review of the system concept, there is one common denominator: the basis of the review is the documentation of the work reviewed. If not documented, it cannot be of much worth to anyone.

Dramatis Personae   Besides quality, the principal persons involved at each review should include the originator(s) of the work reviewed, those whose earlier work provided the basis for the work now being reviewed, and those who will be responsible for the effort performed in response to the documentation under review. In addition, it may be advisable to include peripherally involved people, where applicable. It may even be efficient to include persons who will ultimately use the software.

All this sounds more complicated than it really is. We shall take an example based on the following premises:

1. The software will be embedded in an instrumentation system being developed under contract.

2. Sales engineering (SALES) is responsible for the preliminary analysis and concept.

3. Systems engineering (SYST) defines the software requirements.

4. Software designers (DSGN) perform the top-level design.

5. Programmers (PROG) perform the detailed design and code.

6. The test group (TEST) prepares the test plans and procedures, other than those prepared by quality.

7. The configuration manager (CM) prepares the configuration management plan.

8. Hardware designers (HDWR) design the equipment surrounding the processor.

9. Quality (QUAL) is responsible for conducting reviews and writing the minutes.

10. The customer (USER) hopes all these folks are talking to each other.

Given this cast, we can now move the players on and off the stage in accordance with Table 9-1.

TABLE 9-1. Functional Representation at Reviews

Review	Sales	Syst	Dsgn	Prog	Test	CM	Hdwr	Qual	User*
Concept	X	X						X	X
Requirements definition	X	X	X				X	X	
Top-level design		X	X	X†	X		X	X	
Detailed design			X	X				X	
Code			X	X	X			X	
Unit test plans			X	X	X			X	
Unit test procedures				X	X		X‡	X	
Integration test plans		X	X		X			X	
Integration test procedures			X		X		X‡	X	
Configuration management plan		X	X	X		X		X	

*Optional.

†Key programmers, only.

‡If end-product hardware is required.

Reviews are conducted to detect errors that have been committed: errors in design, errors in planning, and errors in control. Software quality assurance, standing farther from the project than the other members of the review team, will probably find fewer errors than will the others; in our experience, roughly a quarter. Software quality assurance's most important job, then, is to keep the review structured to provide the opportunity for errors to be detected. These meetings are not forums for the discussion of design approaches, but panels to answer questions of the kind previously listed.

The actual meeting of the reviewing team takes place after each reviewer has read through the subject material. In our experience few review meetings have exceeded two hours, and few have been concluded in as little as one hour. Preparation is another matter. One might require three days of study to prepare for a requirements definition review for a medium size program, but only two hours for a configuration management review if the plan is based on well-founded standards.

At no time should software quality assurance permit a review meeting to take on the coloring of an adversary proceeding. This is especially true of reviews of design work, regardless of level. Although it seems obvious that the interests of software quality assurance are no different from those of software development, that any defects found through software quality assurance–led reviews are problems that will, if found later, pose more severe consequences to the development people, it is all too easy for authors of work being reviewed to feel that they are the targets of gratuitous criticism. As we stressed in Part 2, computer programming is the mapping of one's cognitive processes into a working product. One can be unreasonably protective of one's style of solving problems. If the review degenerates into sniping at unimportant matters, the author of the work may come to regard the reviewers as belligerents.

Even the sensitive reviewer may encounter an attitude of hostility among development people. The value of objectivity that an independent auditor can bring to a review may escape the development team that recognizes that it may not be perfect but would just as soon hang the family laundry indoors. This is where enlightened development leadership can be very helpful, and, indeed, frequently is. Even a decade ago, the notion of functionally independent contributions to software quality was favorably received by some software managers. Although this is perhaps more applicable to defect collection and analysis, which we shall come to shortly, it is appropriate to note remarks published in 1973 by Harlan Mills, a highly regarded spokesman for creative software management: "A key step in development accounting is to provide independent accounting facilities and safeguards themselves. . . . Such personnel must be reliable agents of management, just as financial accountants, to ensure accurate and complete reporting of the development and inspection history."[4]

Structured Walk-Throughs   If development management is not supportive, or fails in conveying its feeling of cooperation to the analysts, designers, and coders, one possible solution applicable to design reviews is to hold them within the format of structured design walk-throughs. These are peer reviews, with no management attendance, in which the author of the design serves as the de facto chairman and delivers a step-by-step exposition of the design. This form of show and tell is not quite the same thing as directing a review to the determination of whether design objectives can be met and implemented, but if, within the context of a walk-through, software quality assurance can get the answers it needs to make these judgments, it is better than attempting to engage in the counterproductive arena of suspicion and hostility.

Workbook Inspections   Software development workbooks have been described in Chapter 8. The contents of these can form the basis of reviews even as can more formally defined documents. Although we have used the term "workbook inspections," reflecting the name frequently used, they cannot be inspections by software quality assurance alone if they are to also serve as the subject of milestone reviews. The other members of the review team are still required.

Top-Down Programming   In its purest sense, the top-down technique permits the design, code, unit test, and integration of portions of a program before the design of other modules has even been started. Moreover, the top-level design, as we have defined it, may identify but few of the modules that will finally appear in the upper hierarchical tiers. Top-down programming forgoes the benefits of the iteration inherent in the systematic development approach we have been using for illustration, but it does permit early evaluation of the solutions to critical problems — moreover, within the control structure that will govern the execution of the solutions. Thus, it has gained numerous adherents.

Where the top-down approach is employed, reviews as we have defined them can no longer conveniently serve as control points. That is, the overall design and test scheme evolves over the entire period of development and must be evaluated and reevaluated at each major increment to the system. Moreover, detailed design reviews may no longer encompass the full structure of their subjects, since modules that are destined to become parents of multitier submodule hierarchies may be coded prior to the design of their subordinates. There is nothing to do but to rely on more frequent reviews of lesser scope, scheduled on short notice.

Review Aftermath   In a format amenable to corrective action, software quality assurance's minutes of each review should highlight each deficiency that was found. The organizational function, or even better, person, responsible for each of these action items should also be identified. It may appear that the correction ball should always be in the court of the author of the work reviewed, but this is not quite true. For example, a discrepancy between detailed design and the requirements for the module reviewed may be more easily reconciled by modifying the top-level design. If such a judgment is made at the review meeting, it is the designers, not the programmer (using the function classifications of Table 9-1) who will be responsible for taking the corrective action.

In the aggregate, the list of deficiencies found in the minutes form the log of correction items that must be maintained by software quality assurance. The log will be a mixed bag of changes and requirements for further work. Some items need not be corrected in short order but can be deferred until more urgent matters are attended to. Other log entries will refer to documentation changes only, reflecting solutions arrived at during the review meeting. Reviews are for the purpose of finding defects, not solving them, but if the solution is obvious, there is no point in not recording it in the log. The log will also note deficiencies that should be cleaned up before further work can proceed. Most of the defects logged can be expected to occupy the middle ground of requiring correction before the next phase is completed, but not before it can be started. It is important that software quality assurance publish the updated log periodically to remind responsible persons of open items.

Occasionally, a review will raise doubts concerning schedule, staff, or resource planning. For example, a review of an integration test plan may expose the need for a driver program much more extensive than had been anticipated. If there is any doubt that the driver can be completed in time for the start of testing, the problem — though not a defect — should be prominently noted in the minutes, and appropriate management should be placed on the distribution list for the report. This serves the purposes of both the development personnel and management. If it is necessary for development to delay the start of test or to increase staff, management, while not pleased by this information, will at least know that the required action is unavoidable. The software quality assurance "inspectors" are given the task of preventing errors, or at least their further propagation; they are not corporate finks.

Along the same lines, one must not forget that new support software identified in the test plans will also have to be reviewed. Consider that a test plan identified, but did not further specify, the use of a scenario generator to provide test data. When available, the requirements definition and design of this program will be reviewed by software quality assurance. Further, software quality assurance should qualify the program on the basis of its own tests.

Auditing Tests

There are three missions that software quality assurance can fulfill during unit, integration, and — if applicable — system integration testing. Software quality assurance can verify that procedures are being followed, that the recorded output (where not machine generated) is accurately logged, and that, as previously discussed, library control procedures are properly observed. Verification of the execution of tests as planned, and authentication of the results apply only to those tests for which procedures actually exist; that is, validation tests and not the development tests that are executed prior to validation.

Do these responsibilities mean that software quality assurance must be present during all such tests? We think not. The issue is not the honesty of the development or test people, but the extent to which test discipline attends to meticulous adherence to procedures and data recording practices. It is all too easy to find shortcuts that appear harmless. "Why bother to run the test with both an odd number and an even number of records? If it works for one it will work for the other."

Or, "Did anyone note that failure in the defect log? No? Oh well, it's locked up for the night now. Someone remind me Monday morning."

Or, "Don't waste your time trying to measure the peak amplitude on the face of the 'scope. You can tell by the pattern it's okay. Just write down the expected value."

Someone has to be able to attest to the fact that test management is not permitting the gradual erosion of standards of precision, that a product was tested as management and maybe even the user expected it would be. Occasional visits by software quality assurance during these operations will help to provide this reassurance, even if software quality assurance does no more than to draw the testers' attention to the extent of their departure from standards. The frequency of these visits will, of course, depend upon the people involved, both managers and testers. One will learn the appropriate average interval only from experience.

Qualification and Acceptance

Software quality assurance's responsibility for these tests is quite unlike its role in other tests. Here, it acts as the receiver of goods, the judge of whether the product has been built in conformity to its specifications. Thus, to ensure that the software product can be demonstrated over the full operational range, software quality assurance must either prepare the test plans and procedures or work closely with those who do. Recalling Chapter 7, these tests will need not only to evaluate performance at each corner of the specification, but to make extensive use of random input in an attempt to gauge the extent to which faults lie dormant within the software.

Prior to each day of testing, or prior to each test run after a change has been made, software quality assurance should validate the program load to make certain it contains the correct code. In order words, during these formal tests, library control is not a matter of spot audits, but a process of nearly continuous monitoring. After each modification made to the program, software quality assurance must order regression tests. There may be some that can be waived, but these should be considered as exceptions. For example, a change made to the output format of a financial report should not require reevaluation, over the full range, of the accuracy of a root-solving algorithm used in computing true rate of return. Either the rate of return is computed accurately at one point — any point — or it has been clobbered.

Finally, we note that software quality assurance either logs the results or supervises all logging. In short, it runs the tests and, figuratively, buys the software.

Formal Changes

In its position on the change board, software quality assurance will review change requests based on new or revised requirements or on program trouble reports, one of the several popular names given to formal defect reports. (Software quality assurance should also be a direct recipient of these reports, since their content should be incorporated in software quality assurance's yet to be discussed defect collection system.) Change requests to correct faults that prevent completion of qualification or acceptance may be reviewed simply for feasibility, or, if reviewed after the fact (a reasonable expedient), to make certain that the change does not unwittingly compromise the program's responsiveness to its requirements specification. Change requests having to do with documentation, enhancements, the liberalization of limitations and constraints, minor defects in the code, and other improvements that may arise during operations and maintenance must be viewed with a further purpose. Before the change board can approve these, it must know the total cost of the change. We would not expect that a change board will be endowed with the authority to commit company funds, but it can make certain that management will be provided with an accurate cost estimate on which to base its decision. Too frequently, the cost of a simple change, as estimated by software, ignores the cost of revising documentation and of retesting.

Major modifications that have been approved will be handled much as are development projects. That is, the reviews of Figure 9-1 will still be relevant. On the other hand, minor modifications may require only qualification testing. Whatever the disposition of the change board, software quality assurance should make it its business to follow the matter through to its completion, applying the mechanisms of verification and validation and defect collection where they fit.

Vendor Surveillance

We have referred a number of times to the development of software under contract. What if one is not the contractor, the posture of the previous references, but the buyer? To make certain that the software contracted for is what is needed, the procurement specification should be reviewed in much the same fashion as the review of the requirements definition outlined a few pages ago; perhaps a bit more critically if one is to avoid haggling over the costs of later "changes of scope." In one sense, especially if performance in accordance with the specification is to be quoted by several potential contractors, this review will differ from those of requirements specifications that will be fulfilled by in-house development: the future designers of the software will not be present at the review. Software quality assurance will have the additional task of acting as their surrogate.

It is advisable for software quality assurance to provide, as an accompaniment to the performance specification, an acceptance test plan. Alternatively, the potential (or preselected) contractor can be requested to provide a plan shortly after award of contract. In either case, software quality assurance should make certain that the contract includes delivery of acceptance test procedures at the earliest possible time after award.

The contractor's own software quality assurance program obviously is of interest to software quality assurance, and the contract should include delivery of the software quality assurance plan shortly after award. If the contractor has yet to discover the merits of software quality assurance, then the contract should call for documentation of whatever control system is in effect. Of course, if the subject software represents a small development effort — one or two people over a short period of time — software quality assurance plans or other controls are of minimal interest.

The software quality assurance plan and the acceptance test procedures should be reviewed by software quality assurance. The plan, or other control technique, can best be examined in light of what it can actually do to minimize delivery and performance risk. The closer it adheres to the precepts of this chapter, the more acceptable it is. The acceptance test procedures are, of course, reviewed in terms of the demonstration of full conformance to the procurement specification. However, we might note that the test procedures are more than a definition of how well the software will be tested. They also demonstrate the contractor's understanding of the performance requirements. Thus, they should also be reviewed by those who wrote the performance contract.

During the course of development, software quality assurance should, in a noninterfering way, audit the contractor's prosecution of the documented control plan. We do not mean to suggest a doubling of the quality assurance effort; simply assurance that the documented procedures are being followed. There are two principal fears that the buyer must respond to: late delivery that can jeopardize the success of a project far more costly than the software being contracted for, and tests directed only at getting the software through acceptance, with little regard for the myriad of defects that might have been detected with adequate testing at the knowledge-of-the-code end of the strategic test space. A secondary concern is that the software will not be maintainable, even by the contractor. It is hard to conceive of software that will never be modified.

If a considerable amount of contracting is the practice, software quality assurance would do well to maintain a file of vendor performance history.

Off-the-Shelf Software

Purchases or leases of proprietary software should not be ignored. In addition to reading the sales literature describing the glories of what the software can do, software quality assurance should study the users' manual. Is it clear? Does it bear out the claims of the performance brochure? The purchase order should establish the acceptance criteria that will be employed prior to payment, and software quality assurance should perform or oversee the evaluation of compliance to those criteria. If installation services are required, software quality assurance will want to make certain these are specified in the purchase order, and that the software supplier provides either a fixed price to get the program operational on the intended computer system, or a rate for on-call services.

Independent Verification and Validation

The ultimate in achieving independence of software verification and validation is to hire an outside contractor to perform the review functions with minimum involvement of the development people. The process is costly, since the full burden of finding defects is assumed by the reviewers.

The contractual point of contact with the independent verification and validation contractor ought not be the development or maintenance organization. Program management (if a separate function) or product assurance are better choices. One wants to avoid a conflict of interest even where an independent contractor is used.

The interface between the independent verification and validation contractor and the office responsible for configuration management must be carefully drawn. One wants to reduce to a minimum the in-process proprietary documentation that will be under the control of outsiders. On the other hand, internal configuration management may not be qualified for software configuration control.

For the reasons that we have been developing since Chapter 5, independent verification and validation, no less than verification and validation performed by in-plant personnel, must mesh with development or maintenance. Only by coincidence can an effective verification and validation program be achieved with a "boiler-plate" software quality assurance program offered by an independent contractor. To avoid this, a software quality assurance plan can be prepared for quotation by prospective independent verification and validation contractors, or they can be asked to propose a software quality assurance plan designed to the software specifics and development and maintenance standards in use. Since the substance of these standards should also be a software quality assurance interest, we see that in neither case does independent verification and validation totally relieve the problem of competent internal control. Nevertheless, it can go a long way toward doing so.

In addition to maximum independence, independent verification and validation provides another benefit. With the seemingly endless shortage of capable software people, it can be most difficult to staff a qualified software quality assurance function. More of this in Part 4. Independent verification and validation is one approach to solving the immediate needs of control and product quality.

Tailoring

The verification and validation program we have outlined should be cost effective for medium to large programs (say, over 64,000 binary locations), or for programs whose performance may exert considerable risk beyond the scope of the software itself. As examples of the latter, we have almost any program to be frozen in ROM, or programs of any size that will be used in medical life support systems.

But what of smaller or less critical programs? Short cuts may indeed be appropriate for these. In a program of some 10,000 binary locations, it may be quite adequate for the detailed design reviews to be no more than audits to establish that modules have in fact been designed before being coded. It may often be reasonable as well as expedient for qualification to be the last steps of integration testing, with a single plan sufficing for both.

Discretion and previous software experience are required in the process of determining where to relax the standards of verification and validation. The dominant consideration must be one's problem history. For this, a defect data base is quite nearly imperative. But this fills a far greater niche in the software quality assurance program than simply as an aid to tailoring.

QUALITY IMPROVEMENT: DEFECT MEASUREMENT, ANALYSIS, AND FEEDBACK

Up to this point, each of the software quality assurance activities that has been discussed has addressed issues peculiar to individual projects. Except for the occasional references to standards, we could have been outlining a one-time software quality assurance program fashioned for a single software system. One must go beyond present projects to get to the real purpose of quality: helping to prevent future problems by building on the foundation of earlier work and measuring that work.

Software quality assurance must develop a history of defects based on all work done to a given set of standards, present that history in a manner that will allow identification of the effects of altering the standards, and continuously improve software quality and productivity by offering evidence for adjusting the standards. This, incidentally, is yet another reason for software quality assurance's interest in the establishment of standards.

There is a further reason why defect history is of paramount importance. If a company knows that the *recent* history of the development of software of a given type is characterized by n defects per 1000 lines of delivered code, then it can roughly assume the number of defects in a new program. This number can then be used as a guide to the cost of defect removal during operation and maintenance. For example, if history indicates 2 defects per 1000 lines of code, and a budget is being generated for what is estimated to be a 60,000-line program, then the budget for postdelivery support defect removal (whether in the interest of good will, satisfaction of internal users, or compliance with a warranty) should be on the order of that required to remove 120 defects.

Note the emphasis on *recent* history. We would like to assume that at one time the defect level had been measured at 5 defects per 1000 or higher — a time before software quality assurance began its quality improvement program.

Thus it is important to consider how defects may be logged to support quality improvement. For this it is time to sharpen the definition of words previously used in more casual ways. The IEEE software glossary defines the following words:

Error   A conceptual, syntactic, or clerical discrepancy which results in one or more faults in the software.

Fault   A specific manifestation of an error. A discrepancy in the software which can impair its ability to function as intended. An error may be the cause of several faults.

To these, Lloyd and Lipow add the following:

Failure   A software failure occurs when a fault in the computer program is evoked by some input data, resulting in the computer program not correctly computing the required function in an exact manner.[5]

In short, errors create faults that cause failures. Parenthetically, we note that testing is performed with the purpose of inducing failures at the earliest possible time in the life cycle of the software.

We define *defect* as either a fault or a discrepancy between code and documentation that creates mischief in the testing, installation, maintenance, or use of software.

Classifying Defects

One can simply tally all defects and use the trend of the project-by-project total to determine whether quality improvements are having the desired effect. This will provide some information, but a finer-grained defect data base is much more useful. Specifically, it is far better to be able to identify one's problem areas and to more accurately identify the results of implementing new tools and techniques. If two new approaches are introduced for the same project, more than a grand total defect tally is needed to differentiate between their efforts.

Classifying by Phase in Which Error Is Introduced   Simply knowing in which of the phases of development defects were caused is of inestimable value. This can immediately provide a clue to those aspects of development that are proving most troublesome. Consider that one has accumulated the following data:

TABLE 9-2   Defects Classified by Time of Introduction

Phase in which defect was introduced	Percent of all defects
Inadequate or incorrect requirements definition	45%
Inadequate or noncompliant top-level design	20%
Errors in detailed design	10%
Coding errors	20%
Other	5%

Without further elaboration, this says that while improvements may still be considered for the design and coding stages, one must concentrate on finding ways to improve the specifications that are used as the basis for design. Deeper investigation is, of course, required to specifically locate the area or areas of weakness. Has inadequate analysis resulted in code that is noncompliant with respect to the real need? Is the documentation of the requirements confusing, thin in detail, skimpy in the presentation of the total picture? Are the interfaces ill-defined? Whatever the problems, their source, at least, is better focused by the information of Table 9-2.

Let us assume that it was determined that the worst of the problems was that the requirements specifications were being written in such ponderous and interminable text that the members of the design staff were falling asleep halfway through the material. Improved techniques were introduced along the lines of those suggested in Chapter 5: structured requirements languages, data dictionaries, and the like. At its completion, the next project, undertaken with the new techniques, was found to have the following distribution of errors by source:

TABLE 9-3   Defects Classified by Time of Introduction

Phase in which defect was introduced	Percent of all defects
Inadequate or incorrect requirements definition	15%
Inadequate or noncompliant top-level design	30%
Errors in detailed design	15%
Coding errors	35%
Other	5%

With this data, one switches interest from the requirements definition to the top-level design and coding phases. Eventually, as improved practices reduce the significance of these two phases, the requirements definition may once again be a prominent focus of attention in the never-ending iterative cycle of quality improvement.

The sensitivity of the distribution of defects by phase to specific local practices can be seen in the next two tables. Both represent IBM experience, but a continent apart. The data on which Table 9-4 was based was normalized by its

TABLE 9-4   Defects Corrected per Thousand Lines of Code

Phase	8K Program	64K Program	512K Program
Functional spec	6	8	12
Logic spec	4	7	13
Code	5	6	10

author, Capers Jones, to three nominal sizes of programs. All three show a similar distribution.[6] Table 9-5, published by W. F. Baker, also of IBM, but of another division of that corporation, shows a very different distribution.[7] The reader will note that we have equated the terms "Functional Spec" and "Logic Spec" in the one set of data to "Requirements" and "Design," respectively, in the other.

Jones' west coast data show no statistically significant prominence by source phase. Baker's east coast numbers unmistakably illustrate each development phase as a greater source of defects than its predecessor.

Before leaving this type of classification scheme, we note that while Table 9-4 demonstrates that defect rates increase with program size, the distribution by source reflects the consistency one would expect from a common methodology. Moreover, it shows the leveling out of error sources that one might expect from a mature development system, given a sufficiently large data base.

TABLE 9-5   Defects Corrected in a "Large" Project

Phase	Defects
Requirements	663
Design	993
Code	2526

Classifying by Fault Type   Recall that we found from the initial collection of hypothetical data that our major problem was the requirements phase. We then had to find out what was going wrong in that phase. To assist in this, why not collect defect data descriptive of the fault that was found independently of when the error that caused it was made? Lest it be felt that distributions of generic faults do not reflect the standards in practice, Table 9-6 syn-

TABLE 9-6   Distributions of Defects by Generic Faults

Fault Type	Lipow	Mendis and Gollis	Craig et al.*
Computational	9%	24%	19%
Logic	26%	38%	16%
I/O	14%	4%	19%
Data handling	18%	10%	16%
Interface	16%	20%	16%
Data base and data definition	10%	0%	10%
Other	7%	4%	4%

*The Craig report included data from more than one project. The above data derive from their "Project 3," the one from which the greatest number was harvested.

opsizes three sets of previously published statistics. The sources are data presented by Lloyd and Lipow,[10] investigations by Ken Mendis and Martin Gollis,[8] and by G. R. Craig et al.[9] To fit all three sets of data in a common format, we reduced the finer-grained material of Mendis and Gollis and the finest-grained breakdown of Craig et al. to that of Lipow, ignoring certain ancillary categories (e.g., documentation), and combining others. Also, for commonality, all three sets of data are expressed in the form of percentages, rather than actual numbers.

All three sets of data were for real-time embedded software. The dissimilarity of the three is yet another indication of the effects produced by specific software development practices.

Defect Collection

As useful as defect data may be, one is unlikely to find it currently being collected by the development and maintenance teams. Software people, whatever their merits, have historically been unconcerned with this kind of bookkeeping. As we had stated early in this chapter, despite the large part of software activity concerned with exposing and correcting defects, few records have ever been kept. Thus, we look to software quality assurance to not only perform the analyses of these data, but to amass them as well.

This, not unlike the reviews held by software quality assurance, requires considerable sensitivity. It is difficult to envision professionals displaying enthusiasm for the efforts of outsiders in reporting defects in the fruit of their labor. Once the use of program trouble reports, or some other formal defect reporting method, is invoked, there is no problem in capturing data. But formal reports have no role in development, and most defects (we certainly hope) will be found prior to qualification, the earliest time for such accounting. Unless software quality assurance maintains a one-on-one staffing with software during development testing, a decidedly costly arrangement, the defects will actually have to be recorded at the site of their finding by the individuals who perform the development tests and find the faults underlying the observed failures. In the absence of an independent test team, this implies that the raw defect data will be recorded by the individual or individuals responsible for putting the defects in the program in the first place. In short, programmers will be given an opportunity to attest to the number of errors they make.

To many programmers, this is tantamount to asking them to forgo their annual merit increase. Here, we find further virtue in the concept of independent software quality assurance. If the recorded data is collected by software quality assurance, and only by them, and reported only when totaled with other data, the anonymity of the individual is ensured. Interestingly, no one benefits more from the analysis of defects than those who produce them. What we have is an example of software quality assurance's acting directly in support of the software community.

Figure 9-2 illustrates a form that testers can use to tally the number of defects they find each day. Each of the boxes in the main part of the form would be filled in with a numeric total, except for the columns marked "other." One always needs an "other" category, if only to acknowledge the limits of one's own imagination. However, such a category encourages the person filling out the form to be lazy about making a more difficult judgment. By asking for a description of "other," such a tendency can be countered.

Note also that this sample form includes only causes of faults and not the fault types. What is suggested is that one start with sources of error only, later

SOFTWARE DEBUG AND TEST LOG

CHECK TEST TYPE: □ UNIT ☒ SOFTWARE INTEGRATION □ SOFTWARE/HARDWARE INTEGRATION □ QUALIFICATION OR ACCEPTANCE   DATE 05 / 04 / 80

Units of CPU time used [3][2]

CAUSE OF PROBLEM

CASE NO   62/1261

MODULE NAME	INCORRECT OR INADEQUATELY DEFINED SOFTWARE REQUIREMENTS SPEC	INCORRECTLY OR INADEQUATELY DEFINED SOFTWARE SYSTEM DESIGN	INCORRECT MODULE DESIGN	CODING ERROR	SOURCE DATA ENTRY ERROR	BINARY (PATCH) DATA ENTRY ERROR	HARDWARE CAUSED ERROR	COCKPIT ERROR	SUPPORT TOOL ERROR	OTHER (Explain)
ALPHA				2						
BRAVO	1									
CHARLIE					1					
DELTA			1							
ECHO		2								LIBRARY CONTROL
KEYIN	1									DOCUMENTATION

FIGURE 9-2 A Defect Collection Form.

adding fault-type information. The former is the more significant for implementing quality improvement, and is also somewhat easier to classify. When the defect collection project is well established, cooperation in acquiring the additional information may be more readily achieved. Actually, a substantial amount of fault-type data can be gathered even with the form of Figure 9-2. If a module is an I/O module, by definition we can consider the defect to be an I/O fault. With a bit more interpretation, if the module is one heavy with logical operations, and if the defect is attributed to the detailed design, we will probably be correct in labeling the defect under the logic category.

The sample form also includes the identification of the type of test in which the defect was exposed. This data is used much as the statistics on when defects are created. If one finds few errors caught in unit testing relative to the number found in integration testing, it may mean that module-to-module interfaces were poorly defined, but it may also mean that the techniques or tools of unit testing will bear considerable improvement. As was treated at some length in Chapter 7, the measure of a good test is not so much the number of defects found, but the ratio of that number to the number found plus the number that remain hidden.

The column headings relate in part to the description of design phases as we have been defining them throughout this book, but also extend to other causes of real or apparent failures. Source data entry errors (typographical errors in entering source code into a data file) may seem trivial, but are among the more common causes of faults. Another trivial but prevalent opportunity for error arises in the entry of binary patches. The actual errors in both of these cases may be far removed from the nuances of software engineering, but the loss of productivity that they can create is as significant as the weightier matters. Moreover, the encoding of both source code and patches can be accomplished in a variety of ways and with a diverse assortment of tools; thus it is a proper subject for quality improvement. Of course, should the number of defects attributable to these causes become insignificant, the column headings can be changed to error sources suspected of being more troublesome; say, library control or specific software support packages.

Continuing, we see three columns associated with problems external to the program being tested that can cause tests to fail. These are "Hardware caused error," "Cockpit error," and "Support tool error." These, too, have an adverse effect on productivity, even on defect exposure, and can profitably be the focus of quality improvement.

We have already dealt with the ubiquitous evasion, "Other."

Summarizing, while we can not presume a set of categories appropriate to all development environments, the ones of Figure 9-2 do illustrate the two basic causes of failures:

- Built-in defects

- Defects in the test environment

The Start of Defect Collection   Precisely when it is that one should begin to collect defect statistics is somewhat open to question. Surely, one does not want to include defects found by the compiler, but how about those uncovered in code inspection, static analysis, or exercises in formal correctness proofs? How about the defects found in the first few hours of testing? The question can be resolved in terms of the statistical significance of these defects. To evaluate the efficacy of unit testing, one looks at two sets of numbers: the defects found in unit testing and all those found afterward that apply to the design, code, or source entry of the subject module. Thus, one would want to start collection as soon as the program is compiled.

On the other hand, the attitude of the programming staff may be that of private ownership of code until it is handed over for integration. These entrepreneurs, of course, are not likely to take kindly to code inspection, either. We see a clear call for software quality assurance's entering into some missionary work with the help of software management. Nevertheless, in the face of resistance, there is nothing to do but choose some arbitrary time — say, four hours — after the start of unit test to begin data recording. The first few hours of unit testing generally reap a bountiful harvest of bugs. The cost of removing them is so slight that little is lost if they are not accounted for.

Error-Prone Modules

In addition to the uses previously implied for tabulating errors by individual module, there is another, gloomier, purpose. It seems that some modules start out in misery and never get much better. Whether caused by poor internal structure, or the distraction of the programmer while writing code, or whatever, these modules are so ridden with defects at birth that each remedial action seems only to create as many new defects as it cures. As soon as one tabulates defects per module, the extent to which some are more error-prone than others becomes obvious. In 1975 Albert Endres published, among other defect analysis data, a distribution of the number of errors per module in a single large system.[11] Figure 9-3, a logarithmic graph of his tabulated data, illustrates the skewed distribution of errors among individual modules.

Of a total of 422 modules, 220 had no errors at all. The three modules with the greatest numbers of errors (28, 19, and 15) were three of the largest modules in the system. However, the fourth place "winner," with 14 defects, was one of the smaller modules. This is a module that should be identified as error-prone.

Our own experience has repeatedly demonstrated statistics much like Endres'. A small number of modules, readily identified by tabulating defect totals, contributes to the number of observed failures far out of proportion to their size. These modules are candidates for further analysis to determine if the most appropriate action would be to redesign and code them from scratch. If a module can be redesigned, coded, and unit tested within two weeks, the overall productivity of testing may be improved over the passive alternative of leaving the module in the system, where it might prolong testing by two months. Of even greater importance, the likelihood is eliminated of the error-prone module's continuing to create failures during operation and maintenance.

One may wonder if software quality assurance's identification of error-prone module, subsequently followed by a recommendation to return it to the drawing boards, does not violate the shield of anonymity software quality assurance places between the recorders of defects — assuming a separate test team is not used — and their supervisors. In a statistical sense, this dichotomy will infrequently arise, since most of the time an error-prone module will not be identified as such until integration testing, when persons other than or in addition to the module's author will be engaged in the testing and defect recording activity. Moreover, the basic cause for an error-prone module may be traceable to reasons beyond the programmer's domain, for example, an unstable requirements specification. Still, these are technicalities. The use of defect collection will from time to time be responsible for indirectly identifying the producer

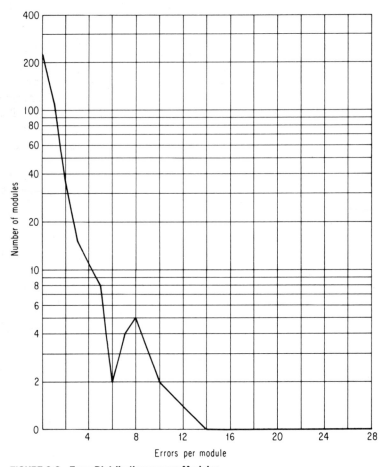

FIGURE 9-3   Error Distribution among Modules.

of a bad job. Software quality assurance may occasionally have to compromise the precept of anonymity in the interests of quality, and no amount of tact can disguise this fact.

Defects Versus Time

There is a further application for defect recording, one similar to the identification of error-prone modules, that relates not to quality improvement, but to the quality of the program for which data has been gathered. Much can be learned from the plot of defect exposure versus time. Analysis of the rate at which defects are found is the substance of time domain reliability modeling, treated more fully in Part 5. However, we have previously touched upon this in Chapter 7 in regard to using, as a criterion for acceptance, the time between failures induced by random stimuli.

For certain reliability models, calendar time may be used as the rate reference. Other models require actual computer, or test, time. For acceptance using the simple time between failures of Chapter 7, only actual computation time makes sense. This is the reason Figure 9-2 includes the block labeled "units of CPU time."

Let's Hear It for the Users

Consider that you, a designer of hydroelectric power plants, have just purchased a software package for analyzing stream flow problems. You take the magnetic tape you received in the mail to the computer room and ask the shift supervisor to install it. The shift supervisor loads it on disk and tries to run the sample problem. It doesn't. The two of you spend the better part of a day trying to figure out why, and finally call for help. One week later a systems engineer shows up, and after two fruitless hours (read $90) admits to never having seen the package before. ("Yeah . . . well, I was scheduled to be in the area, so they thought maybe I could help you.") Eventually, with more $45 per hour assistance, you discover that the software had never been run under the ACME COMPUTER COMPANY FOS/1 software system (yours, of course), although the salesperson had assured you over the telephone that it had been qualified under FOS/1.

Another round of telephone calls, two weeks further delay, and then a patch arrives in the mail. *Mirabile dictu*, it runs! Now you try your first application, the determination of the effect of various underwater temperature layers on surface flow, and discover that at the surface the water in your river runs uphill at 6 meters per hour. More telephone calls before you learn that there is an undocumented restriction on the maximum temperature gradient. You get that straightened out, but give up on trying to figure out how to set up the model for eddy currents. You might have tried harder if the documentation spoke your language and not that of the programmers.

Consider yourself lucky. At least you have been getting the updates you contracted for. Your closest competitor has not, although the competitor has been getting patches for a program that translates dress patterns into instructions for cloth-cutting machines.

At this point you feel you have met, via telephone, the entire staff of your software supplier. If your case is typical, however, not one person there knows of all the problems you have, although your attitude toward the company has become quite well known.

Your problems, whether in documentation, code, or service, are nothing less than defects. Part of software quality assurance's job in defect collection is to speak with customers (and in-plant users, as well) to learn more about the quality of goods and services as perceived by users. Where formal evaluation is conducted through early release of new software to selected users, software quality assurance should take an active part in collecting user feedback.

The problems most important to prevent are the ones that reach users, notwithstanding the fact that they may be no different in kind from the ones found during testing. By gathering these defects and feeding them back to the appropriate functions, software quality assurance serves not only the user, but the producer as well.

Feedback

Incredible as it may seem, we have heard of defect collection systems in which the data were dutifully analyzed, plotted, and transformed into fact-filled presentations, but never fed back to the software development people! Except as used for reliability models or acceptance criteria, collected and analyzed defect data serve no purpose other than the reduction of defect production and the improvement of defect detection methods. If the test results are not used to change the standards, nothing useful is accomplished.

There are two basic ways that the results of analysis can be fed back. At the conclusion of each project, the results should be compared, category by category, against the previously accumulated set of means. An attempt should be made to note, in each class, new techniques and tools that applied to the subject project but not the reference means. Similarly, changes in the efficacy of each test phase* are compared to previous measurements with attention drawn to techniques and tools implemented for the first time in the new program. To accommodate comparisons, most people normalize defects to the number found per 1000 lines of code.

The real world is not always accurately described by statistics. Seeing the normalized number of defects attributable to detailed design drop from a previous average of 15 to 5 on Project ALPHA, for which the previous standard use of flowcharts was replaced by PDL augmented by flowcharts, does not quite prove that PDL should get all the credit. Even if there were no other changes in techniques and tools, the program used as the guinea pig may have

---

*For the purpose of measuring this, defined in Chapter 7 as

$$100 \times \frac{\text{defects detected}}{\text{defects detected} + \text{defects remaining}}$$

we can assume that all defects will be found during testing, even though this is not quite true. One can then work back from the defects found in the last phase to those found in unit testing in order to provide the number remaining after each test sequence.

had inherent characteristics that, at the detailed level, led to straight-line design with few of the logical loops and conditional branches that PDL forces into a structured implementation. Nevertheless, one starts with evidence and goes from there. Defect collection and analysis provides the only evidence that can close the loop for quality improvement.

EDUCATION

The history of software development and maintenance has been so fraught with monumental cost overruns and schedule delays, by programs too defect-ridden to be relied on, by programs that could not be maintained, and by programs that solved all problems but the one at hand, that it has become conventional wisdom in many management circles that software cannot be controlled.

Stuff and nonsense. There is nothing of human origin that cannot be managed. Management must be given to understand that software is no exception; that the controlled sequence of development, estimating and reestimating practices (see Chapter 5), configuration control, and the use of historical data (not just defects, but costs and user feedback as well), will achieve effective software control. Thus, we find that in those organizations where management has been beaten into accepting lesser standards of performance from the software community than from other functions, software quality assurance has a tacit responsibility to encourage management to take a top-down approach toward software's responsiveness to the larger needs.

There is another side to this coin. Management must understand that software is not built in the same way that other products are. Management must not attempt to pressure software into producing code, the most recognizable software product, prematurely. Management must be convinced that software needs capital to spend, much as any producing function. The tools used by software are scarcely as imposing as a five-ton drill press or a new corporate jet, but they are no less necessary to the cost-effective pursuit of its business. Management must learn that software needs adequate lead-time; that doubling the staff may be of no help in meeting an unrealistic schedule, and that the mandated generation of optimistic plans — regardless of the subtlety of the demand — is, in fact, counterproductive.

Helping management to learn to enjoy life with software is not the only educational role software quality assurance can play. In companies other than those that produce software as a principal product, we find many people in the middle-management ranks who find it difficult to adapt to the effects of the suddenly ubiquitous world of computer software. Some cases in point follow.

We talked with a representative of a government purchasing office who insisted on having binary hard-copy listings of the contents of each PROM that is mounted in equipment delivered to him. He was indifferent to the argument that nobody was ever going to read them with a sufficiently low error rate to be able to put the listings to any useful purpose. Readable copy has always been the way he defined what he was buying, and that was the way it was going to be. In time, he allowed that a machine-readable definition of the PROM contents would be permissible, but it was clear that he was not comfortable with the idea.

It was a matter of weeks before we were able to get a configuration manager to accept the idea of a product that undergoes metamorphosis, assuming forms that change with time; in his case, compile time, link edit time, and PROM-burn-time. During the period of our acquaintance, for some mysterious reason, he kept likening computer software to instruction manuals, declaiming that "*They* never change shape!"

A manager of test engineers, preparing for factory tests of equipment embedding computers, became irate when told that in general there is no way to determine which instruction in memory has gone sour* when a front panel display failed to register the expected output. His previous experience had left him unprepared to accept the absence of a one-to-one relationship between computer instructions and events.

Each of these cases involved issues that are within the purview of quality control: product or service salability, product definition control, and product testing. It seems natural for the role of education to fall on the shoulders of software quality assurance in helping others to meet the new software-based technologies.

Finally, we have quality assurance, the lamplighter. We hope this role seldom needs to be filled. Reviews and audits assure order and thoroughness. But order and thoroughness are no guarantee of built-in quality. Defect collection and feedback of analysis provide a basis for improvement of productivity and reliability, but only if good use is made of the digested information. Thus, decomposition of complexity, structure, tools, and the other substance of this chapter must remain the foundation upon which quality software is built. Knowing this, where the practices of software engineering are ignored, software quality assurance must act to proselytize those who continue to embrace archaic methods. It is not in quality's tradition to curse the darkness.

Spreading the Word

One of the most effective ways that software quality assurance can carry out its programs of education is through the use of outsiders. Even where the credentials of the software quality assurance staff are not in question — which for certain matters may well be the case — the credibility of personnel from the world without somehow seems to find greater acceptance.

---

*He was also convinced that semiconductor memory was always on the verge of dropping bits. They do, but memory is the last place we would look when a problem develops in factory test.

Thus, the use of paid lecturers is an effective technique. Software quality assurance can organize in-plant seminars designed for the purposes of management or software (probably not both at the same time). In addition to customer-designed tutorials, software quality assurance would do well to look at symposia offered to all comers at large metropolitan centers. Some of these can be transported for in-plant training. Best of all is the consultant who is given adequate time to learn the client's business and the current standards, and then provides a lecture series, heavy on motivation, directed squarely at the problems as the consultant perceives them and at approaches to their solution.

STANDARDS

Much of what has been presented in Part 3 revolves about the matter of standards. The effectiveness of software quality assurance depends on the existence of development standards and the usefulness and efficacy of those standards. Quality improvement is the improvement of standards, as determined by analysis of their measured effect.

If software development is concentrated in one department, it will probably have a set of well-documented standards. If not, software quality assurance, as its first priority, should urge the software manager to have the standards formalized. What about the organization in which software development is decentralized? Most likely, there is no set of standards common to all departments, possibly none in individual departments. Given this not unusual circumstance, software quality assurance has yet one more responsibility: working with all the software managers to establish documented standards exhibiting as much commonality as possible.

Software quality assurance, of course, needs standards of its own: a boilerplate software quality assurance plan — or, if the diversity of software produced is great enough, set of plans — that will provide much of the background for its specific project plans, and a set of procedures outlining the manner in which software quality assurance carries out each of its activities. The plans and procedures will reflect the local approaches to software development, and as the development standards are modified in response to defect and productivity feedback,* they, too, will be updated.

It is probably a mistake for software quality assurance to attempt to impose a complete quality system all at once. It should not urge revolution in software development methods, but it can outline a progressive evolutionary plan. Where there had been no requirements definition in earlier use, software quality assurance ought not expect the first ones to be as comprehensive as the ones to follow; it takes people time to accept documentation requirements.

---

*We assume software management will maintain productivity records. If not, software quality assurance can compute them as a ratio of labor hours found in accounting records (we refuse to accept the condition of no labor accounting per project) to delivered lines of code.

This applies to all subsequent documentation as well. We want the best, but we can accept monotonic improvement. Similarly, we cannot expect all the tools that one will ever want to be acquired at one time. In addition to the problem of confusion, we would lose the advantage, as noted in Chapter 8, of stepwise refinement of the tool characteristics best suited to the development environment. Indeed, in no respect should software quality assurance try to do it all at once. Hardware quality engineering took a couple of years to get going when it was introduced, and there is no reason to believe that software quality assurance will do better.

There is one other danger in attempting to establish instant total software quality assurance: before seeing how things are working out, software quality assurance might find it has inadvertently established an overly rigid set of standards. All quality solutions, including those shaped by our own discussions of analysis, design, code, configuration control, and testing, are formalized by standards. Nevertheless, the fact that standards are documented, sealed with executive wax, and promulgated does not mean that they cannot be tailored up or down for smaller or larger, simpler or more complex, projects. Indeed, they should be, and the software quality assurance standards must embrace sufficient flexibility to do so.

> A bureaucratic approach to software quality assurance is not a quality solution. Effective software quality assurance is the synthesis of the technology of software engineering and the methodology of quality assurance.

SUMMARY

1. There are three distinct facets to software quality assurance:
   (a) It is a management tool for control and visibility.
   (b) It is the in-plant representative of the user community.
   (c) It is an agent for the improvement of productivity, reliability, and maintainability.

2. Software quality assurance must mesh closely with development or maintenance. Therefore, each software quality assurance plan must track the corresponding development or operational support plan.

3. Software does not lend itself to numerical standards of quality, save for those relating to reliability. One cannot determine the acceptability of a design by the number of unconditional branches or the module size or the like. Software quality assurance must be more than a bean-counting function.

4. Verification by software quality assurance that the results of each phase of development are satisfactory must be accomplished prior to—or very

shortly thereafter — the start of the next phase. This assures visibility, precludes the telescoping of the separate phases, and guarantees a continuity of problem decomposition.

5. If for no other reason, design reviews are cost-effective if they can catch errors before these errors can be propagated to the next phase of development. The cost of removing defects increases nonlinearly with the "distance" between the commission of error and the act of detection.

6. A schedule of reviews appropriate for many environments includes the following:
   System concept
   Requirements definition
   Top-level design
   Test plan
   Test procedures
   Configuration management plan

7. Audits assure conformance to plans and procedures.

8. Review meetings entail representation of several functions. Sensitivity is required to maintain a constructive atmosphere.

9. Finding deficiencies does not end software quality assurance's responsibility. The matter is not closed until corrective action is taken.

10. Qualification is software quality assurance's validation by test.

11. It is essential that software quality assurance be represented on the software change board.

12. Software quality assurance activity in vendor surveillance parallels that of hardware quality assurance.

13. Independent verification and validation provides both independence and a partial solution to the problem of staffing with qualified personnel.

14. Defect measurement, analysis, and feedback is the mechanism by which software quality assurance uses the experience of previous projects to improve future productivity and quality.

15. To be useful, defects must be collected in categories that can lead to inferences of needed improvement. Classifying in terms of the phase in which defects were introduced is one such way. Classifying by type of fault is another.

16. The software community has done little defect measurement of its own. Software quality assurance should undertake both the collection and analysis activities.

17. Defect measurement also leads to the identification of error-prone modules, those modules so riddled with defects that it is easier to rewrite them than to attempt to correct them.

18. The defect collection system must extend to the inclusion of problems reported by users.

19. Software quality assurance can perform an educational role in helping management and development to understand each other's needs. Software quality assurance can help to introduce others (e.g., equipment test engineers) to the facts of life with software. If necessary, software quality assurance can champion the cause of software engineering to a development community clinging to archaic methods.

20. Software quality assurance cannot be effective in the absence of software development or maintenance standards. Quality improvement is the improvement of standards, as determined by analysis of their measured effect. If such standards do not exist, software quality assurance must urge their codification. Software quality assurance's own standards must be flexible enough to accommodate projects of various sizes and degrees of complexity.

REFERENCES

1. M. Shooman, "Software Reliability: Measurement and Models," *Proceedings 1975 Annual Reliability and Maintainability Symposium*, IEEE Cat. 75CH0918-3RQC, pp. 485–489.

2. B. Boehm, "Software Engineering," *IEEE Transactions on Computers*, Vol. C-25, December 1976, pp. 1226–1241.

3. M. E. Fagan, "Design and Code Inspection to Reduce Errors in Program Development," *IBM Systems Journal*, Vol. 15, No. 3, 1976, pp. 182–211.

4. H. Mills, "On the Development of Large Reliable Programs," *Record, 1973 IEEE Symposium on Computer Software Reliability*, IEEE Cat. 73CH0741-9C, pp. 155–158.

5. D. K. Lloyd and M. Lipow, *Reliability, Management, Methods and Mathematics*, 2d ed., published by the authors, 1977, p. 489.

6. Capers Jones, *Technical Report: Program Quality and Programmer Productivity*, TR 02.764, IBM General Products Division, January 1977, p. 51.

7. W. F. Baker (IBM), *Software Data Collection and Analysis: A Real-Time System Project History*, Final Technical Report RADC-TR-77-192, Rome Air Development Center, Griffiss Air Force Base, New York, June 1977, p. 28.

8. K. S. Mendis and M. L. Gollis, "Software Error History and Projection, A Case Study," *Proceedings, NSIA Software Conference,* National Security Industrial Association, February 1979, pp. 30–37.

9. G. R. Craig, W. L. Hetrick, M. Lipow, T. A. Thayer, et al., *Software Reliability Study,* Interim Technical Report RADC-TR-74-250, Rome Air Development Center, Griffiss Air Force Base, New York, October 1974, pp. 4-12–4-17.

10. D. K. Lloyd and M. Lipow, *Reliability, Management, Methods and Mathematics,* 2d ed., published by the authors. 1977, p. 503.

11. Albert Endres, "An Analysis of Errors and Their Causes in System Programs," *1975 International Conference on Reliable Software,* IEEE Cat. No. 75CH0840-7CSR, pp. 327–336.

Part Four
Implementation

Chapter 10

Selling and Staffing

The primary requisites for the achievement of software quality goals are (1) a basic understanding of the problems of software and the solutions, the substance of the earlier chapters; and (2) management acceptance of the quality issues — an acceptance accompanied by the institution of a constructive quality program meant to be taken seriously.

Management acceptance will stem from a philosophical point of view for which we may well look to Japan. There, quality control is considered a cost-saving measure; in the United States, it is generally regarded as a cost. The key to selling a software quality assurance program is its potential for reducing costs. This is what the software quality assurance salesperson must emphasize.

Software development and maintenance efforts have a history of cost over-runs and schedule slippages. Management, now painfully attuned to the problem, has demanded status reporting to provide insight into progress, cost, demands on capital, and expectation of completion. Although these seem to offer apparent visibility, as projects move downstream, and especially during integration, the old problems seem to reappear. What is missing?

Regrettably, status reports provide no assurance that work is being performed to quality standards. Here we can draw a parallel to hardware quality control. For the production of hardware, an independent organization, quality assurance, verifies that each of the items specified, procured, developed, manufactured, or assembled will perform as intended when finally tested or used in its application. This is the control that is necessary to the process of acquiring or maintaining software; perhaps even more important in the software environment, wherein the final products are all but invisible.

Depending on the industry one is in, the need for enlightening management may be moot. In those industries dealing with the U.S. Department of Defense and its branches, the decision to rely upon software quality assurance has already been made. In most cases, it is a contractual requirement — indeed, a prerequisite for the award of contract.

Elsewhere, however, it may be necessary to sell management on the need and payoff of software quality assurance, a task made difficult by the relative infancy of the discipline and the concomitant paucity of payoff documentation. There is nothing to do but present a logically drawn argument that can lead directly to the formulation of a formal program of software quality assurance activities. This argument must encompass the following points:

- Software quality is built in; neither a product of inspection nor an addition to work previously accomplished.

- Objectivity is attained only by organizational independence.

- The software quality assurance function can be competently staffed despite the critical shortage of qualified personnel.

THE CASE FOR SOFTWARE QUALITY ASSURANCE

The arguments for software quality assurance have, in fact, been presented in earlier chapters. We recast them here in the sense of a brief designed to appeal to management.

For all elements of our economy, the cost of acquiring computer software has increased dramatically in recent years. In certain industries, we see a striking example of this: where the major expenditures for design and development have in the past been directed toward the hardware aspects of new products, a significant shift to software design and development has taken place. Even now, for military avionics equipment, we see a fifty-fifty split between hardware and software development, with software continuing to grow. In the consumer and industrial equipment fields, the proliferation of microprocessors is pacing a similar acceleration of the influence of software. In more traditional applications of computation, data base systems, word processing, and telecommunications networking are demanding further explosion of software development and modification.

The message is clear. For manufacturers of equipment, the cost of software development for new products will increase to the point where it will be the major cost contributor to many new product development projects. For users of electronic data processing, the message has already been received that their software costs can exceed the costs of their computing hardware. Even the largest of these find that the acquisition of new software is fraught with problems. It has been reported* that the federal government was urged by the General Accounting Office (GAO) to implement guidelines to assist agencies contract-

*Electronic News, May 26, 1980.

ing for software development. The government spends over $10 billion a year for computer hardware and software. In its study of nine software development contracts, the GAO found only one case in which the software could be used "as delivered." It also found that the "combined total costs and development times of the cases increased from estimates of $3.7 million and 10.8 years to an actual cost of $6.7 million and 20.5 years."

Development is only part of the problem. Like the purchaser of a new sailboat, the recipient of new software can look forward to a total cost of ownership perhaps twice the cost of development. During their lifetime, programs are subject to a continuing cycle of changes. Even programs embedded in equipment are not immune. The reasons for this are several:

- Removal of latent defects — During the test phases one removes most of the built-in faults, but not all.

- Changes to or additions of functional requirements — Anything easy to change will be changed. Also, for many applications, one of the chief reasons for using a computer is to allow for change, so it can be expected to happen.

- Change of computer hardware — If the machinery is changed, as so often happens, reprogramming of the software may be necessary. Software portability is more often myth than fact.

- Change of software operating system — The installation of new supervisory software is often attended by instant obsolescence of productive programs.

Software changes mean cost. If a relatively small software quality assurance cost spent up front — in the development phase that represents the first third of the life cycle cost — can substantially reduce the remaining two-thirds of the total cost, the return on investment is evident. *And a substantial cost reduction is possible.* We expect the number of latent defects in new software to decrease monotonically in time as they are found and removed. However, if software fixes and revisions introduce an untoward number of faults, the net number of defects can actually increase, possibly to the point where the decay of quality makes complete reprogramming the only feasible alternative. Such is the inevitable consequence of poor program documentation, unnecessary complexity, code which is simply not understandable, and inadequate configuration control. All of these causes can be markedly ameliorated by an aggressive software quality assurance program.

Of course, even the initial number of latent defects can be lessened by such a program. Although software quality assurance cannot guarantee the total absence of bugs — simply because there is no way of testing more than a small fraction of the total number of discrete states that a program can assume — it can make the development environment hostile to the commission of errors. One does not have to be concerned with a bug that never got into the code. Going a step further, software quality assurance not only strives to prevent faults from getting into the delivered code, it wants to find them as early in the development phase as possible. An error caught during integration may cost five times as much to remove compared to the cost if found during design; if first encountered during formal testing, perhaps ten times as much.

In the long run, software quality assurance has to pay for itself. The 6 percent or so of the software costs attributable to quality assurance are self-liquidating and yield significant dividends to those organizations that implement a thorough software quality assurance program.

In addition to orally presenting the brief, one must submit to management a concrete proposal delineating what the software quality program will encompass. Since we expect that such a proposal is more likely (although not necessarily) to originate in the quality organization, the following specimen memo proposal is one that might be presented by the manager of quality:

TO: (President)

SUBJECT: Software Quality Assurance

With the rapid expansion of the use of embedded processors in our equipment, support of computer software must be considered and controlled in the same way as other delivered products. The techniques applied by quality assurance to assure delivery to our customers of conforming hardware products should also be applied to the control of deliverable software. Further, our increased dependence on data base systems for the operation of our business prescribes the requirement of support and control of this software as well.

In the recent past, cost penalties, schedule slippages, and general problems have been experienced. The cumulative negative impact of these on our company can be ameliorated by the positive application of quality assurance techniques and principles to software development and production.

Institution of a software quality assurance function will enable the establishing and auditing of a standard policy and procedures for control of the development, production, and configuration management of computer software. It will further provide independence in the final decision to deliver software to a customer.

The major areas and points of control in which software quality assurance should be actively participating will be set forth in software quality assurance program plans. In conformance to these plans, specific contract requirements and personnel responsibilities for providing effective management of software quality will be established. Planning will encompass development and implementation of each system, including practices and procedures to ensure compliance with all software requirements of the contract or internal project. Plans will provide for software support, task control, tool certification, configuration management, documentation, reviews of designs and audits of procedures, testing, corrective action, subcontractor control, and qualification.

Finally, it will be the role of software quality assurance to assure our customers that we are taking the initiative in the development of software practices and management techniques which most directly affect software quality.

_____

Manager: Quality Assurance

Selling a program is only the first step in implementing it. Let us look at some of the specifics that remain.

SOFTWARE QUALITY ASSURANCE AND THE DEVELOPMENT COMMUNITY

Software development strives to provide computer programs in a timely manner, within cost, and to specified performance requirements.

The purpose of software quality assurance is to assure the acquisition of high-quality software products on schedule, within cost, and in compliance with the performance requirements.

That the objectives of both of these disciplines are common, may, in many organizations, cause a problem. The software group can feel that software quality assurance is redundant, unnecessary, and, in fact, an infringement upon their domain. Such feelings must be overcome prior to the implementation of a productive software quality assurance program. Detailed discussions with development management must take place to permit quality management to explain the discipline of software quality assurance, to convince development that rather than a bureaucratic impediment, software quality assurance is a constructive facet of software engineering itself. Together, development and quality can outline the general terms of a software quality assurance program, leading to the drafting of specific procedures that both groups can work with.

Once the fears engendered by territorial imperative are stripped away, it is clear that software quality assurance is actually supportive of development. An example of how the independent posture of software quality assurance can directly abet the interests of development is found in the following memorandum, prepared with the cooperation of development management to dispel the trepidation of the development staff concerning the institution of a defect reporting system.

    I Why?

    As we continue to develop internal standards related to the manner in which we carry out our business of building computer software, we shall want to know in what areas of activity we need to concentrate our efforts at finding better ways. Specifically, we are concerned with the efficiency with which we, as a company, are able to produce deliverable, usable code. If we can identify the principal sources of the difficulties attending our development of software, we can then address the areas where we shall want to consider the use of new techniques and the acquisition or development of new tools.

We can, of course, speculate on the sources of problems. Many feel that the requirements definitions given development leave much to be desired. Some wonder if a more iterative problem decomposition procedure would not lead to more straightforward program structures. Others feel that where assembly language is used, an untoward number of coding errors is created. And so it goes. The simple fact is that we do not really know where we must concentrate our improvement programs, because we have never attempted to quantify our problems.

To quote Lord Kelvin, "When you can measure what you are speaking about, and express it in numbers, you know something about it; but when you cannot measure it, when you cannot express it in numbers, your knowledge is of a meager and unsatisfactory kind."

In an analogous way, we don't know if we are testing as efficiently as we should. The "goodness" of a test is measured by the number of problems it can expose. Those left behind will remain in the system that much longer, with the potential for creating other problems and for finally causing a failure at a time when the bug will be more difficult to isolate. Simply put:

$$\text{Test goodness} = \frac{\text{number of bugs squashed}}{\text{number squashed} + \text{number left alive}}$$

Thus, we should want to quantify not only the sources of bugs, but the test stages in which we detect them, so that we can know where we should address methods of making each stage more effective.

Summarizing thus far, as professional software engineers, we have an interest in continuously improving the methodology and technology that we employ, and to do so we need information. Hence, the software debug and test log.

The log is a bean-counting form in which each person engaged in testing can keep a continuous tally of the number of bugs of various source categories during each day of testing. The log also has boxes to be checked off that apply to the test environment. This will provide a data base useful for evaluating the effectiveness of our testing methods.

The last item on the log is the name of the module to which various problem counts apply. Knowing the generic type of module (e.g., interrupt handler, number cruncher, display formatter) and the principal source of problems relating to that module, we can hope to infer futher specifics concerning the potential for improvement. For example, if we find that for display formatting routines, one of the strongest sources of bugs is module design, we may want to consider development of a tool for automatically generating graphic output.

A second reason for wanting to know to which module a line of bean counts applies is found in the measurement of the efficacy of our bug-catching procedures. Knowing to which modules we applied bug-catching techniques and tools will allow us to measure the degree to which these are effective — or will, once we have a large enough data base to smooth the effect of the number of bugs with which each module is initially endowed.

In short, we want to get better; to know where to expend labor and money. For this we need data, and in sufficient quantity to be able to use statistical inference.

II How?

Pads of forms, illustrated in Figure ____, will be held in the software department stationery supply cabinets. Each member of the staff actively engaged in testing is asked to complete one form each day, whether or not problems were found. We ask that people in a joint testing effort communicate with each other to make certain that they don't duplicate data. At the end of each week, the forms should be mailed directly to software quality assurance, which has the responsibility for making sense out of all the data that will be generated. Incidentally, all reports generated by software quality assurance will be made available to all members of the software staff. We expect everyone will be interested in the analyses.

Software quality assurance has this responsibility for three reasons: (1) it wants to do it, (2) the bookkeeping associated with quality improvement programs is a traditional quality engineering activity, and (3) any person who fears self-incrimination can be assured that in no way will source information be revealed to anyone who can influence an individual's health, happiness, or coming merit review.

A Matter of Policy

The need for direct cooperation between development and quality and the light tone of the above memo may lead one to feel that software quality assurance can be established on an informal basis. Not so. The role of software quality assurance must be explicitly drawn and made clear to everyone concerned. The proper instrument for documenting the ground rules of a software quality assurance program is a policy on software quality assurance. In addition to framing the scope of its activity, the policy should clearly establish software quality assurance as that part of the organization which is charged with the responsibility and endowed with the authority for assuring the quality of software developed in-house or procured from outside sources. Even at so general a level (as compared with operating procedures), policies must reflect the business environment in which they will be used. Nevertheless, Chapter 11 presents an illustration of the contents appropriate for many policies.

Once agreed to, the policy should be promulgated by upper management — preferably by the president or general manager — to ensure that all affected functions will adhere to it.

STAFFING AND ORGANIZING

To implement an effective software quality assurance program one needs to understand more than the symptoms of poor quality; one should be well versed in the elements of good quality. In this sense, software quality assurance is no different from the quality assurance of hardware. More than it is in the case of hardware, however, quality assurance is concerned with built-in quality, rather than quality derived from inspection or other after-the-fact techniques. Thus, quality assurance must be intricately involved in the various phases of software design. In short, the software quality assurance function must be staffed by persons holding a comprehensive understanding of software engineering; in fact, by software professionals.

We are not suggesting that the department has to be fully staffed with software professionals. With the program set up by those who know software engineering, quality engineers can be trained to augment the activities of the software professionals; bringing to them any matters about which they are uncertain. This in turn means that explicit procedures are required. In time, we can expect that the quality engineer trained in software quality assurance will become reasonably independent, but at least one software professional is required at the start to help lay out the program and to serve as a software quality assurance "cadre."

Among the set of procedures that seem appropriate for much of industry, we would expect to find the following:

- System design review
- Software requirements specification review
- Top-level design review
- Module design review
- Review of integration test plan
- Code inspection
- Review of test procedures
- Documentation standards audit
- Configuration control audit (including library control)
- Test audit
- Standard for qualification plan
- Defect collection, analysis, and feedback
- Quality evaluation
- Tool certification
- Vendor survey and surveillance

- Disposition of program trouble reports
- Record retention and control

Help Wanted

Unfortunately, there is a scarcity of competent software engineers,* and quality is competing with software development in the open market for those available. The competition is an unfair one, since development offers the opportunity to build software, rather than control it — an offer clearly more attractive to the majority of technically oriented and eager software practitioners. Moreover, development offers a more obvious career path. In this regard we note that qualified software engineers command salaries substantially greater than those of quality engineers.

Despite the one-sided contest, there remains the opportunity to hire software professionals for software quality assurance. All software engineers are not alike, and as their number increases, so will the minority who will be attracted to a career of furthering the quality aspects of software engineering.

The most effective means of obtaining the software professional is through the transfer of a well-respected and competent person from the development group. This has many advantages, most notably, familiarity with the type of software developed and procured, insight into known weaknesses, rapport with in-house designers, and the knowledge of how to operate within the organization.

If internal transfer fails, one can attempt to hire from the marketplace at large. Again, one runs into the same problems, mitigated only by the size of the population being tapped. Hiring from without will require an aggressive recruitment program, a committed management, and competitive salaries.

Whether acquired from within or without, one must be careful to distinguish between software professionals who, by disposition and knowledge, are software engineers (as we defined them in the closing pages of Chapter 3, and whose practices are described in Chapters 5–8) and those who are not. The great majority of software people are not software engineers, and a routine programmer is not the person to fill the software quality assurance slot.

This slot must, of course, be defined. Below is a job description illustrating the specific responsibilities of the position and the educational requirements of potential candidates. This job description is necessarily general, and must be tailored to the specifics at hand.

---

*It is possible that the shortage of software professionals is partly artificial. In a poorly controlled environment, they are less productive than they can be. Also, and especially in the world of electronic data processing (commercial computing), many switch jobs so often that they never complete anything useful. Again, a controlled development process reduces the risk that upon the programmer's leaving, the work accomplished by one of these itinerant professionals will have to be scrapped.

FIGURE 10-1   Job Description: Computer Software Quality and Reliability Manager

---

Function

Provides counsel and guidance to company management with regard to the quality and reliability of in-house- and subcontractor-developed computer programs used in conjunction with specific equipment categories and company systems. Establishes criteria which will permit the computer programming personnel to structure computer programs (in terms of language, problem decomposition, data validity checks, etc.) to optimize the reliability of said programs. Establishes standards which will permit the quality department to exercise its responsibility to assess the reliability of a specific computer program and its suitability to its intended use.

Specific Duties

1. Provides consultation for programming, engineering, logistics support, and other cognizant personnel of the company in all central, branch, and field locations.

2. Confers with responsible technical personnel to determine scope and magnitude of the effort involved in complying with contract or self-generated requirements affecting computer software.

3. Collaborates with personnel of cognizant departments to determine and/or recommend methods, procedures, and operations to be exercised for the efficient conclusion of contractual or self-generated requirements relative to computer software at all locations.

Let us now consider the situation where there is an immediate need to establish a software quality assurance function and all efforts to bring a software professional on board have failed. Given these circumstances, it will be necessary for the quality department to utilize the services of a consultant to set up the program and to train the assigned quality assurance engineer(s) in the prosecution of that program. This is not the final resolution of the need for a software professional, but it allows for an interim solution until the professional is found. It also forms the foundation for an eventual training program to convert quality engineers into software quality engineers.

One of the situations wherein the requirement for "instant software quality assurance" is most likely to arise occurs when a company receives its first U.S. government contract requiring software quality assurance. Unless the quality department is made aware of the requirement sufficiently early, the services of a consultant may well be procured through the actions of the systems engineering or software development functions. This is undesirable, since (1) the software quality assurance program will be fashioned on a specific project basis

4. Participates actively and early in design reviews to set down the computer software concepts, method of execution and implementation, and integration into operational equipment.

5. Develops test and assessment criteria for checking software and the integration of hardware and software.

6. Provides inputs to technical and cost proposals relative to the company's participation in computer software quality and reliability.

7. Remains abreast of advances in computer software techniques and quality and reliability enhancement and assessment by attending outside symposia, conferences, and meetings related to assigned responsibilities.

8. Keeps management aware of the status of software development projects during design, development, and test.

Qualifications

Education: B.S. or advanced degree in computer science, mathematics, or any of the engineering or natural science disciplines.

Experience: Ten years of broad and diversified computer programming experience, five of which should have been in a supervisory position. Experience should include extensive application of the technology and methodology of software engineering.

Knowledge required: Advanced and comprehensive knowledge of software engineering, including test methods and system integration procedures.

without concern for the long-term needs, and (2) the independent position of software quality assurance will be compromised.

SOFTWARE QUALITY ASSURANCE IN THE ORGANIZATION

The need for independence cannot be stressed too highly. Even where the disciplines of software engineering are in effect, seemingly making the services of the quality organization unnecessary, a number of events seem to conspire to defeat the interests of quality. All too often, software is produced under the most trying of schedules. Receipt of the order may be late, completion of the system analyses required to define the overall hardware-software configuration may slip, hardware availability and the readiness of new support software may be delayed. Only one thing never changes: the end date. Under these circumstances, the seemingly more vulnerable of the scheduled activities become the target for assault. There is pressure to skimp on test planning, various documentation of the design, library control procedures, test documentation, and so forth. Even those who know that herein lies madness may succumb to the temptation to meet that end date no matter what. Only the single-minded devotion to quality of a functional activity independent of the design group can act to brake the excesses of those who might compromise quality in an ill-conceived attempt to recover schedule slippages or cost overruns. Independence is the key. The responsibility for assuring quality must be vested in the quality department.

In this regard, we note that quality must always report at the same level as those departments which it must evaluate and audit. Quality must be autonomous, and its management must have the same organizational status and access to top management as have the other functions. Figure 10-2 illustrates

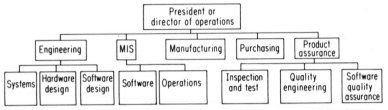

FIGURE 10-2 Software Quality Assurance in the Design and Manufacturing Organization.

this doctrine as expanded to include software quality assurance, as it might apply to a manufacturing concern.

We have discussed the requirement that software quality assurance be undertaken by persons who know software. Figure 10-2 suggests that they know something else, also. Nowhere is this other attribute better described than in Crosby's *Quality is Free:*

> Every successful quality program I ever saw was headed by an individual who knew how to communicate with, and even discipline, management groups without antagonizing them. Successful quality managers know that the way to make people quality conscious is to make them comfortable with the concepts of quality, and show them how to recognize what they can receive from loyalty to the concept. But quality is unique in that all the successes as well as failures are caused by people in other operations. The product or service is quality because of other people's fingers and minds, and the quality managers must be able to work with those people in order to handle the function properly.[1]

In the area of software quality, this is especially true, since quality will be working with a group which has always been independent, not used to people overseeing its efforts, and — until recently — not controlled by specific procedures and guidelines. This makes the organizational structure and the people within it of paramount importance in ensuring the implementation, direction, and control of the software quality program.

TRAINING

Although we have scarcely ignored the missionary work required to sell the concept of software quality assurance, it remains that the toughest part of implementing a software quality assurance program is staffing it. Even if one uses a consultant to get the program started, ultimately one will want a team of software quality assurance engineers on the payroll. Beyond question, the greatest hurdle to be overcome is that caused by the limited availability of personnel with the requisite skills in computer applications, software development (and maintenance), *and* the practice of quality assurance. It is difficult to find people with the necessary training and experience in any of these fields, nearly impossible to find candidates at the appropriate levels of ability in all. This problem is not unique to industry. It has also been faced by the U.S. government.

The Defense Logistics Agency (DLA) has been a major force in establishing and formalizing those quality and reliability requirements which are now universally recognized and contractually invoked. In its Defense Contracts Administration Services, the DLA has long maintained a force of quality representatives whose mission it is to audit the adherence to quality procedures of the government's suppliers. The DLA has continued its trailblazing efforts by zeroing in on the problem of obtaining personnel to staff their software quality assurance responsibilities in the procurement of software and firmware.

Training the Quality Engineer

The DLA's problems, and its solutions, apply equally to industry. Software professionals are in short supply. Quality engineers are in short supply. But the shortage of software people is the greater. The DLA's approach is to take existing quality assurance personnel with an electronics background (and a potential for learning) and provide them with the necessary training in the technology of computers and software. The DLA's own quality specialists teach the courses, using materials prepared by professional industrial education firms. As originally launched in 1977 under the designation S-36, the program was made available throughout the DLA's regional jurisdictions for presentation to selected personnel. The curriculum, structured on the premise that the personnel to be trained had an electronics background but knew little about computer software, included the following:

- Computer systems and programming fundamentals
- Computer structured programming
- Procurement quality assurance of computer software

- Defining the software quality program requirements
- Evaluating the software quality program
- Review of the software documentation
- Software testing

Since industry, in general, faces the same problems and decisions regarding its present quality personnel and their level of training in computer software technology, a similar approach can be taken. The outline of a comprehensive training program for industry follows. It is assumed that the trainees have had some exposure to the disciplines of computer technology.

1. INTRODUCTION
   - Influence of software on company's business
   - Why programs fail

2. CHARACTERISTICS OF COMPUTER PROGRAMS
   - Scope of computational activity
   - Data dependency
   - Time dependency

3. DEVELOPMENT METHODOLOGY — MANAGEMENT ASPECTS
   - System concepts and analysis
   - Development and design
   - Operation and maintenance as an iteration of development
   - Product approaches versus management information system approaches

4. DEVELOPMENT METHODOLOGY — TECHNICAL ASPECTS
   - Language
   - Structured design
   - Modularity
   - Etc.

5. SPECIAL PROBLEMS OF MICROPROCESSOR PROGRAMS
   - Cross-assemblers and cross-compilers
   - Simulation and emulation
   - Hardware test fixtures

6. CONFIGURATION MANAGEMENT
   - Release and change control
   - Library control
   - Firmware control

7. REVIEWS AND AUDITS

8. QUALITY ASSURANCE ROLE IN CERTIFICATION AND TESTING

9. DEFECT COLLECTION AND ANALYSIS

10. TOOLS FOR SOFTWARE QUALITY ASSURANCE
    - Library control
    - Static analyzers
    - Dynamic analyzers

11. RELIABILITY MODELING

12. DOD STANDARDS (applicable to industries engaged in the development and production of military products)

Training the Software Engineer

Although we may expect that ultimately most of the software quality assurance personnel will come from the quality community, we do not want to ignore those who are lured from the ranks of software, especially since we expect that it will be software people who inaugurate software quality assurance functions. The training of software professionals is the easier of the two, since they will be operating within an environment of quality professionals and supported by well-documented standards and procedures. The software engineer, entering the environment of quality assurance, will be expected to acquire a working knowledge of those aspects of quality assurance which are as valid for software as for hardware:

- Design review and audit

- Configuration control

- Test controls

- Documentation

- Supplier and contractor control

- In-process and functional audit

- Corrective action

- Cost of quality

- Retention of records

GENTLY BUT FIRMLY

The process of convincing management to institute a software quality assurance program (developing a policy, staffing with qualified personnel and qualifying others through training, and working out the operating procedures with the software development and maintenance groups) may take from one to three years depending on the priorities established. In any case, it must be built on a sound foundation, building slowly, and assuring that each element, when thought out and implemented, is understood and accepted by the other affected functions. We may then expect that the discipline of software quality assurance, properly instituted and carved out in a constructive spirit, will result in the production of quality software within the schedule and cost constraints that were budgeted.

SUMMARY

1. Management acceptance of a software quality assurance program will derive from an understanding of software quality assurance's ability to control and reduce cost.

2. Status reports that provide no assurance that work is performed to quality standards do not offer real visibility.

3. Design and development costs, currently split evenly between hardware and software, are continuing to shift in the direction of software.

4. The cost of ownership of software greatly exceeds the development costs. This can be reduced not only by software quality assurance activities during the period of operation and maintenance, but even more markedly by ensuring design, code, and configuration control practices consistent with the subsequent, and inevitable, cycle of changes.

5. Latent defects can be greatly reduced — and cost-effectively detected earlier — by an aggressive software quality assurance program.

6. Software quality assurance pays for itself in the long run.

7. The common goals of software development and software quality assurance may be the cause of conflicts between them. Working with development management, the software professional representing quality must resolve these. Mature development management should recognize that software quality assurance can be supportive of them.

8. The role of software quality assurance should be set forth in a software quality assurance policy endorsed by the highest level of general management.

9. Quality must engage the services of a software engineer to institute a software quality assurance function. This can be by internal transfer, hiring, or employing the services of a consultant. The first two may prove difficult, since the demand for software engineers far exceeds the supply.

10. Software production is often conducted under adverse cost and schedule constraints. Software quality assurance must have the mandate to exercise independence from those who would throw caution to the wind in employing counterproductive approaches to meet these constraints. Software quality assurance must be part of the quality organization.

11. Until recently, software managers have operated without interference from other functions. Software quality assurance personnel must possess sufficient sensitivity to this and must be supported by an organizational structure which assures the same access to all management levels enjoyed by development.

12. Training programs can be employed to permit the use of quality engineers in staffing the software quality assurance function once it has been established. Software professionals entering the quality community have much to learn, too.

REFERENCES

1. Philip B. Crosby, *Quality Is Free*, McGraw-Hill, New York, 1979, p. 70.

Chapter 11

Standards, Policies, and Plans

We have stated several times that the software quality assurance program must be intertwined with the development or maintenance program. Since there is great diversity in the types of software developed or maintained and equal diversity in the technological and managerial approaches used, there can be no single set of development or maintenance standards or policies of managerial purpose. Accordingly, there can be no one set of software quality assurance operating guidelines. Nevertheless, at the highest level, it is possible to define the responsibilities laid upon software quality assurance and the authority with which it should be endowed.

PUBLISHED STANDARDS

There are several standards for software quality assurance that are currently in use, and, as we shall shortly see, they exhibit sufficient commonality to support our claim that at the highest level, the function of software quality assurance can be defined. Of the six standards that we shall compare, all but the one published by the IEEE have been issued for the purpose of imposing software quality assurance programs on contractors or for auditing the contractors' compliance with standards. The exception is actually a standard for the preparation of software quality assurance plans. The six standards are as follows:

Mil-STD-1679 (Navy) Encompasses all aspects of software development, with emphasis on software quality assurance.

Mil-S-52779A (Tri-Service) The basic software quality assurance specification for U.S. military procurements.

FAA-STD-018	Software quality assurance standard of the Federal Aviation Administration.
AQAP-13	Allied Quality Assurance Publication (NATO) for software quality assurance of NATO procurements.
DLAM-8200.1	Defense Logistics Agency Manual (DOD), which, among other types of procurements, instructs Defense Contract Administration Services representatives in the auditing of contractors' software quality assurance activities.
IEEE-P730	IEEE's trial use standard for software quality assurance plans.

Table 11-1 summarizes the scope of these documents. It is evident that, in the large, they share a common philosophy regarding the role of software quality assurance.

The DOD, FAA, and NATO standards are similar in their basic requirements, but each provides unique inputs to the establishment of a software quality program. The standard of the professional society, IEEE-P730, proposes uniform minimum acceptable requirements for the preparation and content of software quality assurance plans, thus indirectly implying a standard for software quality assurance. Beyond the illustration of the commonality with which management planners view software quality assurance, we reference these standards because they have formed the bedrock from which most of the procedures and plans for software quality programs, both in the U.S. and internationally, have been developed. Moreover, the extent of agreement among them is indicative of the coming of age of software quality assurance. We choose one of these, the one that we believe has received the greatest use, as a specific illustration of the requirements for a software quality program that might be imposed by contract. Following is a paragraph-by-paragraph synopsis of Mil-S-52779A, *Software Quality Assurance Program Requirements.*

SCOPE

When made applicable by contract reference, this specification mandates the establishment and implementation of a software quality assurance program by the defense contractor. Tailoring is intended. The specification applies to independent software, software embedded in a system, and, unless specifically exempted, nondeliverable software (e.g., support tools) developed under the contract.

TABLE 11-1

Program requirements and elements	Standards for implementing and monitoring				
	AQAP-13	Mil-S-52779A	FAA-STD-018	DLAM8200.1	IEEE-P730
Quality planning	X	X	X	X	X
Software support (tools, techniques, methods)	X	X	X	X	X
Work instructions	X	X	X		
Configuration management	X	X	X	X	X
Software documentation	X	X	X	X	X
Design reviews and audits	X	X	X	X	X
Testing	X	X	X	X	
Corrective action	X	X	X	X	X
Subcontractor and supplier control	X	X	X	X	X
Computer library controls	X	X	X	X	X
Preparation for delivery and storage	X	X		X	
Records			X		

REQUIREMENTS

Software Quality Assurance Program

Upon award of contract, the contractor will plan, develop, and implement a software quality assurance program. Documentation of the program will be in the form of a software quality assurance plan. The remaining paragraphs under the REQUIREMENTS heading refer to specific requirements that the plan must address.

Tools, Techniques and Methodologies

The plan will identify the tools, techniques, and methodologies to be used which will support quality assurance objectives, and will describe how their use will support objectives and requirements of the quality assurance program.

Computer Program Design

The plan will include procedures for design documentation review and the evaluation of design logic; fulfillment of requirements; completeness; and compliance with specified standards.

Work Certification

The plan will identify procedures for approving or certifying the description, authorization and completion of work. Monitoring to assure compliance with the procedure is required.

Documentation

The plan will state or reference documentation standards for deliverable software; specify procedures to assure delivery in accordance with the standards of correct documentation and change information; provide periodic independent review of documentation.

Library Control

The plan will identify and establish procedures and controls for the handling of source code, object code, and related data to ensure accurate identification of each program, including modifications, and to make certain that only the proper software is submitted for testing.

Reviews and Audits

The plan will describe or reference procedures for review and audit to establish traceability of initial contract requirements through successive baselines, and will provide quality assurance measures to ensure these procedures are being implemented. The plan will include the schedule for reviews and audits.

Configuration Management

The plan will specify the relationship between the software quality assurance and configuration management programs. The procedures for assuring that the objectives of the configuration management program are being attained will be referenced or documented.

Testing

The plan will identify procedures to accomplish testability, review of test plans and procedures, review of test requirements and criteria, verification that tests are conducted in accordance with plans and procedures, certification of test results, review and certification of test reports, and assurance of the control of media and documentation to allow repeatability. Assurance is required that support software and hardware are acceptable.

Corrective Action

The plan will delineate procedures which assure documentation and reporting of deficiencies to appropriate management; analysis of defect data, problem reports and trends; and review of corrective measures for adequacy.

Subcontractor Control

The plan will describe methods for subcontractor control to assure receipt of procured software in conformance to contract requirements and the requirements of the software quality assurance specification.

The remaining paragraphs of the specification refer to contractual matters and the delivery of data and programs.

A SOFTWARE QUALITY ASSURANCE POLICY

As we had stated in Chapter 10, a company that will be producing computer software must formulate a policy of action and responsibilities for the control of quality of the product. To a large extent, such a policy can be derived from the standards just discussed. Indeed, for many companies, it is appropriate to refer to these standards in the policy. In any case, a software quality policy will reference — or possibly document — higher-level management directives which in broad terms describe the responsibilities, authorities, functions, and operations of the functional organizations of a company concerned with the production of software and the establishing of a software quality assurance program.

Promulgated by upper management, the policy will provide an ex cathedra summary of actions germane to the function of software quality assurance as prescribed by modern management practices, contractual requirements, and where applicable, external specifications (e.g., Mil-S-52779).

The policy will require that verification of each defined activity against the system requirements and the work previously performed is necessary to provide a reliable base of written documentation for the start of each progressive phase in the development of software. The policy will insist on adequate planning to minimize problems in the later stages of the development of software which may result in inefficiencies associated with testing, or may even require the reprogramming of portions of the software. The policy will be unequivocal in the establishment of software quality assurance as an integral part of the quality organization, charged with the mission of assuring the adequacy and quality of software design, documentation, test, and control in accordance with defined requirements and applicable specifications. It should be made clear that the satisfaction of these responsibilities will include the monitoring of design and test efforts, review of all formal documentation, and ongoing surveillance of software configuration control.

Beyond establishing that the prosecution of software development in conformance to the policy is intended to minimize costly rework and concomitant delays, the policy should include certain specific definitions of the software quality assurance activity. It should state that the adoption of cost-effective practices and procedures applies to all phases of software development and maintenance, including the establishment of the stability of support hardware and software resources. In the following example of how these specifics may be outlined, we have assumed an organization in which (as in Chapter 10) deliverable software is developed by engineering, and internal data processing systems by management information systems. We further assume, as is a common practice, a program management organization, independent of both engineering and management information systems, but responsible for the release of funds and cost control applicable to both.

1. System Design: A program requirements specification prepared by engineering or management information systems will be reviewed for completeness by software quality assurance prior to the onset of software design. This requirements specification will include, among other information, detailed hardware-software interface data, processor characteristics, identification of all processing tasks, equations, algorithms, accuracies, and processing response times, as applicable. Software quality assurance will document the findings of the review, report them to program management and engineering or management information systems, and follow up all deficiencies.

2. Software Top-Level Design: Software quality assurance will advise program management whether this phase should continue beyond 20 percent of its allocated funds pending corrective action on program requirements specification deficiencies.

   Design documentation that provides the basis for the top-level design review will include, as a minimum, a hierarchical decomposition of appropriate depth for each complete executable program, requirements specifications for each module so identified, memory and execution load budgets by module or function, and an outline of global data. Software quality assurance will document its findings, report them to program management and engineering or management information systems, and follow up all deficiencies.

3. Detailed Design: Software quality assurance will advise program management whether detailed design should continue beyond 20 percent of its allocated funds pending corrective action of the top-level design documentation deficiencies. Detailed design documentation, which forms the basis of the detailed design review, will principally be the exposition of the design of individual modules, including memory and load estimates and an analysis of computational accuracy, but will also include refinement of the data structure. Software quality assurance will document its findings, report them to program management and engineering or management information systems, and follow up all deficiencies.

4. Coding: Software quality assurance will advise program management whether coding, as applicable to each module, should continue beyond 20 percent of its allocated funds pending corrective action on the applicable detailed design review deficiencies.

   For the most part, software quality assurance will review coding only for compliance with coding standards and conventions. However, for modules critical to the success of the project, software quality assurance will conduct code inspections to affirm compliance with the design documentation. Software quality assurance will document its findings, report them to program management and engineering or management information systems, and follow up all deficiencies.

5. Test Plans and Procedures: Test plans will be reviewed by software quality assurance prior to the start of testing. Integration test procedures will be reviewed by software quality assurance prior to the start of integration. Qualification test procedures will be prepared by software quality assurance. The review of the integration test procedure will stress sufficient detail to permit the tracking of progress against quantified, planned milestones. In general, test plans and procedures will be reviewed to provide assurance that hardware and software resources are available, that system-build activities will be methodical, and that tests will be repeatable. Software quality assurance will document its findings of these reviews, report them to program management and engineering or management information systems, and follow up all deficiencies.

6. Testing: Software quality assurance will advise program management whether applicable test activity should commence pending corrective action on deficiencies found in the review of the plans and procedures pertinent to the test.

   During testing, other than qualification tests, software quality assurance will witness certain tests, certify that the tests were conducted in accordance with the procedures, and attest to the authenticity of recorded data. Software quality assurance will conduct qualification tests. Software quality assurance will follow up all deficiencies and their correction.

7. Defect Data: A starting test point will be established for each project, from which software quality assurance will collect defects and analyze trends, partly to determine progress in testing. To aid in the improvement of productivity and products, software quality assurance will evaluate the defects and classify

them by cause and type. Such classification will then be used by software quality assurance as the basis of quality improvement programs.

8. Configuration Control: Software quality assurance will review the configuration management and library control plans and will audit the actual configuration management and library control records to ensure traceability of tested and delivered programs back to source code and design documentation. These reviews and audits will also ensure consistency among design documents. Software quality assurance will document the results of its reviews and audits and will follow up all deficiencies.

The above example of the specifics to be included in a software quality assurance policy contained more detail than we hope will normally be necessary. Where the development and maintenance standards are properly documented, it is sufficient to simply state that conformance to these will be reviewed or audited. For example, rather than establishing the minimum contents of top-level design documentation, a policy can merely charge software quality assurance with the review of these per Standard Practice _____ .

With the establishment of a software quality policy to represent the committed support of top management, it becomes essential to initiate standard procedures for the application of software quality assurance disciplines designed to assure the implementation of the goals of the policy. In addition to documenting the mode of operations of software quality assurance, the procedures establish a common ground upon which software quality assurance and development can cooperate.

In Chapter 10, we identified a set of procedures representative of those that describe the day-to-day operations of software quality assurance. The content of these would be based on the concepts of Chapter 9, fashioned to conform to the type of software with which one is concerned and the development or maintenance practices in use. The procedures would, of course, reflect not only software methodology, but the traditional disciplines of quality control. The initial void which may have existed between the classically hardware-oriented quality control concepts and techniques and the newer field of computer software quality assurance has been bridged through the transfer of the methods of hardware quality assurance to those of software quality assurance. This is seen in the organization of the body of software quality concepts, techniques, and responsibilities into a set of procedures.

SOFTWARE QUALITY PLANS

With the issuance of a policy on software quality and the drafting of a set of software quality assurance procedures, software quality assurance knows what it has to do and the ground rules under which it will operate. Equally important, so does everyone else. Now it remains to do it. In the methodical tradition of quality, the means of implementing the policy and procedures is set forth in a software quality assurance plan for each project undertaken.

The software quality assurance plan will be a formal, planned approach to the application, for a specific project, of the established concepts, measures, and management requirements of software quality, to assure with sufficient confidence that system software will meet requirements at an established cost.

As we have previously stated, we do not presume to present a plan suitable for all types of software or development or maintenance environments. Still, it is possible to define the contents of a plan, even if only in a general way. These contents, which we are about to describe, are based on the preceding chapters of this book, but are couched in language and format derived from published standards — those listed a few pages ago as well as others (e.g., data item descriptions) published in support of these standards.

We would have a typical software quality plan encompass the following concepts and requirements:

General

Each of the software items to which the plan applies should be listed. For example, deliverable programs, support programs, deliverable documentation, test data. Applicable documents should be noted.

Definitions

The plan should provide adequate definition of nomenclature it will use which is peculiar to the plan, not universally known and understood, or susceptible to other valid interpretations. Examples of such are the terms "firmware," "test specification," and "module."

Quality Planning and Organization

The initial effort in setting up a software quality assurance program for a project will be directed to quality planning and organization. Accordingly, the responsibility and authority of personnel performing software quality functions and those responsible for liaison with customer or user representatives will be clearly defined. If at all possible, personnel will be named.

Software Support

The plan will describe provisions for identifying, documenting, and validating applicable software support tools used in development or maintenance. Positive control will be established over development processes and resources utilized. Examples of support tools are compilers, link editors, simulators, static analyzers, dynamic test probes, and library control tools.

Task Control

The plan will identify procedures to be used in preparing and issuing work instructions for all software tasks to be accomplished. Procedures to track work progress against approved schedules and resource allocations will be referenced in the plan. Typically, the procedures will include the following:

- Description of work to be performed
- Control of authorization for initiation of work
- Criteria for evaluation of work performed

Configuration Management

The plan will identify the configuration management procedures to be applied to software during all operations from the generation of the first documentation through completion. The procedures, which if not available for reference should be described in the plan, include the following:

- Identification of software documents and code files
- Release procedures
- Procedures for initiating changes
- Control of masters and validation of copies
- Storage and handling of software media
- Control of support software
- Provisions to ensure that nonconforming software is not integrated into the overall system
- Release of new versions and revisions
- Control of test materials and files
- Auditing of all configuration management procedures
- Constituency of the change control board

Software Documentation

The plan will identify the software documentation standards, coding conventions, and practices to be used. The plan will reference or describe the procedures by which documentation and code are reviewed for conformance to standards.

Design Reviews and Audits

The plan will reference the procedures to be used for design reviews and audits to evaluate design concepts and logic; ensure the fulfillment of requirements, completeness, and compliance with specified standards; and establish the traceability of initial stipulated requirements through successive design phases. A schedule for reviews and audits will be referenced or established in the plan. The procedures referenced or described will include the following:

- Descriptions of the objectives of each design review or audit

- Correlation of each review and audit with milestones established in the development or maintenance plan

- Methods for specifying nonscheduled reviews and audits

- Identification of personnel involved

- Identification of the specific material reviewed

- Provisions for the recording of minutes

Testing

The plan will identify all software quality program requirements related to software testing and integration. To satisfactorily control the quality of testing, it is essential that test documentation such as test plans and procedures be employed. The elements of test planning include the following:

- Definition of the levels of testing that will be used, and the objectives of each. Typically, these may include unit tests, integration tests, qualification tests, system level tests, and acceptance tests

- Determination of the criteria to be used for declaring tests complete

- Procedures for scheduling and conducting tests

- Retention of the results of tests

- Identification of hardware and software resources and techniques that will be used

Software quality program measures will include the following:

- Review of test requirements and criteria for adequacy, feasibility, and traceability

- Review of test documentation to determine compliance with contractual or internal requirements

- Verification that tests are conducted in accordance with approved test plans and procedures and that the software is of the correct version and revision

- Provision for witnessing tests and/or certifying that recorded data were valid

- Review of test procedures to assure repeatability

- Provisions for regression testing after changes

- Provision for review and certification of test reports

- Direction of qualification testing activities

Corrective Action

The plan will reference or document procedures for the prompt detection, documentation, and correction of software problems and deficiencies. The procedures will provide for the following:

- Documenting and reporting problems and deficiencies to appropriate software personnel and management

- Analysis of data and examination of problem and deficiency reports to determine their extent and cause

- Analysis of trends in performance of work to ensure compliance with standards

- Review of corrective measures to ensure that problems and deficiencies have been resolved and that such resolution is correctly reflected in appropriate documents

- All necessary retesting to validate modifications to any item of software as a result of corrective action. This includes regression testing as noted under *Testing*, above.

Acquisition Control

The plan will reference or document the procedures to be implemented to ensure that all software acquired from suppliers conforms to applicable requirements of the contract or internal standards. The plan will identify "off-the-shelf" purchased software that will be validated prior to use, the provisions for so doing, and the associated documentation that is subject to validation. For software acquired under contract or subcontract, the plan will identify the methods and procedures used for the following:

- Control of acquisition documentation (e.g., purchase order provisions)

- Evaluation of facilities and capabilities to determine selection of suppliers. This includes evaluation of software quality assurance programs.

- Surveillance of contractor or subcontractor operations

- Evaluation of acceptability of software delivered by the contractor or subcontractor

Records

The plan will describe the records to be established and used to provide objective evidence and traceability of operations to assure and demonstrate compliance with contractual or internal requirements. The description will include the procedures and responsibilities for initiation, validation, and retention of such records.

It may appear that the preparation of a software quality plan requires an untoward amount of effort and the production of too many pages of information. Actually, much of the plan for a given project will be common to a whole family of similar projects, and a significant amount of the plan can be copied from boiler plate. Also, well-documented operating procedures allow a considerable part of the plan to consist of little more than an identification of where in the development or maintenance phase they will be used. Finally, there is nothing to suggest that a large part of the information that should be documented cannot be presented graphically.

The Plan as a Working Document

Let us summarize the chain of documentation defining software quality assurance. We may, or may not, have an externally applied specification (e.g., Mil-S-52779A) to define the software quality assurance requirements. In either case, there should be a policy outlining the scope of software quality assurance, conforming, if applicable, to the external specification. The policy, in turn, inspires a set of operating procedures to be shaped by quality plans for application to specific projects. This is summarized in Figure 11-1.

In Chapter 10, we listed a set of operating procedures appropriate to many environments. We list them again, but with the addition of identification numbers, which we shall need shortly.

SP 1   System design review

SP 2   Software requirements specification review

SP 3   Top-level design review

SP 4   Module design review

SP 5   Review of integration test plan

SP 6   Code inspection

SP 7   Review of test procedures

SP 8   Documentation standards audit

SP 9   Configuration control audit (including library control)

SP 10   Test audit

SP 11   Standard for qualification plan

SP 12   Defect collection, analysis, and feedback

SP 13   Quality evaluation

SP 14   Tool certification

SP 15   Vendor survey and surveillance

SP 16   Disposition of program trouble reports

SP 17   Record retention and control

A plan prepared along the general lines just presented, referencing the above procedures, was the basis for the software quality program in support of the development and initial operational phase of a military system in which the role of embedded software was prominent.

Figure 11-2 depicts this program. The major milestones are shown in circles. There were, of course, milestones less significant to the overall project, but key

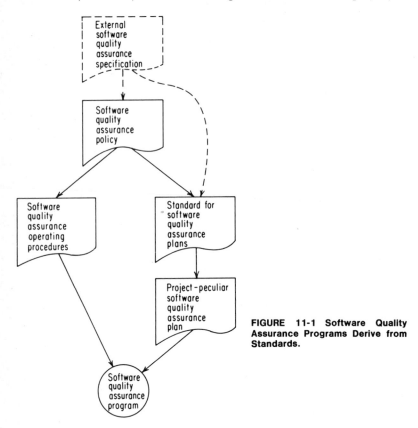

FIGURE 11-1 Software Quality Assurance Programs Derive from Standards.

to the tracking and auditing of software progress. These included the design of the major components of the software, incremental stages of integration, and the like. In Figure 11-2, the software quality assurance operating procedures (underscored) were applied where shown. It may be noted that the requirement for some support software, most expediently available from subcontractors, was anticipated in the proposal phase and more accurately defined during the system design phase. The early recognition of the requirement came in response to a question raised by software quality assurance.

A more complete diagram of the project would have shown other activities as well: hardware design, changes to design documentation during testing, the

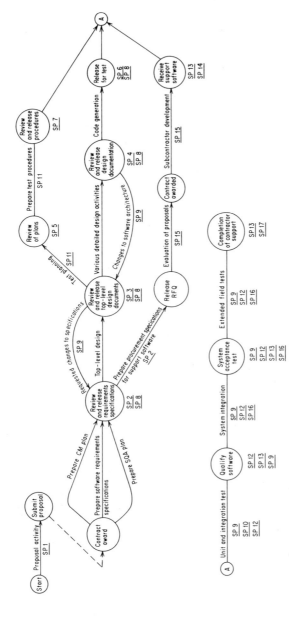

FIGURE 11-2 A Software Quality Assurance Program Applied to Embedded Software.

293

application of the software quality assurance procedures to modification cycles (which iterate the development cycle) during field test, and incremental record retention prior to delivery.

Of all the concerns of software management, the one for which it can most look for help from quality is that of planning and the subsequent adherence to plans. This requires documentation: standards, procedures, and the actual plans. Software quality assurance's documentation of its own activity serves the further purpose of leading by example.

SUMMARY

1. Software quality assurance requirements have been formally defined by the DOD and its branches, the FAA, NATO, and the IEEE. There is considerable commonality among these standards, symptomatic of software quality assurance's evolving maturity.

2. Upper management can document its expectations of software quality assurance and of the cooperation of other functions in a policy expressly defining the responsibilities and authority of software quality assurance.

3. Software quality plans implement the purposes of management's policy in the prosecution of specific projects. A standard for the contents of a plan is also a further definition of the role of software quality assurance.

4. Software quality plans and procedures are realized in a software quality program through the methodical application of the precepts of software quality assurance.

Part Five
Toward Quantifiable Standards

Chapter 12

Reliability and the Measurement of Goodness

Among the attributes of computer software, the first that commands the attention of quality is the degree to which the software can be depended upon to perform its function. We shall label this attribute, "reliability." Until a new operating system is fixed so that it no longer causes disk read-write heads to crash against the mechanical stops, the console operators think of the software as being unreliable. An airplane pilot who discovers that the recently installed (and software-driven) area navigation system gives course fixes that are in error by as much as 5 mi regards that system as unreliable. The extent to which software is not reliable is a function of the bugs embedded within it or the inconsistencies between it and the purposes for which it was intended. In short, unreliability is an effect of defects.

Thus, quality has an interest in measuring reliability, and not just assessing it qualitatively (good, adequate, poor, disastrous). Seldom, however, can reliability — or some quantity related to reliability — be arrived at simply by counting the number of defects in the software, for the simple reason that known defects are generally removed at or shortly after their discovery. Moreover, even if we were to know precisely the number of defects, we might not know the frequency with which the code segments harboring them were exercised, thus making reliability — in the sense of the distribution of the frequency of failure — an inexact calculation. Nevertheless, defects, and the history of the detection of defects, open the door to the quantification of what it is that we intuitively consider as software reliability.

This business of quantifying the characteristic of software that is most identified with its quality is of considerably more than casual interest. If the reliability of software can be described by a simple number, or set of numbers, or an equation for generating an indefinably large set of numbers, we should be able to determine its acceptability as a completed product in much the way we accept (or reject) other products. If we define the reliability of a complex system (i.e., one comprising many individual parts, as does a pinball machine, a computer, or a jet engine) as the probability that it will operate successfully during some interval of time, then it is possible, based on the tests made of it, to use standard techniques of statistical inference to calculate the confidence* one has that the reliability lies between some predefined minimum value and 1. If one has, say, 20 percent confidence that the minimum has been achieved, one is disposed to reject the item. If one has 98 percent confidence, it is reasonable to accept it. One can go further and define a middle ground which calls for further testing; delaying the accept or reject decision, or in the specific instance of software, giving further opportunity to detect and remove defects.

There is a recursive quality to the reference to complex systems just presented. What if a complex system contains both hardware and embedded software? The classical method of predicting hardware reliability entails the summing of failure rates† for each of the elements (motors, electronic components, microprocessors, etc.) of the system. To properly estimate the reliability of systems in which processors are embedded, however, one cannot ignore the potential for failure of the software resident in the processors. If we define the reliability of the system as the probability that it will perform its intended function over a specific operating time in a specified environment, we may compute its value as the product of the reliability of the hardware and the reliability of the software. The bulk of this chapter is concerned with techniques for quantifying software reliability. They should be of special interest to those whose responsibilities currently include the estimation of the reliability of complex systems.

Independently of the use of software reliability estimation in calculating systems reliability, there is much value in quantifying reliability for the development of software acceptability standards. In Chapter 7 we offered a simple technique to determine when sufficient testing had been done to establish the acceptability of software. We suggested that the criteria include the achievement of some minimum elapsed time between several successive failures, given random data as test stimuli. While this is a more thoughtful technique than is usually applied, it lacks any semblance of having a mathematical or scientific foundation. The fact that the software passed the test gives us no quantifiable confidence of its reliability or of the number of defects that it may still contain.

Whether for the determination of the reliability of complex systems, the acceptability of software, or of the need for further testing, attaching reliability numbers to a computer program requires an estimation of the probability den-

---

*On the bayesian face of the coin, some might prefer to think in terms of pure probabilistic determinations.

†MIL-HDBK-217C,[23] which we shall return to in the discussion of the nonhomogeneous Poisson process, is a common source of published failure data.

sity function of its failure modality; in other words, the construction of a failure model for the software. (In fact, as we shall see, most of the models that have been developed are actually descriptive of defects, not failures, but for the moment this is of small importance.) Thus, we find that the search for quantifiable standards of software reliability is inextricably bound with the modeling of software. As will become apparent, for a variety of reasons, abstracting software behavior in the form of a model remains an inexact science. This is curious, since modeling is one of the historical uses of computers. For as many years as we have had computing machinery, we have had software models developed for the purpose of investigating physical, biological, economic, and psychological processes. Of greater pertinence, we have had models that provide information to assist in arriving at management decisions. Software itself seems to be the least modeled of the likely subjects.

The models that are of primary interest to us are those that are founded on the failure history of software, and, in particular, those that model failure in the time domain and without regard to the structure of the software. However, before introducing these we shall consider models of other types, each of which bears upon the problem of reliability in one manner or another, and which, taken in the aggregate, provide useful background to the problem of estimating reliability from actual test data. It should be noted that in our exposition of these, and the later models as well, we make no attempt to provide all of the information available for each model. Our purpose is to acquaint the manager with the scope, constraints, and application of the models. Ample references are given to allow readers to gather information adequate to help them use any model that seems appropriate to their needs and programming or testing environment.

MODELING WITH KNOWLEDGE OF THE CODE

We have previously stated that complexity is inconsistent with software quality. Much of Chapter 5 was given to an exposition of the approaches to attacking complexity. The salient effect of complexity is its encouragement of the implantation of hidden defects. If one has a measure of complexity, one also has grounds for improving the estimates of the amount of time that should be allocated for the test and debugging effort. Further, programs that have a greater measure of complexity than their size would suggest are good candidates for unusually intensive testing at the nodes and paths end of the strategic test space.

McCabe's Complexity Model

To model complexity, it is first necessary to define the earmarks of complexity. Thomas McCabe[1] has couched the concept of complexity entirely within the decision structure of a program. This has considerable intuitive appeal and also correlates well with experience in defect-prone programs. The model that represents complexity is expressed by the simple equation

$$V(G) = e - n + 2p$$

where $V(G)$ = the cyclomatic number of classical graph theory, and, as used here, is the measure of complexity
e = the number of edges in the program
n = the number of vertices
p = the number of connected components

These terms bear further definition. The *vertices* of classical graph theory are translated into the processing nodes, including decision points, of software. The *edges* represent the paths between the nodes, and are directed (i.e., unidirectional). That is, if program flow can be bidirectional between two nodes, they are connected by two edges. We may consider each module in a program as a unique component. To illustrate the model, Figure 12-1 presents the cyclomatic number for three familiar constructs.

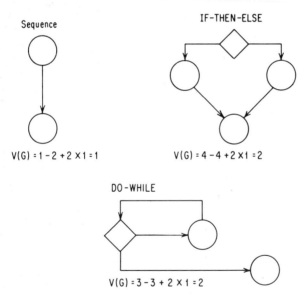

FIGURE 12-1 **McCabe Cyclomatic Numbers.**

As one of the uses of his cyclomatic model, McCabe suggests a criterion for maximum module complexity. As we had stated back in Chapter 5, there is a disquieting trend toward limiting module size to some arbitrary number of statements, a move founded in the erroneous belief that this will achieve true modularity. As a much more reasonable alternative, McCabe recommends that modules be limited to cyclomatic complexities of 10.

McCabe's is one of many models presented in summary form in a publication of the Data and Analysis Center for Software (DACS) of Rome Air Development Center.[2] Although the report does not attempt to provide more information than the bare facts of each model, its 150-odd pages represent a comprehensive survey of cost, complexity, and reliability models. A survey restricted to reliability models is that of Swearingen and Donahoo.[3] Unlike the DACS report, this is less an outline of the models than an attempt to provide some insight into their properties.

Halstead Measures

The model developed by the late Maurice Halstead provides several outputs useful for predicting the course and consequences of software development.[2,4] There are only four parameters that form the basis for the model:

n_1 the number of distinct operators (instruction types, keywords, etc.) in a program

n_2 the number of distinct operands (variables and constants)

N_1 the total number of occurrences of the operators

N_2 the total number of occurrences of the operands

Halstead defines the *vocabulary* of a program to be

$$n = n_1 + n_2$$

He defines the *observed length* of the program to be

$$N = N_1 + N_2$$

Several of the model outputs are based on the *volume V* of the program (the number of bits required to specify it),

$$V = N \log_2 n$$

Halstead's concept of software science includes the mental processes of computer programmers. He defines a parameter E as the number of discriminations made in the preparation of a program, and E_0 as the mean number of discriminations made between the commission of errors.

Combining E_0 with V, we find the estimated number of bugs resident within the program prior to testing:

$$\hat{B} = K \frac{V}{E_0}$$

where K is a constant.

Independent estimates have empirically estimated that E_0 ranges between

3000 and 3200.[5] The use of a single point constant such as this, uncalibrated for a specific programmer working on a specific type of application in a specific programming environment, does not recommend $\hat{B}$ for use as a determinant in seeking bugs. We would not expect to see the responsible project manager order that the testing continue until the last of the $\hat{B}$ bugs has been exposed. Nevertheless, it is a useful number for roughly estimating the length of time over which debugging will take place. If experience indicates that bugs are removed at the rate of, say, 300 per month, then given a $\hat{B}$ of 600, we can suspect ahead of time that the two weeks allocated for development testing will be woefully inadequate.

As an alternative formula for estimating $\hat{B}$, one not requiring an estimate of K, we have

$$B = \frac{E^{2/3}}{E_0}$$

To estimate E, we first define V' as the volume of the most compact (highest language level) representation of the program. The Halstead model includes the calculation

$$E = \frac{V^2}{V'}$$

Statistical Prediction

Models have also been developed for presumptive prediction of defects based on more detailed characteristics of the program, specifically, characteristics measured in terms of the frequencies of statement types. The method followed in both studies described next was to tabulate the failure history of actual programs and their characteristics (size, number of I/O statements, etc.), and to then perform multiple linear regression analyses to isolate the key factors and to use their regression coefficients in the final linear equations.

In research conducted by R. W. Motley and W. D. Brooks[6] on a large set of data samples, regression analyses were performed for the prediction of the number of faults in a program and also for the fault occurrence rate per program. The study produced far too many sets of output of varying consistency to summarize here, save to note that fault prediction was more nearly successful than that of rate. Also, considerable variation from program to program suggests that functional differences among the programs, programming language, the test environment, and the overall personnel-management environment influence the effect of the structural elements used as independent variables.

In another study, Lipow and Thayer[7] used nine independent variables. These did not include the total number of statements, since the researchers were more interested in the variables that constituted the total number. In the following list of the variables used, all but the first four were not quickly eliminated on the basis of statistical zero influence coefficients:

- Number of branches

- Number of calls to application routines

- A complexity measure based upon the number and levels of nesting of IF statements

- Number of assignment statements not involving arithmetic operations

- A loop complexity measure based on the number of levels of nesting

- Number of calls to system or support routines

- Number of I/O statements

- Number of assignment statements involving arithmetic operations

- Number of nonexecutable statements (but not including comments)

R^2, the square of the multiple correlation coefficient, was calculated as .967 when using only the first four variables. Using a stepwise minimization process, Lipow and Thayer then reduced the number of variables to just the first one, with R^2 reduced by only .088 to a value of .959, thus suggesting that the number of branches alone provides a good predictor. Indeed, it appeared to be a better predictor than the total number of statements, for which the researchers computed an R^2 of .941.

Although the number of faults and a measure of complexity are not the same thing, they are related, and it is instructive to compare Lipow and Thayer's conclusion with McCabe's premise that complexity is a function of only the decision structure of a program.

It is difficult to conclude from these two studies, or from other research on the subject that we have seen, more than is intuitively apparent. Nevertheless, it is quite possible that analysis of a large body of data pertaining to one's unique and stable software environment might offer a basis for statistically acceptable early indications of the debugging effort that will be necessary.

Further Modeling of Structural Properties

Although much of the modeling interest at the level of knowledge of the code is concerned with complexity and its consequences or with correlation between statement types and the commission of errors, some thought has also been given to the failure generation process in terms of software architecture.

As an example of this, we have the models developed by B. Littlewood that consider the reliability of individual modules and of the switching between them.

Littlewood assumes the failure process of each module to be Poisson,* that transfers of control between modules are subject to failure, and that these transfers can be described in terms of Markov processes. Although his earlier work considered the transfer between modules i and j as finite state Markov processes with constant transition rate, the semi-Markov model[8] permits the sojourn time within a module to be a random variable of any appropriate distribution characteristic of that module and the destination module.

Given the reasonable assumption that there will be many transfers between successive program failures, Littlewood posits a failure point process that is asymptotically a Poisson process, for which the rate parameter can be computed. The variables in the computation for the rate parameter include the following:

- The probability of transfer from module i to module j

- The probability of failure of that transfer

- The failure rate of each module

- The mean of the sojourn time distribution of module i prior to invoking module j

These input parameters are not easily estimated, at least not to a credibility sufficient for use in accept or reject decisions. What we find most interesting, however, is the development of a rationale for using the Poisson failure law for software, without regard to the input data stream. For the most part, work in reliability modeling has been oriented toward real-time computation,† in which one could quite easily model Poisson processes based on the random nature in regard to time of the input data. However, Littlewood's work suggests that the Poisson failure law may be more generally applicable to any modular software. To the extent that the individual modules of a software system may be likened to the components of a large hardware system, Littlewood points out that we can view his results as analogous to the arguments of hardware reliability theory for justifying exponential failure laws for certain complex devices.

---

*This assumption is shared by most models, at the level of the entire program, usually as a result of the input data stream randomness. More, shortly.

†A list of references at the end of this chapter indicates that much of the work accomplished has been sponsored by the Rome Air Development Center, whose primary interest in software is in the programs embedded in military instrumentation systems.

MODELING THE SOFTWARE BLACK BOX

The models that are of direct interest to software quality assurance are those whose parameters can be estimated on the basis of the previous failure history of the software in question. Such models require no presumptive knowledge of the failure mechanisms peculiar to the program. The proof of the pudding is derived solely from its performance.

The basis of such faithful models is the expectation that the complex stochastic process from which failures arise can be described with a (necessarily) limited set of descriptors deducible from performance alone. This is expecting quite a bit, even if one is not so optimistic as to hope to find a single model applicable to all programs. Nevertheless, the models look at macroscopic failure parameters, with each model founded on a set of premises purported to predicate the failure history. Common to all of these models is the one premise that software failures can be described by a probability distribution. We have, then, models of a number of distinct types, representing diverse assumptions of software fault exposure and of the testing and debugging environment. Underlying most of these is the confidence that as testing continues, reliability grows, although several of the models we shall introduce can reflect a less constructive debugging process.

Some researchers choose to distinguish estimation models from measurement models. They consider estimation as a result that can be obtained by tracking and abstracting failure history during development, measurement as an activity that takes place in the program's operational environment or, perhaps, during formal test and evaluation. We see the essential difference in the evaluation of the input data used to generate failures; models designed expressly for measurement will emphasize realistic representation of the operational input data space. Nevertheless, considering the present status of model development and the appropriate management of test planning, we do not see why estimation or reliability growth models cannot be considered as instruments for measurement. Indeed, as a class, these models are the ones furthest developed, and are the only ones we shall discuss in any detail.

As the models are described, it may be noted that a one-to-one correspondence appears to be implied between software failures and software faults (or defects). That is, removal of a single defect will prevent a specific failure from recurring. This is somewhat incorrect. Our experience has shown that from time to time a given defect can cause two quite different failures in the same run. We have also seen failures that result from the concerted mischief of two independent defects. For those models that estimate reliability solely on the number of defects detected, the implication of one defect per failure and one potential failure mode per defect would appear to be a source of estimating error. However, considering the approximations inherent in most of the premises on which the models are founded, the occasional departure from single-defect–single-failure causality will exert a secondary effect, at most.

All models require input. Among the set of input data that these models operate on are the failure history as a function of calendar time (hours, days, etc.) or operational time (basically the same as computer time), debugging times, estimated initial fault counts, fault correction rates, error generation rates, and other data reflecting the software or the debugging environment. The various outputs are even more diverse. They include the number of remaining defects, number of initial defects (or an update of an initial estimation), probability density function for failures, reliability as a function of time, calendar time to remove the remaining faults, MTTF, and other statistics reflecting the capabilities of the individual models.

That an abstraction of the failure process of a program in a given test management milieu can produce a numeric result is not quite the same as proving the statistical validity of that result. Since these models operate on observed behavior alone, and not on the fault mechanisms of the software, results that are not solely recapitulations of the observations must be subject to interpretation, none more so than MTTF. We use it as an example. Mean time to failure is a single number of venerable importance in the material world where there are random physical or biological processes (molecular migration, the feeding habits of termites, etc.) that in the aggregate can govern observed failure phenomena. There are also systems of so great a number of independent parts, each subject to failure from latent defects or stress, that they, too, fail in accordance with well-behaved (Poisson) statistical patterns. However, software failures, especially at such time as the defect population has been reduced to the relatively small number we would expect when we might become interested in using time-to-failure as an accept or reject criterion, are another matter. Some might argue that the number of discrete states the software is capable of remains enormously high regardless of the number of faults, but each state is subject to failure only if it can be adversely affected by a defect. In short, the use of any single-point statistical inference drawn from these models must be used with care in order not to impute to it more significance than the number really has.

With this caveat, we are almost ready to look at representative models, which, taken as a group, reflect the state at which reliability modeling has arrived. A matter of notation first, however. For those models incorporating both calendar time and computer operating time, we shall use t to denote the former and τ, the latter. This is opposite to the notation used by Shooman, who has contributed to several of the models that will be described, but will permit consistency with all of the first group of models — of which the Shooman exponential model is the only one accommodating operation time — without intimidating the nonmathematically disposed reader with an excess of Greek letters.

Shooman Exponential Model

This is not only one of the earliest reliability models, it is also one that has influenced the development of several others. Further information can be found in a number of sources.[2,3,9–12]

Shooman suggests that the failure data be gathered in test series run every week or so, starting at the beginning of the integration phase.* Thus, the model's application does not require continuous defect collection during debugging.

The model assumes that each fault is corrected within the interval in which it is detected, and that no new defects are introduced. The total number of machine instructions remains constant, permitting the model parameters to be normalized to the size of the program, an implication that the model is suitable for programs of all sizes.

The *hazard function* (failure rate) from which the model is developed is

$$z(\tau) = C\epsilon_r(t)$$

where τ = operating time
t = elapsed time (development or debugging time)
ϵ_r = the number of faults remaining

In other words, the hazard function assumes that failure rate is proportional to the number of remaining faults. This is arguable. It is true if there are a large number of bugs and they are randomly distributed throughout the program with respect to the input data. However, as integration proceeds and most bugs are flushed out, it is unlikely that practical experience can be depended upon to consistently bear out the premise in a test environment of limited input data space.

We shall also define, for this and other models as well, some more terms:

- Reliability: $R(t) = P\{$no failures in interval 0 to $t\}$
- Cumulative distribution function of failures (cdf): $F(t) = 1 - R(t)$
- Frequency, or probability density function (pdf): $f(t) = \dfrac{dF(t)}{dt}$

And more rigorously, we define the hazard function $Z(t)$ to be the probability density function of time to failure, given the fact that failure did not occur prior to t. The condition on prior failure distinguishes $Z(t)$ from $f(t)$. From these,

$$Z(t) = \frac{f(t)}{R(t)} = -\frac{1}{R(t)}\frac{dR(t)}{dt}$$

*Although, unlike Shooman, model-makers have generally neglected to say so, the estimation models really apply to programs with all their working parts in place.

From which

$$R(t) = \exp - \left[\int_0^t z(x) \, dx \right]$$

Normalizing ϵ_r to the number of instructions (I_T),

$$\epsilon_r(t) = \frac{E_T}{I_T} - \epsilon_c(t)$$

where E_T = total number of faults at $t = 0$
 $\epsilon_c(t)$ = number of faults corrected in the interval t, normalized with respect to I_T
 $\epsilon_r(t)$ = normalized number remaining

Substituting the equations for $\epsilon_r(t)$ and $Z(\tau)$ into the expression for the reliability function, Shooman derives

$$R(\tau, t) = \exp \left\{ -C \left[\frac{E_T}{I_T} - \epsilon_c(t) \right] \tau \right\}$$

Further, defining MTTF $= \displaystyle\int_0^\infty R(t) \, dt$, he derives

$$\text{MTTF}(t) = \frac{1}{C[(E_T/I_T) - \epsilon_c(t)]}$$

Note that MTTF is a function of elapsed time only.

The reliability function shows reliability to decrease exponentially between debug intervals. To some, this may seem contrariwise to intuition, which suggests that the longer one observes failure-free performance, the more trust one has in the software (or, for that matter, hardware). On the other hand, given the expectancy that there are faults still hidden in the program, a plausible argument can be raised that the longer one tests with random input, the closer one comes to the time that one of the defects must be exposed.

It remains to estimate the constants E_T and C. Generally, the constants that must be calculated in the reliability models are found by curve fitting techniques or by maximum likelihood estimation (MLE).* The MLE equations

---

*The use of MLE is a common practice of reliability engineering.[13,14] For the purpose of definition, we consider the case of estimation of a single parameter. Given a random sample $x_1, \ldots, x_n$ from a population of pdf $f(x, \theta)$, one seeks an estimator $\hat{\theta}$ for the parameter θ. The *likelihood function of the sample*, defined as

$$L(x_1, \ldots, x_n; \theta) = f(x_1; \theta) \ldots f(x_n; \theta)$$

is the a priori probability of obtaining the x_i that constitute the observed sample. MLE then resolves to the determination of that θ that maximizes L.

used by Craig et al.[12] in their study are

$$\hat{C} = \frac{\displaystyle\sum_{i=1}^{k} n_i}{\displaystyle\sum_{i=1}^{k} [\hat{E}_T/I_T - \epsilon_c(t_i)]\, H_i}$$

$$\hat{C} = \frac{\displaystyle\sum_{i=1}^{k} n_i/[\hat{E}_T/I_T - \epsilon_c(t_i)]}{\displaystyle\sum_{i=1}^{k} H_i}$$

where there are k ($k \geq 2$) tests following the debugging intervals $(0, t_1)$, $(0, t_2)$, ..., $(0, t_k)$, n_i is the number of runs terminating in failure in the ith test, and H_i is the total time of all runs in the ith test.

Jelinski-Moranda De-eutrophication Model

Another of the early models, one which also has given rise to several others, is the de-eutrophication model,[2,3,11,12,15,16] so named for the estimation of reliability during the period in which the software is cleansed — of bugs, presumably, rather than of algae and water lilies. Unlike the Shooman model, the Jelinski-Moranda model requires removal of each defect as soon as it is detected. Like the Shooman model, indeed most of the models, it assumes all the bugs in the program are equally likely to cause a failure in the testing environment.

The model also assumes that the failure rate is a Poisson process and proportional to the number of remaining defects. Finally, as do most models, this one assumes no new defects will be introduced.

The hazard rate, constant between failures, is

$$Z(t_i) = \phi\, [N - (i - 1)]$$

for the time between the $(i - 1)$st and ith failures. N is the initial number of faults and ϕ is a proportionality constant. Both ϕ and N must be calculated (estimated).

The reliability function is

$$R(t_i) = \exp\,[-\phi(N - n)\, t_i]$$

where t_i = elapsed time between $(i - 1)$st and ith failures
$\quad\quad n$ = number of defects removed by $(i - 1)$st interval

As in the Shooman model, this is of the form $R(t) = e^{-\alpha t}$, from which $MTTF = 1/\alpha$, or

$$MTTF = \frac{1}{\phi(N - n)}$$

N and ϕ can be estimated by MLE with the following equations:

$$\sum_{i=1}^{n} \frac{1}{\hat{N} - (i - 1)} = \frac{n}{\hat{N} - \left[\sum_{i=1}^{n}(i - 1)X_i\right]\bigg/ T}$$

and

$$\phi = \frac{n}{\hat{N}T - \sum_{i=1}^{n}(i - 1)X_i}$$

where $X_1, \ldots, X_n$ are the elapsed times between successive failures and $T = \sum_{i=1}^{n} X_i$.

On a suggestion of Lipow, Alan Sukert modified the model to permit the detection of more than one fault in a given debugging period. This changes the MLE solution[2] to

$$\sum_{i=1}^{M} \frac{m_i}{\hat{N} - n_{i-1}} = \sum_{i=1}^{M} \hat{\phi} t_i$$

and

$$\frac{n}{\hat{\phi}} = \sum_{i=1}^{M}(\hat{N} - n_{i-1})t_i$$

where M = total number of time intervals
$\quad m_i$ = number of defects found in ith time interval
$\quad n$ = number of defects found to date
$\quad n_i$ = cumulative number of defects found through ith interval

Although in the early stages of debug and test, defects are nearly always removed directly after they have made their presence known, the assumption of more than one failure per time interval reflects practices where a program is restarted directly after a crash, as in evaluation testing or any testing where failures are not observable except by analysis undertaken after the conclusion of the test interval. Thus, the Lipow-Sukert modifications of this model and of two yet to be introduced contribute to the usability of the basic models.

Geometric De-eutrophication Model

Many persons may choose to quarrel with the last model's assumption of equal likelihood of detection of all faults and of a constrained number of initial defects. These are partially alleviated by assuming that the failure rates of successive time intervals will decrease geometrically, rather than by a constant amount. The difference between the de-eutrophication model and its geometric variant[2,3,11,16] is illustrated by Figure 12-2.

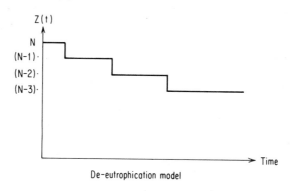

De-eutrophication model

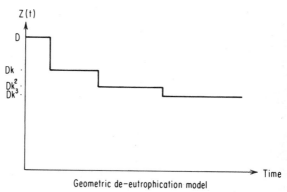

Geometric de-eutrophication model

FIGURE 12-2

The decrease in step size reflects the premise that the bugs detected earlier tended to be located in the more frequently traversed paths, thus being vulnerable to exposure.

To reflect the geometric progression, the hazard rate is defined as

$$Z(t) = Dk^{i-1}$$

for the ith interval. D and k, the initial failure rate and failure rate step ratio, respectively, are to be calculated (estimated) from the collected data.

This leads to a reliability estimate

$$R(t_i) = \exp(-Dk^n t_i)$$

where t_i = elapsed time of ith interval
$\quad\quad n$ = total number of time intervals

Also derived is

$$\text{MTTF} = \frac{1}{Dk^n}$$

It is observed that the initial number of defects does not enter into the calculations.

The MLE calculation of D and k is given by

$$\frac{n}{\hat{D}} = \sum_{i=1}^{n} \hat{k}^{i-1} t_i$$

and

$$\frac{1}{k \sum\limits_{i=1}^{n} (i-1)} = \hat{D} \sum_{i=1}^{n} (i-1)\hat{k}^{i-2} t_i$$

where t_i is the length of the ith interval, as before.

As was the case with the basic de-eutrophication model, the geometric model has been modified by Sukert[17] to permit more than one fault detection per time interval.

Schick-Wolverton Model

There are several similarities between the Schick-Wolverton[2,3,11,18] model and the Jelinski-Moranda de-eutrophication model. Both assume a fixed number of initial defects (no new ones may be introduced during debugging), and both assume but one fault detection per time period. However, whereas the Jelinski-Moranda model assumes that the time between failures is exponentially distributed, the Schick-Wolverton model assumes a Rayleigh distribution. This derives from the hazard function

$$Z(t_i) = \phi[N - (i - 1)]t_i$$

where t_i is the duration of the ith interval.

This is identical to the Jelinski-Moranda function, except for the additional factor t_i. (For that matter, it is quite nearly the same as the Shooman hazard function, save for the inclusion of t_i.) Whether or not having the failure rate increase as the time between the $(i - 1)$st and ith failure is more plausible than a constant hazard rate may be argued. Nevertheless, the Rayleigh distribution of debugging intervals to which it gives rise does more nearly reflect the experiences of many of the effects of nonconstant staffing levels during defect removal.

The reliability function is

$$R(t_i) = \exp\left\{-\phi\,[N - (i - 1)]\,\frac{t_i^2}{2}\right\} \qquad \text{(Rayleigh)}$$

and

$$\text{MTTF} = \left\{\frac{\pi}{2\phi[N - (i - 1)]}\right\}^{1/2}$$

N and ϕ can be found by MLE from

$$\hat{N} = \frac{2n/\phi + \sum\limits_{i=1}^{n} (i - 1)t_i^2}{\sum\limits_{i=1}^{n} t_i^2}$$

and

$$\hat{\phi} = \sum_{i=1}^{n} \frac{2}{N - (i - 1)} \frac{1}{\sum\limits_{i=1}^{n} t_i^2}$$

for n time intervals.

The time required to find all of the remaining faults is given by

$$\hat{T} = \frac{\sum\limits_{i=1}^{N-n} 1/i}{\phi}$$

with variance

$$\hat{V} = \frac{\sum\limits_{i=1}^{N-n} 1/i^2}{\phi^2}$$

As he did for the Jelinski-Moranda de-eutrophication and geometric de-eutrophication models, Sukert, on a suggestion by Lipow, modified the Schick-Wolverton model to permit more than one defect removal per time period.[2] The assumption that each interval is marked by a single failure is replaced by the assumption of a constant hazard rate during the time interval, with the rate proportional to the number of defects in the system at the start of the interval and the cumulative test time through half of the interval. This last comprises the total test time up to the interval start, plus a representation of the average search time in the current period. Thus,

$$Z(t_i) = (N - n_{i-1}) \left(T_{i-1} + \frac{t_i}{2} \right)$$

where n_{i-1} and T_{i-1} are the cumulative number of defects found and the time consumed prior to the current interval.

This leads to

$$R(t_i) = \exp \left[-\phi(N - n) \left(T_{i-1} t_i + \frac{t_i^2}{4} \right) \right]$$

The MLE solution for N and ϕ is

$$\sum_{i=1}^{M} \frac{m_i}{N - n_{i-1}} = \sum_{i=1}^{M} t_i \left(T_{i-1} + \frac{t_i}{2} \right)$$

and

$$\frac{n}{\phi} = \sum_{i=1}^{M} (N - n_{i-1}) t_i \left(T_{i-1} + \frac{t_i}{2} \right)$$

with m_i and M defined as in the extended Jelinski-Moranda model.

Musa Execution Time Model

The model[2,3,18,19,20] is based on the premise that reliability estimations in the time domain can be based only on actual execution time, as opposed to elapsed, or calender time, since it is only during execution that software is exposed to failure-provoking stress. Actually, the model consists of two components: one in execution time to model failure probability, and one in calendar time for estimating correction and further test activity relative to planning constraints. In its basic form, Musa recommends that the model not be applied until integration has been completed, that is, when all the modules are in place.

Execution Time Component The key assumptions are, in the main, familiar. Failure intervals are s-independent and Poisson-distributed. The execution time between failures is piecewise exponentially distributed, and the failure rate is proportional to the number of remaining defects. There remains one important assumption that introduces a new concept: Defects do not have to be corrected at the same rate, or at the same average rate, as failure rates occur. Musa does, however, assume a constant ratio of the two rates, which he calls the *fault reduction factor B*.

Ignoring, for the moment, the creation of new faults, the hazard rate is

$$Z(t) = fK(N_0 - n)$$

where f = average instruction execution rate divided by total number of instructions

$\quad$ K = proportionality constant to relate defect exposure frequency to instruction execution frequency

$\quad$ N_0 = initial number of faults

$\quad$ n = net number of corrected faults

The correction rate, then, is

$$\frac{dn}{dt} = Z(t) \qquad (t \text{ in execution time})$$

Another variable, the *testing compression factor C*, is defined as the average ratio of the rate of detection of failures during test to the rate during normal use of the program. With this, and reintroducing the fault reduction factor,

$$\frac{dn}{dt} = BCZ(t)$$

Equating M_0, the total number of failures required to remove the N_0 initial defects, to N_0/B, and defining T_0 as the MTTF at the start of test, Musa derives the *s*-expected value of the net number of faults that will be detected and corrected:

$$n = N_0 \left[1 - \exp\left(\frac{-Ct}{M_0 T_0} \right) \right]$$

M_0 can also be considered as the number of all the failures that it is possible to detect from the start of testing to the point at which further defect removal is abandoned.

MTTF displays an exponential increase with execution time:

$$T = T_0 \exp\left(\frac{Ct}{M_0 T_0} \right)$$

Defining m, the *s*-expected value of the number of failures that will occur, we have

$$m = \frac{n}{B} = M_0 \left[1 - \exp\left(-\frac{Ct}{M_0 T_0} \right) \right]$$

This leads to the calculation of the number of failures that will have to occur to increase MTTF from T_1 to T_2:

$$\Delta m = M_0 T_0 \left(\frac{1}{T_1} - \frac{1}{T_2} \right)$$

The additional execution time to experience Δm is

$$\Delta t = \frac{M_0 T_0}{C} \ln \frac{T_2}{T_1}$$

Finally, the reliability for an operational period t' is

$$R(t) = \exp\left(-\frac{t'}{T}\right)$$

We have previously commented on reliability functions that decrease with time.

Calendar Time Component   The suppositions underlying the correlation of execution time to calendar time are related to the constraints on the pace of testing imposed by the avilability and efficiency of use of personnel to identify failures, personnel to remove defects, and computer time. Since the results depend on record-keeping and dynamic interrelationships among the constraints far more complex than is evident in the equations, we shall not discuss them in any detail, save to note that while the correction rate may be exponential in execution time, the model demonstrates that the various real world aspects of software development create a correction rate in calendar time (the time domain in which management observations are made) of many possible shapes.

Nonhomogeneous Poisson Process (NHPP) Model

This model[21,22] differs from the earlier ones in two key respects. Rather than a fixed number to be calculated, the number of initial defects is a random variable (anticipating the bayesian models, of which, more shortly). Also, the time before the ith failure, rather than being s-independent of all other times to failure, is assumed dependent on the time to the $(i - 1)$st defect. The number of failures in nonoverlapped intervals are assumed independent of each other. That is, given the intervals $t_1 \ldots t_n$, the counts $N(t_1)$, $N(t_2) - N(t_1)$, $\ldots, N(t_n) - N(t_{n-1})$ are s-independent, where $N(t_i)$ is the cumulative number of failures to time t_i.

With $\lambda(t)$ as the NHPP intensity function (essentially, the hazard function), the defining NHPP criteria are as follows:

- $N(0) = 0$

- $N(t)$ has independent increments over all t

- $P\{2 \text{ or more events in } \Delta t\} = 0(\Delta t)$

- $P\{\text{exactly 1 event in } \Delta t\} = \lambda(t)\,\Delta t + 0(\Delta t)$, where $0(\Delta t)$ denotes a term such that $0(\Delta t)/\Delta t$ becomes negligible as $\Delta t \to 0$

The number of software failures in any time interval is assumed proportional to the remaining number of defects, as in earlier models. Defining $m(t)$ as the cumulative number of failures (the mean value of the NHPP) and a as its limit [the mean of the distribution of $N(t)$ as $t \to \infty$], the model posits the intensity function

$$\lambda(t) = abe^{-bt}$$

where b is a proportionality constant.

Short of the limit, the mean value function is found from

$$m(t) = a[1 - \exp(-bt)]$$

For $t \geq 0$, $N(t)$ is Poisson-distributed with the s-expected value of $E\{N(t)\}$ = $m(t)$, and, in general,

$$P\{N(t) = n\} = \frac{[m(t)]^n}{n!} e^{-m(t)} \qquad n = 0, 1, 2, \ldots$$

Letting $N'(t)$ represent the number of defects in the system at time t,

$$E\{N'(t)\} = a \exp(-bt)$$

If n defects have been found by t, the model yields, as the conditional distribution of $N'(t)$ and its expectation,

$$P\{N'(t) = x \mid N(t) = n\} = \frac{a^{x+n} e^{-a}}{(x+n)!}$$
$$E\{N'(t) \mid N(t) = n\} = a - n$$

We also have the distribution of $N(\infty)$:

$$P\{N(\infty) \to n\} = \frac{a^n e^{-a}}{n!}$$

which recalls the earlier definition of a.

Finally, the conditional reliability: for the next failure occuring at t, given that the last was detected at time s,

$$R(t \mid s) = \exp[-a(e^{-bs} - e^{-b(s+t)})]$$

Note that the reliability is not an express function of the number of bugs found (although, as we shall see, that number enters into the estimation of a and b). This should find favor with those who may find it difficult to accept the notion that the number of discovered or remaining defects is the direct determinant of the reliability of the software.

It may also be observed that there is nothing in the model that implies data entry of either execution or elapsed time. However, the illustration in Reference 21 of the model's application was in calendar time.

The variables a and b can be estimated by MLE. Let s_k = the time of the kth software failure; $k = 1, 2, \ldots, n$. Then, the equations are

$$\frac{n}{a} = 1 - \exp(-bs_n)$$

and

$$\frac{n}{b} = \sum_{k=1}^{n} s_k + as_n \exp(-bs_n)$$

Reliability engineers employed in the development of electronic hardware for military applications have, for some time, been complying with the guidelines for assessing reliability found in MIL-HDBK-217.[23] Rome Air Development Center has proposed that a similar handbook be developed for software reliability.[22] The NHPP model will be the basis for the initial, interim version of the handbook.

Weibull Distribution (Wagoner)

We have seen models adopted from the exponential and Rayleigh distributions of classical (hardware) reliability theory. Both of these single-paramenter distributions can be considered special cases of the two-parameter Weibull distribution, also used for reliability modeling of hardware.[13,14] The credit for recognizing its potential for software is given[2,11,18] to W. L. Wagoner, who, with good results, applied the model to the failure incidence of a 4000 statement FORTRAN program.

The hazard function is

$$Z(t) = \frac{\lambda}{\sigma} \left(\frac{t}{\sigma} \right)^{\lambda - 1}$$

where σ = scale parameter
λ = parameter to squeeze or stretch the shape of the distribution curve

In Wagoner's work, all time is in units of CPU time.
Reliability and MTTF:[11]

$$R(t) = \exp \left[-\left(\frac{t}{\sigma} \right)^{\lambda} \right]$$

$$MTTF = \frac{\sigma \Gamma(1/\lambda)}{\lambda}$$

A least squares solution is available for σ and λ.[2]

Gompertz Distribution (Nathan)

If software reliability modeling can profit from hardware forms, why not from those of other disciplines where statistical inference has proven successful! Irwin Nathan[24] has demonstrated the feasibility of this by developing a model based on the work of Benjamin Gompertz, a nineteenth-century actuary concerned with the prediction of survival rates of males of a given age.

Of the models noted thus far, Nathan's is the first to consider correction, or defect removal rate, independently of failure rate.* The model does not attempt to predict failure rate during testing, but the cumulative number of corrections that will have been made and verified at some time in the future. The premises are that the initial number of problems are finite and that

P {that at least one more problem will be corrected during

development}

depends solely on a function of the number of remaining problems and the proven defect removal rate. For

$N(t)$ = cumulative number of verified corrections
C = initial number of defects
$\ln A$ = correction rate
B = a function of number of corrections made prior to completion of first test interval $N(0^+)$
$N(t) = CB^{A^t}$ (t in calendar time)

This describes an S-shaped curve with a point of inflection at $N(t) = C/e$. B is actually an early (in the life of the development project) measure of the rate of corrections relative to the number of defects:

$$B = \ln \frac{N(0^+)}{C}$$

That $N(t)$ should be so sensitive to one historical datum is mathematically disquieting, and we should be surprised that the fit of data to the model resolves for all data histories with any consistency as the predictions are updated. Nevertheless, using a nonlinear regression fit in a least squares sense on monthly summary data, Nathan has applied the model to several case histories with remarkably good fits.

Trivedi and Shooman Markov Model

Unlike the Littlewood Markov model presented earlier, the states of this model[3,25,26] do not relate to those of the modules constituting the program, but the condition of the software's being either "up" or "down." The program is considered to have a sequence of states $n, (n-1), (n-2), \ldots$, in which it is up, and a sequence $m, (m-1), (m-2), \ldots$, in which it is down. The general state is given by $(n-k)$ if the $(k-1)$st detected defect has been corrected but the kth failure has yet to happen, or $(m-k)$ if the kth failure has occurred but the underlying fault has not yet been fixed.

---

*The Musa model also included the concept of correction rate apart from detection rate, but assumed a constant ratio of the two.

Clearly, testing stops directly after a failure and is not resumed until the correction has been made.

Transitions between states are modeled as a Markov process, with transition probabilities $\{\,p_{ij}\,\}$ (probability of transition from state i to state j). P_{ij} is a function of either λ_j the failure rate or μ_j the correction rate. That is,

$$P\,\{\text{transition from state } (n - k) \text{ to } (m - k)\} = f(\lambda_{n-k}),$$
$$P\,\{\text{transition from state } (m - k) \text{ to } (n - k - 1)\} = f(\mu_{m-k})$$
$$k = 0, 1, 2, \ldots$$

The reliability function for a general hazard function $\lambda(k, x)$ is

$$R_k(\tau) = \exp\left[- \int_0^\tau \lambda(k,x)\,dx \right]$$

Beyond this general definition of reliability, Trivedi and Shooman developed the model only for a constant failure rate between each defect correction and the subsequent failure; that is, $Z(\tau) = \lambda_k$. For this case,

$$R_k(\tau) = \exp\left[-\lambda(k)\tau\right] \qquad (\tau \text{ in operating time})$$

This represents a family of exponential curves, similar to those of the Shooman exponential model.

To go further with the model, one should want to develop general equations for the calendar time state probabilities $P_{n-k}(t)$ and $P_{m-k}(t)$, given expressions for λ and μ in defects found (removed) per calendar unit. As Trivedi and Shooman point out, unless λ and μ are assured constant, the model does not lend itself to this. Thus, they provide a method, which they refer to as the "numerical solution," for arriving at the determination of the probablities in terms of the actual number of defects removed or remaining. This, an iterative solution of difference equations, accommodates piecewise definition of λ_k and μ_k.

Shooman-Natarajan Model

With the last two models, we have seen that abstractions of the test and debug process can encompass correction process parameters of failure; at least with regard to the rates of each. Parenthetically, it may be observed that in the earlier test stages, failure rates (in execution time) and correction rates are both high. Later, failure rates are low — or at least we hope so — but the types of defects found often require major rewrites of the code, so that the correction rate slows down also. In brief, the two rates may be s-independent, but nevertheless both show similar distributions with time.

The modeling of the correction process can be made even more realistic by accepting the unpleasant fact known to every programmer: one not only removes defects in the debugging process, one also introduces new ones. This capability is provided by the models of Shooman and Natarajan.[2,3,27] For $n(t)$ = the number of defects in the program at debug calendar time t, Shooman and Natarajan state the basic premise that

$$\frac{dn}{dt} = r_g(t) - r_c(t)$$

where r_g = generation rate of new defects
     r_c = correction rate for all defects

The hazard function is basically that of the Shooman exponential model. In the interval $\Delta\tau$ of operating time,

$$z(\tau)\,\Delta\tau = k\epsilon_r(t)\,\Delta\tau$$

where ϵ_r = number of remaining software faults
     k = constant of proportionality

In the manpower-limited version of the model, the one most fully developed, the researchers define the correction rate as

$$r_c(t) = \begin{cases} k_1 & \text{for } n(t) > n_1 \\ k_2 n(t) & \text{for } n(t) \leq n_1 \end{cases}$$

n_1 is the number of defects in the system at the time t_1 when the correction rate is no longer limited by manpower but by the number of remaining defects.

k_1 is, by definition, the correction rate during the manpower-limited period, and k_2 is a constant of porportionality when manpower no longer determines the correction rate.

The number of defects in the system is

$$n(t) = n_1 \exp\left[(a_1 - k_2)(t - t_1)\right]$$

where a_1 is proportional to $r_d(t)$, the detection rate [also, $r_g = a_1 n(t)$].

Shooman and Natarajan have also developed expressions for $n_c(t)$ for the conditions of debugging instability (the number of defects increases with time), controlled debugging (the number monotonically decreases in an S-shaped fashion with a point of inflection at t_1), and oscillatory debugging (at t_1 the number of bugs increases until some n_2, decreases to n_1 again, ad infinitum).

Bayesian Models—General

Before discussing the next group of models, we interject a few general comments about bayesian reliability.

Reliability estimation can be divided into two camps: classical and bayesian. The classical approaches assume the form of parametric equations, the employment of which is tantamount to estimation of the parameters. In classical reliability, the results are derived entirely from collected data, and the risk of making an incorrect decision is based on the estimation of confidence intervals. Bayesian approaches consider the model parameters to be random variables, postulate *prior* probabilities based on theory or historical data, update these with new data to form *posterior* probabilities, and may lead to judgments of time to next failure that are based directly on the probability distribution function.

Bayesian reliability models have their origin in Bayes' equation for conditional probability. The probability of the simultaneous occurrence of events A and B is that of the occurrence of A, given that B has already occurred, multiplied by the probability of B's occurrence. This is written as

$$P \{A \cdot B\} = P\{(A \,|\, B)\} \, P\{B\}$$

The inverse is also true:

$$P \{A \cdot B\} = P \{(B \,|\, A)\} \, P\{A\}$$

For the purposes of reliability estimation, we are more interested in the equations when combined:

$$P \{(A \,|\, B)\} = P\{(B \,|\, A)\} \times \frac{P\{A\}}{P\{B\}}$$

We may interpret this to mean that the posterior probability of A, given the new data B, is the probability of B, given A, times the ratio of the probabilities of A and B. Another way of looking at it is to say that posterior probabilities are proportional to prior probabilities when multiplied by likelihoods.

In general, bayesian approaches should be able to arrive at reliability estimations of equivalent certitude* to those of classical approaches, using less data than the classical means. In terms of software time-domain models, this means earlier in time.

Goel-Okumoto Imperfect Debugging Model

We have had models that incorporate defect removal at a rate different from defect detection, and one model that admits to the creation of new bugs in the process of fixing old ones. With the Goel-Okumoto model,[2,3,28] we can consider the possibility that an attempt to remove a defect may not have been completely successful; that is, in the interval since the previous observation, the

---

*Observe how cleverly the use of the word "confidence" was avoided. Actually, confidence limits can be applied to bayesian models also, given a fix on the parameters of the distribution.

software system has not really changed.* The model does not, however, accept the generation of new faults. In the real world, of course, one has both new defect generation and unsuccessful removal of old defects.

The other basic assumptions of the model are an exponential time distribution between failures and a constant failure rate parameter. The probability of simultaneous events is negligible, as is the time to perform a correction process.

$$p = P \{\text{of successful correction of a defect}\}$$
$$q = 1 - p$$

The probability density function (pdf) of the time to the next failure for the ith remaining fault [*not* after the $(i - 1)$st failure has occurred] is

$$f_i(t) = i \lambda \exp(-i\lambda t)$$

with cumulative distribution function (cdf)

$$F_i(t) = 1 - \exp(-i\lambda t)$$

In other words, the model postulates i exponential distributions, each of parameter λ.

Given i remaining defects, the time distribution to the next failure (the one leaving j faults), in terms of a semi-Markov process, is

$$Q_{ij}(t) = p(1 - e^{-i\lambda t})$$

The time T_{N,n_0} is the time required to reduce the N initial defects to n_0 remaining ones. Its cdf, defined as $G_{N,\,n_0}(t)$, is found from

$$G_{N,n_0}(t) = \sum_{j=1}^{N-n_0} B_{N,j,n_0} [1 - e^{-(n_0+j)p\lambda t}]$$

where

$$B_{N,j,n_0} = \frac{N!}{n_0!\,j!(N - n_0 - j)!} (-1)^{j-1} \frac{j}{n_0 + j}$$

For large N, B_{N,j,n_0} is difficult to compute. Goel and Okumoto provide[28] a gamma approximation of $G_{N,n_0}(t)$ to ease the pain.

---

*We do not mean to suggest that chronologically this was the earliest model to incorporate uncertainty in the debugging process. The Littlewood-Verrall bayesian model[29] incorporated a set of growth functions to govern the discrete change in reliability when attempting the ith repair. Each of these functions is postulated to be fixed for a given program, programmer, and debugging stage. Evidential approaches to the estimations of these functions are not obvious, leaving a less satisfactory statistical alternative.

From the above, one derives a number useful for planning purposes, namely, the expected time to attain n_0:

$$E\{T_{N,n_0}\} = \sum_{j=1}^{N-n_0} \frac{B_{N,j,n_0}}{(n_0 + j)p\lambda}$$

It may be more useful to know what one may expect for the number of faults remaining at time t:

$$E\{X(t)|X(0) = N\} = N \exp(-p\lambda t)$$

The reliability function between the $(k - 1)$st and kth failure is

$$R_k(x) = \sum_{j=0}^{k-1} \binom{k-1}{j} p^{k-j-1}q^j \exp[-(N - k + j + 1)\lambda x]$$

One may also want to estimate the number of failures that will occur in a time period t. The expected total number is given by

$$M_N(t) = \frac{N}{p}[1 - \exp(-\lambda pt)]$$

To use any of the above, it is necessary to estimate the parameters N, λ, and p. The researchers provided both MLE and bayesian inference procedures. For the latter, the prior estimates for N and λ are given as gamma distributions, while that for p is a beta distribution:

$$P\{N\} \propto N^{\alpha-1} \exp(-\beta N)$$
$$P\{p\} \propto p^{\pi-1}(1 - p)^{\rho-1}$$
$$P\{\lambda\} \propto \lambda^{\mu-1} \exp(-\gamma\lambda)$$

α, β, γ, μ, π, and ρ are assigned as prior parameters. If, however, one chooses to plead "prior ignorance," Goel and Okumoto recommend setting α, β, γ, and μ to zero, and setting π and ρ to 0.5. Using such vague "priors" as they are called, vitiates, but does not invalidate, the use of a bayesian model.

The posteriors, the ones that one uses as the parameters for the model outputs, are found by solving the set of equations:

$$-\lambda \sum_{i=1}^{n} t_i + \sum_{i=1}^{n} \frac{1 - y_i}{N - (i - 1)} + \frac{\alpha - 1}{N} - \beta = 0$$

$$\lambda \sum_{i=1}^{n} (i - 1)t_i - \sum_{i=1}^{n} \frac{y_i}{1 - p} + \frac{\pi - 1}{p} - \frac{\rho - 1}{1 - p} = 0$$

$$\frac{n}{\lambda} - \sum_{i=1}^{n} [N - p(i - 1)]\, t_i + \frac{\mu - 1}{\lambda - \gamma} = 0$$

where n = number of failures that have occurred
t_i = time between $(i - 1)$st and ith failures
y_i = 1 if failure resulted from imperfect debugging
y_i = 0 if failure did not result from imperfect debugging

Littlewood Bayesian Differential Debugging Model

Littlewood has proposed a model[30] in which the defects remaining in a program may each be subject to a different occurrence rate. This reflects the common observation that some segments of code are exercised with greater frequency than other segments, leading to the corollary that a bug within a more frequently entered portion of the program has an inherently higher hazard rate. Thus, the usual assumption that the failure rate is proportional to the number of remaining defects may be a poor approximation of the defect modality. Of course, the heavily trafficked bugs are generally the first to be found, leaving the bugs in the less frequented code areas to be more evenly encountered after the initial debugging stages. If, then, one starts one's modeling process at that time, the assumption of uniform fault occurrence is more reasonable.

Littlewood has also avoided the common assumption of constant hazard rate between failures. Although there is no causal basis for the hazard rate of a program to change except when a defect is removed, the notion of constant rate of failure contravenes the intuitive feeling that the longer the program performs correctly, the more trustworthy it is. The differential debugging model leads to a failure rate as shown by dotted line in Figure 12-3.* If intui-

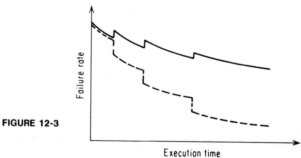

FIGURE 12-3

Failure rate

Execution time

tion is to be properly served, however, one should consider the solid line, which says that as soon as a failure occurs, we lose the faith. (This has also been suggested by G. Myers.[31])

In this model, failure rate becomes a random variable, rather than a parameter. Representing the unknown occurrence rate of the individual defects as $\phi_1, \phi_2, \ldots$, the failure rate, given that i failures have already occurred, can be

*The Littlewood-Verrall model[29] also exhibits this.

thought of as

$$\lambda = \phi_1 + \phi_2 + \cdots + \phi_{n-i}$$

where $N =$ the number of initial defects.

The ϕ_i are, of course, not known, and must themselves be represented by random variables, Φ_i, each having its own pdf. It is assumed that prior to the start of the debugging process, the occurrence rates are given by a Gamma distribution* with parameters α and β:

$$\text{pdf}(\phi) = \frac{\beta^\alpha \phi^{\alpha-1} e^{-\beta\phi}}{\Gamma(\alpha)}$$

which leads to the distribution in execution time of the entire program:

$$\text{pdf}(\tau) = \frac{(N-1)\alpha(\beta + t)^{(N-1)\alpha}}{(\beta + \tau + t)^{(N-1)\alpha+1}}$$

where t represents time to present.

From this equation, Littlewood develops a number of outputs:

- A failure rate function decreasing in time
- Current MTTF
- Prediction of reliability k failures or T units of time from the present, given that I failures have already occurred
- The number of bugs that will have to be fixed to provide 95 percent certainty that the failure rate is less than a stipulated number
- The cdf and mean of the time to detect and remove the last defect

For any of these outputs it is necessary to estimate the parameters N, α, and β. Littlewood[30] gives a somewhat messy MLE method. An approach based on Bayes would appear to be more attractive, and, indeed, was being pursued by Littlewood as a continuing effort.

Thompson and Chelson Bayesian Model

We started this chapter by asserting that software reliability models hold the promise of providing criteria for acceptance of software on measurable grounds of reliability performance. The last model[32,33] we shall introduce is devoted to just that purpose. Although it provides other statistical inferences as well, it is not an appropriate candidate for use during debug and test.

The model was designed for application to software embedded in critical systems, where tolerance to remaining defects is zero. That is, the objective

---

*Littlewood indicates that other distributions might serve equally well, and that, in any case, the dotted line curve of Figure 12-3 is independent of the choice.

(whether realized or not) is to deliver (accept) software containing no defects. To this end, rather than being concerned with the probability of n remaining defects, the model uses a prior p, on the probability that the *software contains at least one error.* One can view the preceding models as treating software for which p is always assumed to equal 1; that is, for which the presence of defects is pessimistically — if realistically — considered a certainty.

A constant occurrence rate λ is assumed, with

$$P\{\text{no event occurring in interval } t\} = \exp(-\lambda t)$$

Both λ and p are random variables. Their priors are determined as follows: Let H denote current test data, consisting of k failures* in T operating hours. The likelihood of H for $k = 0$ is

$$L(H|\lambda, p) = p \exp(-\lambda T) + (1 - p)$$

For $k > 0$,

$$L(H|\lambda, p) = \frac{p \exp(-\lambda T)(\lambda T)^k}{k!}$$

The gamma density function,

$$h(\lambda | T_0, k_0) = \text{gamma}(\lambda | T_0, k_0 + 1),$$

is taken as the prior in λ, where k_0 and T_0 represent previous testing experience and

$$\text{gamma}(\lambda | T, k) = \frac{T(\lambda T)^{k-1}}{\Gamma(k)} e^{-\lambda T}$$

The prior density function of p is assumed

$$g(p | a, b) = \frac{p^a (1 - p)^b}{\beta(a + 1, b + 1)}$$

where both a and b are $> (-1)$, with a representing the number of previous software deliveries containing at least one defect and b representing those in which none were ever found after delivery. λ and p are s-independent. Beyond that, even given $p = 1$, the model does not require an explicit relationship between failure rate and the number of remaining defects. We have seen this in other bayesian models as well. That the reliability can be estimated indifferently to any effect of defect population or failure rate may leave one with a sense of dissatisfaction.

Although the model provides other outputs, we shall concern ourselves

---

*We use the word "failure" despite the insistence of the researchers that software never fails, although the system it serves may fail as a result of the software. See also their comments in Thompson and Chelson.[34] Although we understand the distinction they make, we find it unnecessary, and continue to use "failure" in the sense in which it has become an accepted term within software engineering.

directly with the pass/fail resolution. One does not become interested in this until some time has passed in which no failures have occurred. Now, one wants either to narrowly bound the uncertainty that there are no further defects to be found, or to determine that insufficient test time has taken place on which to base a decision. At this point, the marginal posterior distribution function in λ, as given by Thompson and Chelson, is

$$F(\lambda | H) = \frac{a + 1}{a + b + 2} \text{Gamma} (\lambda | T + T_0, k_0 + 1) + \frac{b + 1}{a + b + 2}$$

where

$$\text{Gamma} (\lambda | T, k) = \int_0^\lambda \text{gamma} (X | T, k) \, dX.$$

Also,

$$E\{\lambda | H\} = \frac{a + 1}{a + b + 2} \frac{k_0 + 1}{T + T_0}$$

There are similar expressions for R, and Bayes' interval estimates may be applied to either. Consider the lower $(1 - \alpha)$ limit* on λ, defined as that λ_α for which $F(\lambda_\alpha | H) = \alpha$. If we define a maximum acceptable λ as λ_a, and an unconditionally rejectable failure rate as λ_r or greater, then one can arrive at the following decisions based on $F(\lambda | H)$:

1. Accept if $F(\lambda_a | H) \geq 1 - \alpha$.

2. Reject if $F(\lambda_r | H) \leq \beta$.

3. Continue testing if neither inequality is satisfied.

As a practical matter, we would expect that the second decision would actually be implemented not as an out-of-hand rejection, but as a mandate for further testing in the expectation that the priors will ultimately be updated to the point that the software can satisfy the acceptance criterion.

It may be noted that the pass/fail policy implicitly accepts the possibility that the intolerable may have to be accepted, namely, that p may be greater than zero.

Validation

Some of the above models, especially those that were developed in the mid-1970s, have been exposed to independent, competitive validation. That is,

---

*Loosely, α represents the risk of rejecting true hypotheses—in our case, of the acceptability of λ. Another quantity, β, represents the risk of incorrectly accepting a false hypothesis. Typical α's and β's used in acceptance testing range from 0.001 to 0.1.

there is a small body of literature describing experiences in applying the same set of failure data to several different models. Results of "fly-offs" have been published.[11,35-38] We shall not summarize these, because the validity of a model is an inverse function of the distance between its assumptions and the conditions under which the data were collected. Sometimes model A looks better than model B, and sometimes model B has its turn in the winner's circle.

None of this is to say that model selection is a horse race. In using a model, one tacitly accepts its premises. If these do not seem to hold, if the parameters change dramatically at each update, one concludes that the premises of the model inadequately reflect the software and testing environment. On to another model. In brief, independently of the validation of other researchers, there is little basis for holding confidence in a model without first validating it for one's own software characteristics, personnel, standards, methods, and tools. Of course, any model used demands input gathered to its own requirements. If a model operates on the number of debug hours to each failure, and data is available only in weekly summaries, the model cannot be used.

MEASUREMENT IN THE DATA DOMAIN

Earlier, we had stated that there is no need to rule out time-domain estimation models as instruments for the establishment of quantitative reliability standards. None of these models, however, have the capability of directly relating failure history with the opportunity for failure that awaits specific defects. The models cannot do so for the simple reason that the defects are unknown until detected. Moreover, even if the source of certain defects might be suspected, the time-domain models described consider the program as a black box, with the structure of the program completely hidden. What the models depend on is a testing history governed by Poisson failure law.

For the purposes of modeling with knowledge of the code, Lloyd and Lipow[14] have developed a set of relationships wherein the input data space is partitioned functionally; that is, relative to the groups of logic paths. The probability of execution of a given logic path is related to the probabilities of a functional partition correctly and incorrectly invoking the path. Reliability, then, is a measure of correct path selection (accompanied by correct path behavior) made by a functional partition. Lloyd and Lipow consider the sampling of the data domain in terms of disjoint subsets of the input data space, leading to a determination of confidence limits on estimations of reliability.

Analyses as these are not easily conducted for large programs and are probably impossible without the use of tools to identify the logic paths. A tool was, in fact, used by E. C. Nelson, whose work is one of the foundations of the methods of Lloyd and Lipow. What these ideas seem to point to is the use of static analyzers and dynamic test probes as a technique to relate the relevance of the sample data space used in testing and evaluation to the entire data domain of a program, perhaps simply to indicate the need for further testing, but possibly also as a way of refining the assumptions of a time-domain model.

SOFTWARE QUALITY ASSURANCE GOALS FOR THE FUTURE

The development of quantifiable, measurable standards of software reliability will dominate the future evolution of the discipline of software quality assurance. However, we recall from earlier chapters that reliability is scarcely the only measure of the quality of the delivered software product. Maintainability is a matter of major, if perhaps not equal, importance. Qualitatively, we have discussed maintainability in terms of program structure, documentation, and a configuration management scheme suitable for the entire life of software. Quantitatively, we have said nothing.

The real measure of maintainability will be in terms of the ability to repair defects that have been detected during operation and maintenance, and in the freedom to undertake program modification without the generation of an untoward number of defects. To our knowledge, no work has yet been undertaken to model the maintainability of a program. Perhaps the direction is to be found somewhere in the work of Goel and Okumoto on imperfect debugging and that of Shooman and Natarajan on the generation of new faults.

Within the technology, methodology, and management controls described in Parts 3 and 4, we know how to produce good software. What remains is the measurement of our success.

SUMMARY

1. Considerable work has been done to quantify the degree to which we can depend on software to work correctly. The dimension we assign to that degree is *reliability*.

2. The calculation of the reliability of a program can be useful to determine whether additional testing is required to expose more defects, to serve as criteria for acceptance, and to complete the estimation of the reliability of complex systems in which software is embedded.

3. Reliability models are the key to determining software reliability. Models also exist for quantification of the complexity of a program and for the pre-test prediction of the number of bugs that a program may contain.

4. The premise that software failure can be described by a probability distribution is common to those reliability models that are based on the observed pattern of defect exposure. Differences among the types is mostly a reflec-

tion of other assumptions that must be made concerning the failure modality of a given defect and the testing and debugging environment.

5. Despite the general acceptance of Poisson failure law for software, the significance of single point statistical inferences (e.g., MTTF) may be less important for software than for hardware.

6. The thirteen reliability models (plus variants) discussed are all representative of estimation based on failure history without regard to the structure of the software. Tools that can relate the opportunity for failure (i.e., the path coverage of the data used) with the history of failure can give greater credibility to the estimations.

7. Although considerable progress has been made in the estimation of reliability, little has been done to quantify maintainability. Within the literature of reliability modeling, however, we may see the germ of the modeling of maintainability.

REFERENCES

1. Thomas McCabe, "A Complexity Measure," *IEEE Transactions on Software Engineering*, Vol. SE-2, No. 4, December 1976, pp. 308–320.

2. Computer Sciences Corporation (under contract to IIT Research Institute), *Software Engineering Research Review: Quantitative Software Models*, SRR-1, Data and Analysis Center for Software, Rome Air Development Center, Griffiss Air Force Base, New York, 1979.

3. D. Swearingen and J. Donahoo, "Quantitative Software Reliability Models — Data Parameters: A Tutorial," *Workshop on Quantitative Software Models*, IEEE Catalog No. TH0067-9, 1979, pp. 143–153.

4. Maurice Halstead, *Elements of Software Science*, Elsevier-North Holland, Inc., New York, 1977.

5. Ann Fitzsimmons and Tom Love, "A Review and Evaluation of Software Science," *ACM Computing Surveys*, Vol. 10, No. 1, March 1978, pp. 3–18.

6. R. W. Motley and W. D. Brooks, *Statistical Prediction of Programming Errors*, RADC-TR-77-175, Rome Air Development Center, Griffiss Air Force Base, New York, 1977.

7. M. Lipow and T. A. Thayer, "Prediction of Software Failures," *Proceedings 1977 Annual Reliability and Maintainability Symposium*, IEEE Cat. No. 77CH1161-9RQC, pp. 489–494.

8. Bev Littlewood, "Software Reliability Model for Modular Programming Structure," *IEEE Transactions on Reliability*, Vol. R-28, No. 3, August 1979, pp. 241–246.

9. Martin Shooman, "Operational Testing and Software Reliability Estimation During Program Development," *1973 IEEE Symposium on Computer Software Reliability*, IEEE Cat. No. 73CH0741-9CSR, pp. 51–57.

10. Martin Shooman, "Software Reliability: Measurement and Models," *Proceedings 1975 Annual Reliability and Maintainability Symposium*, IEEE Cat. No. 75CH0918-3 RQC, pp. 485–491.

11. Alan Sukert, "An Investigation of Software Reliability Models," *Proceedings 1977 Annual Reliability and Maintainability Symposium*, pp. 478–484.

12. G. R. Craig et al., *Software Reliability Study*, RADC-TR-74-250, Rome Air Development Center, Griffiss Air Force Base, New York, 1974.

13. Martin Shooman, *Probabilistic Reliability: An Engineering Approach*, McGraw-Hill, New York, 1968.

14. David Lloyd and Myron Lipow, *Reliability: Management, Methods, and Mathematics*, 2d ed., published by the authors, Redondo Beach, Calif., 1977.

15. Z. Jelinski and P. B. Moranda, "Application of A Probability-Based Model to A Code Reading Experiment," *1973 IEEE Symposium on Computer Software Reliability*, IEEE Cat. No. 73CH0741-9CSR, pp. 78–80.

16. P. B. Moranda, "Prediction of Software Reliability During Debugging," *Proceedings 1975 Annual Reliability and Maintainability Symposium*, IEEE Cat. No. 75CH0918-3RQC, pp. 327–332.

17. Alan Sukert, *A Software Reliability Modeling Study*, RADC-TR-76-247, Rome Air Development Center, Griffiss Air Force Base, New York, 1976.

18. George Schick and Ray Wolverton, "An Analysis of Competing Software Reliability Models," *IEEE Transactions on Software Engineering*, Vol. SE-4, No. 2, March 1978, pp. 104–120.

19. John Musa, "A Theory of Software Reliability and Its Application," IEEE Transactions on Software Engineering, Vol. SE-1, No. 3, September 1975, pp. 312–327.

20. John Musa, "Validation of Execution Time Theory of Software Reliability," *IEEE Transactions on Reliability*, Vol. R-28, No. 3, August 1979, pp. 181–191.

21. Amrit Goel and Kazu Okumoto, "Time-Dependent Error-Detection Rate Model for Software Reliability and Other Performance Measures," *IEEE Transactions on Reliability*, Vol. R-28, No. 3, Aug. 1979, pp. 206–211.

22. Alan Sukert and Amrit Goel, "A Guidebook for Software Reliability Assessment," *Proceedings 1980 Annual Reliability and Maintainability Symposium*, IEEE Cat. NO. 80CH1513-R, pp. 186–190.

23. M1L-HDBK-217C, "Reliability Prediction of Electronic Equipment," April 9, 1979.

24. Irwin Nathan, "A Deterministic Model to Predict 'Error-Free' Status of Complex Software Development," *Workshop on Quantitative Software Models*, IEEE Cat. No. TH0067-9, 1979, pp. 159–169.

25. Ashok Trivedi and Martin Shooman, *A Markov-Model for The Evaluation of Computer Software Performance*, Research Report, Polytechnic Institute of New York, EE/EP 74-0111-EER110, under contract to ONR and RADC, May 1, 1974.

26. Ashok Trivedi and Martin Shooman, "A Many-State Markov Model for the Estimation and Prediction of Computer Software Performance Parameters," *Proceedings 1975 International Conference on Reliable Software*, IEEE Cat. No. 75CH0940-7CSR, pp. 208–220.

27. M. Shooman and S. Natarajan, *Effect of Manpower Development and Bug Generation on Software Error Models*, Technical Report RADC-TR-76-400, Rome Air Development Center, Griffiss Air Force Base, New York, January 1977.

28. Amrit Goel and K. Okumoto, *Bayesian Software Prediction Models*, Final Technical Report RADC-TR-78-155 (5 Vols.), Rome Air Development Center, Griffiss Air Force Base, New York, July 1978.

29. B. Littlewood, and J. L. Verrall, "A Bayesian Reliability Growth Model for Computer Software," *1973 IEEE Symposium on Computer Software Reliability*, IEEE Cat. No. 73CH0741-9CSR, pp. 70–77.

30. B. Littlewood, "A Bayesian Differential Debugging Model for Software Reliability," *Workshop on Quantitative Software Models*, IEEE Cat. No. TH0067-9, October 1979, pp. 170–181.

31. G. Myers, *Software Reliability: Principles and Practices*, Wiley-Interscience, New York, 1976, pp. 334–335.

32. W. E. Thompson and P. O. Chelson, "Software Reliability Testing for Embedded Computer Systems," *Workshop on Quantitative Software Models*, IEEE Cat. No. TH0067-9, October 1979, pp. 201–208.

33. W. E. Thompson and P. O. Chelson, "On the Specification and Testing of Software Reliability," *Proceedings 1980 Annual Reliability and Maintainability Symposium*, IEEE Cat. No. 80CH1513-R, pp. 379–383.

34. W. E. Thompson and P. O. Chelson, "Referee Comments" (to B. Littlewood paper, "How to Measure Software Reliability and How Not To"), *IEEE Transactions on Reliability*, Vol. R-28, No. 2, June 1979, pp. 108–109.

35. R. E. Schafer, J. E. Angus, J. F. Alter, and S. E. Emoto, *Validation of Software Reliability Models*, Technical Report RADC-TR-79-147, Rome Air Development Center, Griffiss Air Force Base, New York, June 1979.

36. A. N. Sukert, "Empirical Validation of Three Software Error Prediction Models," *IEEE Transactions on Reliability*, Vol. R-28, No. 3, August 1979, pp. 199–205.

Index

Index

About the Author

ROBERT DUNN is a Staff Consultant at ITT Avionics Division, where he heads the software quality assurance program. He is a well-known lecturer at conferences and symposiums on software quality control, and has represented industry on select government software planning teams.

RICHARD ULLMAN is Vice President and Director, Product Assurance, ITT Avionics Division. He is responsible for the quality of all products produced by ITT Avionics Division. Mr. Ullman was a U. S. delegate to the NATO Symposium on Quality and Its Assurance in 1977 and 1980.